BRASSEY'S BOOK OF

ESPIONAGE

Also by John Laffin

Military

Brassey's Battles: 3,500 Years of Conflict. Campaigns and
   Wars from A–Z
War Annual 1
War Annual 2
War Annual 3
War Annual 4
War Annual 5
War Annual 6
War Annual 7
Middle East Journey
Return to Glory
One Man's War
The Walking Wounded
Digger (The Story of the Australian Soldier)
Scotland the Brave (The Story of the Scottish Soldier)
Jackboot (The Story of the German Soldier)
Tommy Atkins (The Story of the English Soldier)
Jack Tar (The Story of the English Seaman)
Swifter than Eagles (Biography of Marshal of the R A F
   Sir John Salmond)
The Face of War
British Campaign Medals
Codes and Ciphers
Boys in Battle
Women in Battle
Anzacs at War
Links of Leadership (Thirty Centuries of Command)
Surgeons in the Field
Americans in Battle
Letters from the Front 1914–18
The French Foreign Legion
Damn the Dardanelles! (The Agony of Gallipoli)
The Australian Army at War 1899–1974
The Israeli Army in the Middle East Wars 1948–1973
The Arab Armies in the Middle East Wars 1948–1973
Fight for the Falklands!
On the Western Front: Soldiers Stories 1914–18

The Man the Nazis Couldn't Catch
The War of Desperation: Lebanon 1982–85
Battlefield Archaeology
The Western Front 1916–17: The Price of Honour ⎫
The Western Front 1917–18: The Cost of Victory ⎬ Australians
Greece, Crete & Syria 1941   ⎪ at War
Secret and Special   ⎭
Holy War: Islam Fights
World War 1 in Postcards
Soldiers of Scotland (with John Baynes)
British Butchers and Bunglers of World War 1
The Western Front Illustrated
Guide to Australian Battlefields of the Western Front
   1916–1918
Digging Up the Diggers' War
Panorama of the Western Front
Western Front Companion
Forever Forward: 2/31 Battalion 1940–45
We Will Remember Them: AIF Epitaphs of World War 1

General

The Hunger to Come (Food and Population Crises)
New Geography 1966–67
New Geography 1968–69
New Geography 1970–71
Anatomy of Captivity (Political Prisoners)
Devil's Goad
Fedayeen (The Arab-Israeli Dilemma)
The Arab Mind
The Israeli Mind
The Dagger of Islam
The PLO Connections
The Arabs as Master Slavers
Know the Middle East
Fontana Dictionary of Africa slnce 1960 (wlth John Grace)
Aussie Guide to Britain
And other titles

BRASSEY'S BOOK OF
Espionage

by
John Laffin

BRASSEY'S

London * Washington

First English Edition 1996

UK editorial offices: Brassey's, 33 John Street, London WC1N 2AT
UK orders: Marston Book Services, PO Box 269, Abingdon, OX14 4SD

North American orders: Brassey's Inc., PO Box 960,
Herndon, VA 22070, USA

John Laffin has asserted his moral right to be identified as
the author of this work.

*Library of Congress Cataloging in Publication Data
available*

*Briish Library Cataloging in Publication Data
A catalogue record for this book is available from the British Library*

ISBN 1 85753 144 2 Hardcover

Typeset by Pantek Arts, Maidstone, Kent
Printed in Great Britain by Redwood Books, Trowbridge

CONTENTS

ACKNOWLEDGEMENTS

This is a blanket acknowledgement of thanks for all those personal friends and professional contacts, past and present, 'in intelligence' or with links to intelligence, who have provided me with information. They are in Britain, France, the United States, Australia, Canada and other countries. Not one of them would thank me for being mentioned here by name. I have a reputation, in writing: *War Annual – The World in Conflict* for never disclosing the name of a confidential source and I want to maintain that reputation with this book. See, however, the footnotes, chapter notes and bibliography.

One person must be named and specially thanked – my wife Hazelle. She has helped me immeasurably with the writing and preparation of this book, as with all my other books. She is too much the professional to find the literary work exasperating but on one occasion she said, 'It seems to me that many men and women of intelligence lack common sense.' It is an exquisite paradox.

Hazelle may have been thinking of an experience of mine in the mid-1970s. I had been travelling as a journalist in Beirut, which at that time was possibly the most dangerous terrorist territory in the world, and two members of a western security service – not themselves 'spies' – telephoned to ask if they might interview me about my experiences there. Having established that I would not reveal my sources of information and that I did not want the interview taped, I agreed to what was for me a role reversal – I was more accustomed to doing the interviewing.

One agent was a young man and on this very hot day at a pavement cafe he was dressed in lightweight casual slacks and shirt. The other, was in his fifties, wore a suit and under it a white shirt with a tie and ornate silver cufflinks. I agreed to a request that the younger man could take notes of what was said. But strangely, although my experiences in Beirut and southern Lebanon had been interesting, he made only a few notes. His partner, who asked the questions, kept an elbow on the table and rested his chin in his hand.

It probably took me all of two minutes to realise that the bulbous cufflink had to be a microphone and that my words were, after all, being taped. I was too amused by the pair's professional ineptitude to be angry about the deceit. When I said, 'I admire your taste in cufflinks – do you mind if I take a closer look at them?' the agents knew that the interview had ended. At the time I remarked to Hazelle, 'Those two could risk their lives if they are always as dumb as they were today.'

They had made a series of blunders. The day was too hot to be wearing a heavy suit outdoors; the younger agent, having secured permission to take notes, should have been busy writing them to help cover his partner's use of a microphone; and the older man's awkward position, elbow on table, chin in hand and with an eye-catching out-size cufflink pointing at me were dead giveaways. They were trained and intelligent men but where was their common sense? No older, experienced hardnosed journalist would be deceived by such clumsiness – and neither would an enemy.

❶

FEAR IS THE SPUR

Fear is the predominant cause of the stresses, tensions and wars between nations and between groups within nations. Fear takes many forms. Fear of being attacked, of being invaded, of losing lives, territory, prestige, status, privileges or wealth. Some nations and tribes fear that their religion is under threat, others that their standard of living or their industries are being undermined by foreign competition. More physically and violently, there is fear of genocide, rape and wholesale destruction. Talk politics to people of any nationality, and in most cases fears will quickly surface. In our time, the wars involving Serbia, Croatia and Bosnia, with their volatile mixture of Orthodox, Roman Catholic and Islamic religions as well as complex political groupings, were provoked by *all* the fears I have referred to. And all these fears were sadly proved to have been justified.

However the most common, acute and pervasive fear among leaders and their people, is that of *not knowing*. This anxiety or fear can reach pathological proportions. Throughout history it has been important for every nation, every racial, ethnic, religious or political group and minority to know what is happening 'over the hill', that is, in spheres that affect their interest. 'Intelligence' came into being to fulfil this desperate need for reliable information. In the fifth century BC the Chinese sage Sun Tzu wrote the first handbook on war, *The Art of War*, and in it he says, 'Knowledge is the reason the enlightened prince and the wise general conquer the enemy wherever they move.'

The desire and demand for advance information is rooted in the most basic instinct of all – survival. Prophets, oracles and astrologers

1

were among the earliest sources of 'intelligence'. For ancient rulers, at whatever level of power, it made sense to consult these authorities because everybody understood that the gods knew ahead of time what was going to happen. The wise and holy men were perceived as having a direct contact with the gods, and thus they were men of great power and influence.

On occasions, a ruler went over the heads of soothsayers and took his intelligence concerns directly to the Lord. An anxious David (in the Book of Samuel) seeks military advice from Him: 'Shall I pursue after this troop?'

The Lord answers, 'Pursue, for thou shalt surely overtake them and without fail recover all.' David was victorious and no doubt pleased with his 'intelligence' coup.

When Moses was in the Wilderness with the Children of Israel in about 2,400 BC, the Lord instructed him to send a leader of each of the tribes 'to spy out the land of Canaan'. The overall commander of this mission was Joshua, the son of Nun, and his orders from Moses are set out in the Book of Numbers, Chapter 13: 'Go southward and up into the mountains and see the land and what it is.

- Whether the land be fat or lean;
- Whether there be wood thereon or not;
- Bring in samples of the fruit of the land;
- And the people that dwelleth therein, whether they be strong or weak;
- Whether they be few or many;
- What cities do they dwell in;
- Whether in tents or strongholds.'

This was a specific intelligence briefing and is the first reference in the Bible to spies. Differing reports from the spies led to discord, and among the people no consensus emerged about whether they should go on into Canaan. Many other differences and disputes have occurred in the centuries since Moses but few have been so widely aired as those which followed the spy mission to Canaan.

With such beginnings it can be said that intelligence is an ancient profession. It is conventional wisdom that prostitution is the oldest of all but some would argue that organised fighting or soldiering is the oldest. Leaving that argument aside, intelligence has been closely associated with both fighting and prostitution. A famous harlot,

Rahab of Jericho, was intimately associated with an early spying mission when Joshua sent two agents into the town. Her dangerous conspiratorial collaboration paid off for Rahab, for when Joshua captured Jericho and wiped out its populace Rahab and her family were the only people spared.

Translations of Sun Tzu's book were not available to rulers and generals of the ancient world. Had they been able to read his tome they would have been intrigued by his chapter, 'The Employment of Secret Agents'. Sun Tzu explains that agents are of five kinds: native, inside, double, expendable and living. Native and inside agents are the 20th century's 'agents in place'. A classic double agent is one operating for both sides at the same time, or pretending to do so. Expendable agents are those through whom false information is fed to the enemy, and in Sun's time they were 'expended' as literally – betrayed or abandoned to the enemy – as they sometimes are today. His 'living' agents are today's 'penetration agents', who get into the enemy's official departments and installations and return with intelligence. All these terms are much more fully explained in Chapter 2.

Hannibal, active in the third century BC, did not need a handbook on intelligence to tell him that he needed information about the military strength and placement of his enemies. But he went much further, almost to the point of 20th century requirements. He sought to know details of his enemies' economies, and civilian morale, and the speeches made by the important men opposing him. He and his generals closely studied these speeches to glean intelligence from them.

In one way, Mithridates of Pergamon in the first century BC eclipsed even Hannibal as a military leader. A consummate politician as well, he was master of 22 languages and he knew the local tribes and their customs far more thoroughly than his Roman enemies did. In my opinion, Mithridates was one of the most brilliant intelligence analysts of ancient times and this is why he was able to defeat the power of Rome in Asia Minor.

While leaders of the ancient world in the West practised espionage, they laid out no principles and rules as Sun Tzu did. They published no handbooks to which those who came after them could refer and supplement with their own ideas and experience. In contrast, Sun Tzu's fertile and devious mind set out the first outline for an organised intelligence service. He proffered advice on counter-intelligence, deception, security, disinformation and even psychological warfare.

3

I do not intend this book to cover the history of espionage/ intelligence/spying. It is essentially though not exclusively post–1945 in content. However, it is necessary for modern people interested in 'the great game' to realise that it was not the invention of the British Secret Service and then developed in modern times by the CIA. It did not begin in Czarist Russia, nor was it the scheming of Sir Francis Walsingham who brought it into being for the safety and power of Queen Elizabeth I. In its structured, academic and practical form and in its systematic practice it goes back to the genius of Sun Tzu, nearly 2,500 years ago.

It is not surprising that thousands of years of experience built upon Sun Tzu's system have made Chinese intelligence outstandingly successful. Its international ramifications and massive penetration today are ignored by the rest of the world at its peril. We need to know China's intentions – the intellectual equivalent of finding out what is on 'the other side of the hill'. This will be one of the massive intelligence tasks for many nations and groupings of nations in the 21st century.

②
THE LANGUAGE OF SPYING

It is much easier to understand the way the intelligence/espionage system works if one first understands the terms and definitions used by the people involved in the world of spying and security *against* spying. The language of espionage and its related activities is intriguing and many people involved in intrigues would prefer to keep the details of some of this language to themselves. Used in conjunction with the list of spying organisations in Chapter 3, this chapter is intended to make this book more informative and entertaining. Most espionage books give merely a 'glossary of terms' which stimulates more questions than it answers.

Given the devious nature of spying, it is not surprising that it has developed a language of its own. Agents use words, phrases and terms that are euphemisms often designed to cover a grim reality. One of the best examples is 'wet stuff' – for murder. Very few people in intelligence use the words 'murder' or 'assassination', though they are much less grisly than 'wet stuff', with its connotations of blood and mangled flesh. Not all the terms given here are in daily use. Some have become outmoded, only to be replaced by some equivalent phrase. A few will be familiar to avid readers of spying stories in newspapers and magazines.

Agent: Simply put, an agent is a person assigned to carry out a particular spying task. He/she is not a career staff member of an intelligence organisation, but somebody recruited by a staff officer to operate under cover in his own country. An agent is therefore a traitor. HR (Kim) Philby was a Soviet agent in Britain, Judith Coplon was a Soviet agent in the US and Alfred Frenzl, a German parliamentarian, was a Soviet agent in Germany. Oleg Penkovsky was an agent for Britain in the Soviet Union. A Briton sent to spy abroad is not, strictly speaking, an agent, though the term is sometimes incorrectly used to describe such a person.

Agent provocateur: An *agent provocateur* joins a subversive group and not only spies on it and reports to his controller, but also incites it to take the kind of action which will lead to the arrest of its members or at least badly damage the group's reputation. The *provocateur's* aim is to put out of action an organisation or an individual considered dangerous to his side. Whenever it is reported that an embassy official has been ordered out of a country it is fairly certain that he is the victim of an *agent provocateur*.

Black propaganda: The dissemination of information, true or false, which purports to come from sources other than the real ones. It can be very effective in moulding public opinion, as with forgeries of documents or papers which make them appear to have been produced by the enemy. During the First World War, British Intelligence produced the 'truth' about German atrocities in Belgium by publicising supposed German photographs and leaflets. In fact, they had been printed in Britain. In the Second World War, the Nazi chief of propaganda, Josef Goebbels, repeatedly quoted damaging statements purportly made by Prime Minister Churchill and President Roosevelt. They had never made these statements.

To be blown: To be unmasked as a spy – the ultimate horror for any spy. Even if not caught and punished, a spy who is blown is not much use to his employers, except perhaps as an instructor. In some countries a blown spy has a 'heart attack' (q.v.).

Careless leaks: This probably applies to the Americans more than to the agents of any other important nation. They tend to talk too much, perhaps because they like to impress people with their contacts and knowledge. A former Polish spy told me, 'America is a delightful country in which to carry out espionage. Much of the information that I gained there came to me just because I kept my ears open.'

Case officer: The career professional within the SIS or CIA or other intelligence organisation who directs or 'runs' an agent or agents on the job.

The Company: The term used by CIA employees for the CIA, though sometimes they are referring to the Office of Special Operations within the CIA.

Contrived leak: This usually refers to the intentional disclosure of information without its looking contrived. It is a way of supplying false or misleading information to an enemy. In more recent times a contrived leak has also come to mean the release of important information without the authority to do so. It is an appeal by disaffected subordinates, over the heads of superiors, to public opinion. Contrived leaks have occurred many times in the British Foreign Office and Ministry of Defence, and in the US Ministry of Defence and State Department. Some people regard it as treason, since the perpetrators are breaking the Official Secrets Act, or its equivalent elsewhere, which they had solemnly signed.

Counter-espionage: In the trade, this term refers to the penetration and manipulation of foreign espionage services, but in the popular mind it means finding and neutralising spies at work in the home country. To some extent I use this meaning in my book because of the popular perception. The true objective of counter-espionage is to control the enemy's espionage operations.

Counter-intelligence: This is really security to see that enemy agents – or unauthorised people even if they are not spies – do not have access to prohibited places and material. At its simplest level, counter-intelligence security means alarm systems, security passes and closed-circuit television surveillance. Then there is the security of communications, codes and ciphers, the various systems used to record incoming reports and the storage of classified materials. In order of importance, the classifications for documents and other materials are RESTRICTED, CONFIDENTIAL, SECRET and TOP SECRET. A top secret file will have on it the names of the small circle of people entitled to read it.

Counter-intelligence security staff are involved in a wide range of activities. At a low level, they check that wastepaper baskets are empty and that typewriter ribbons and carbon sheets have been locked away. Spies can glean valuable information from typewriter ribbons. Counter-intelligence staff sweep offices for bugs and they sometimes monitor telephone conversations for what are known as 'indiscretions', meaning careless talk. They are responsible for lie-detector tests and they make random unannounced surveillances or spot-checks of office staff. Senior staff in counter-intelligence write the security rules and they train staff, especially newer members, in security. In short, their duty is to prevent enemy agents from getting into the nation's security system. The CIA probably has the most stringent security rules but it can experience its disasters and none more critical in the 1990s than the damage done by Aldrich Ames and his wife, Soviet agents within the CIA.

Even among experienced, well-trained people accidents can happen. Take the case known to me of a senior person in a ministry of defence who, preoccupied with a marital problem, left a briefcase of TOP SECRET papers in his car, which he forgot to lock. The vehicle was in a much used public car park. Two hours later the official remembered what he had done, rushed back to the car and found the briefcase still there and apparently not tampered with. But he was well aware that he was doing the kind of job that would interest 'the other side', and he sometimes had a tail. The official was in a state of anguish. Had an enemy agent photographed the documents and cleverly left the brief-case and its contents so as to appear untouched? They *looked* all right. Should he report the matter to Security and make himself seem foolish and irresponsible? Or should he assume that all was well? He reported the matter – and just as well for himself because one of his own security staff had spotted the briefcase in the unlocked car and, having telephoned for back-up, was closely monitoring the situation to see what might happen. Had the official not reported the incident he would have been in deep trouble, even at his high rank. 'I was sorely tempted to hold my tongue', he told me after his retirement.

Courier: The courier, who collects reports and passes them on, takes no other part in the spying activities of his network, yet could compromise the entire network. He alone, besides the chief, knows the identities of most of the agents and of the chief himself. For counter-espionage agencies the enemy courier is the main target. The fax machine and computer have to some extent replaced the need for couriers, but the KGB still uses them a good deal. (See *Drops*.)

Cover role: A spy may pose as a journalist, a business executive, a travel agent, a commercial traveller, even as a shoe repairer. Some people get away with this deception for years.

Cut–out: The go-between is an intermediary whose job is to make contact between the network chief and an agent or other supplier of information. He is used to protect – or 'cut out' – the identity of agents so that they are known to only a tight circle of people. A cut-out is different from a courier in that he/she rarely carries written information, plans, photographs and so on. He passes his information by mouth, about a projected meeting perhaps.

Deception: As instructors tell their trainees, 'Our objective in deception is not to create entirely false pictures but to bring about shifts of emphasis that will cause an enemy to modify those of his policies affecting our interests.'

Sometimes the best deception is to provide the enemy with the truth. This apparent paradox makes good sense in application. In the mid-1960s the Soviet Union radically increased the range and intensity of its experiments in biological warfare just as Britain and the US were publicising an end to their experiments. Certainly, these governments had openly fully discontinued their experiments but they could reopen their facilities in two weeks. More than this, they revealed that they had the capacity to wipe out the entire population of Eastern Europe within a week. On top of all this, in a scientific emphasis to the deception, Western experts explained that the West would always be ahead: they had decades ago discovered what Soviet scientists were now finding out. This was entirely or almost entirely the truth, but it was a deception exercise. As a result, the Soviet Union, at the time, was reduced to a worldwide campaign in which it urged an end to biological warfare. The precise benefits to the West from all this was that the USA and Britain had forced a change in Soviet policies and at the same time had strengthened their own position by putting Soviets at a disadvantage. I assume that intelligence instructors use the episode as a classic example in attaining a deception objective.

Deep cover: An agent chosen for illegal work may be sent to live abroad for many years, in *deep cover*, as long as is needed to perfect his knowledge of the language and the way of life of another country. During this period he has no operational mission. When the agent is considered 'ripe' he usually returns to his own country for briefing on a mission, perhaps in the country he has just left, perhaps in another. It does not matter where he goes, for the objective has been attained: he no longer looks and speaks like an Englishman or a Russian or a German. 'Gordon Lonsdale' is a classic example. Actually a Russian, he posed for many years as a Canadian. The annals of British, German and Israeli Intelligence also provide some good examples.

Defector: A citizen of any country who transfers his allegiance to the enemy and thus commits treason; he actually leaves the country to which he owes his loyalty and takes up residence, almost always in hiding, in the country to which he has fled and for which he is going to work in future. It has been argued that by this definition Kim Philby was not a defector because by the time he disappeared from Beirut and flew to Moscow he had been working for the Soviet Union, in Britain and the US, for 30 years. He was thus a Soviet agent and a traitor but not by definition a defector. It is something of a semantic point.

Defector-in-place: In effect, another term for a penetration agent. It refers to a member of any government service who turns against his own country and works for one of its enemies but stays at his original job without suspicion. A defector-in-place is different from an ordinary defector in that he does not cut and run. One of the most significant defectors-in-place in modern times was Oleg Penkovsky. He supplied invaluable information to the CIA and SIS but was found out in 1962. It is not clear whether he was executed or committed suicide.

Diplomatic bag: The sealed pouch, bag or sack of mail that passes between an embassy or consulate and its Foreign Ministry. According to international protocol it cannot be opened by Customs or Police, even if they have reason to believe that it contains weapons. Much confidential information is enclosed in a diplomatic bag. On the whole, nations observe the inviolability of the diplomatic bag, but it has been tampered with on numerous occasions and some bags have 'disappeared' in transit. Miles Copeland, for many years a CIA officer, tells a story of respective CIA and KGB station chiefs who swapped their embassies' bags long enough to allow each to photocopy the contents of the other. Each man believed that his counterpart was acting independently of his HQ and that, therefore, the material in both bags was genuine. They established a reputation for acquiring valuable information, which each openly admitted had come from a breached diplomatic bag. Almost simultaneously, the KGB and the CIA realised that their men were colluding. The American officer was fired without a pension; the Russian vanished without trace.

Dirty tricks: A wide-ranging term to cover the use of methods such as wire taps, bugs, anonymous incriminating letters and the discrediting of a person of high character if he happens to be 'obstructive'. The most extreme dirty trick is murder. It is astonishing how an intelligence agency, even one that considers it has high principles, will justify dirty tricks, even those which call for murdering enemies.

Disinformation: The creation and distribution of what purport to be official documents of an enemy country. Even after the end of the Cold War, Russia kept its disinformation department working. It once produced and cleverly released a document that was supposed to be part of a British cabinet paper. It wholly misrepresented the British (and US) attitude towards trade union policies in Black America and it was designed to cause trouble between the two powers and the Africans. It succeeded.

A KGB training manual states: 'Disinformation is essential in the execution of State tasks and is directed at misleading the enemy concerning the basic questions of State policy; the military-economic status and the scientific-technical achievement of the Soviet Union; the policy of certain imperialist states with respect to each other and to other countries; as well as the specific counter-intelligence tasks of the organs of State Security'.*

Double Agent: A person serving two intelligence services. He/she appears to work for the service of origin but is *doubled* so that he is actually working for an enemy intelligence service. Most double agents are not career or staff officers, but agents in line with the definition given in this book. Philby, Burgess, Maclean, Prime and others were *not* double agents. Both the SIS and OSS recruited agents, trained them and then infiltrated them into Nazi Germany and Fascist Italy,

---

* Cited by the Deputy Director of the CIA in his report, *CIA Study Soviet Covert Action and Propaganda*, presented to the Oversight Committee of the Permanent Select Committee on Intelligence, House of Representatives, 6 February 1986. Author's query: could the CIA report itself be disinformation?

or the occupied countries, where they cleverly persuaded the enemy to employ them as agents and send them back to Allied territory to spy. Through these double agents Allied commanders often discovered enemy intentions and military dispositions.

Drop, also known as Dead Drop: A 'drop' is the leaving of a secret letter or package by an agent in a place where a courier can retrieve it. It is 'dead' because nobody knows about it other than the courier and except in the case of a brush-drop (see below) he does not see the agent. In short, the dead drop is the secure passing over of information – though it is sometimes anything but secure. The term 'dead drop' is frequently used in intelligence terminology.* Of the various types of dead drops, four are most important. They are the city drop, the country drop, the moving drop and the brush drop.

The *city drop* is probably the most frequently used and its advantage is that it is convenient for the agent who leaves the information and the courier who collects it. Another advantage is that a drop in a public place, carried out with skill, is less likely to be observed than a country drop. An envelope, packet or film can be placed under a specified seat in a cinema, behind a mirror in a public toilet, in a library book that is most unlikely to be taken out, in the cistern above the toilet bowl, in a lavatory or in a garbage bin in a public park. The assumption is that the material will be retrieved quickly, but delays can occur. An agent working for the SIS in Amsterdam arranged to collect a thin envelope under a cinema seat occupied by a man who sat through an entire day's showing of pornographic films. After an uncomfortable eight hours he managed to collect the material.

The *country drop* is time-consuming for the agent, who might have to invent an excuse for being absent for some hours. The courier might also find it inconvenient to travel to some distant place. However, a country drop is generally safe since there are thousands of places where the package might be left – in trees, under stones, in derelict buildings, for instance. A large number of searchers would be

---

*Frank Bossard, the British traitor working for the Soviet Union in London in the early 1960s used nine drops with one in reserve designated A to C, E to I and K. He was informed which drop to visit by coded signals broadcast by Moscow Radio at 7.45 am and 8.30 pm on the first Tuesday and Wednesday in each month. Bossard, an MoD scientist, sold to the Russians most of Britain's guided missiles secrets.

required by a security service that suspected a certain person of being an agent operating a country drop. Most discoveries are made not by searches but by tailing the suspect, not an easy task in the country when the agent is experienced.

The *moving drop* is generally secure in that agent and courier are well separated in time and distance and are unlikely to be picked up together, as sometimes happens in city and country drops. A moving drop might be in the toilet of a train or aircraft. Though tiny, an aircraft toilet has many places for hiding secret packets. An agent for the Soviet Union in the USA used to drop his material from a low-flying helicopter whilst ostensibly taking people up for joy rides. The courier would be waiting at the drop zone. The packets were weighted, so that they would drop straight and true and this caused an accident which led to the operations being uncovered: a cylindrical packet knocked out the courier's eye and he was found in great distress by some passing walkers, who also picked up the cylinder. The episode was so odd that they reported it to the police. Most dead drops are discovered through some mishap.

The *brush drop* is favoured by experienced professionals as virtually foolproof even though it is based on the two people concerned, agent and courier, being able to see each other. The brush drop is often carried out as a straight swop, such as the exchange of shopping trolleys in a supermarket or the tactic of swapping identical briefcases in a toilet or at a table that is so popular in spy films. The packet may simply be handed over in a crowd of people packing into a subway or underground. The brush can be open, with an agent tapping his courier on the arm and saying, 'Excuse me, but I saw you drop this', as he hands over a shopping parcel.

There is yet another way of dead-letter dropping that can be carried out by cool, practised agents and couriers. At one time MI5 had under casual surveillance a man suspected of being an agent for the Bulgarian Government, but the watchers saw no suspicious people arrive at his home. Indeed, for an entire week nobody turned up there. By now there were other good reasons to believe that the man was an agent so a team sat down to discuss him and his lifestyle. A sharp-witted older woman controller said to her observers, 'Do you really mean that nobody – nobody – visited the house in a week? What about the postman?'

13

Yes, the postman arrived daily, the observers admitted sheepishly. He was now closely watched through binoculars and his movements were filmed. Twice he rang the bell to deliver a package requiring a signature but this in itself was not suspicious. The postman was also filmed pushing letters through the letterbox in the front door. The watchers, by freezing the film, noticed that sometimes as he put a letter *in* he appeared to draw something *out*, concealed in the palm of his hand. They went back to the film showing a registered delivery; this time enlargement revealed the suspect agent was slipping something into the receipt pad that the postman held out to him. MI5 and Special Branch took no immediate action. If the postman was collecting from one agent he could be the courier for others so he was systematically watched for weeks. No further suspicions were aroused and as it was becoming urgent to stop the agent's activities Special Branch moved in and agent and courier were arrested. The postman was indeed engaged in espionage.

People who visit houses, office premises and shops on a regular basis are generally not suspected of being couriers. A milkman is, well, just a milkman, and a garbage collector is just a garbage collector. One of the best covers for a courier is that of a collector for a charity or a meter reader for an electrical supply company, since he has legitimate reason for entering a house. A computer repair technician is a good cover role because such a person may legitimately stay for hours on a 'difficult job'.

It might be wondered why agents and other people involved in espionage do not more frequently use the normal postal service. The answer is that the mail is often used, especially in the democratic West where security agencies are legally required to have really strong evidence to intercept and open a suspect's letters before they may request permission from the government – in Britain's case the Home Secretary – to do so.

Many intelligence services still distrust the mail for sending secret material, and with good reason. Counter-espionage agents, in Britain as in every other country, do intercept and open mail in what are regarded as important cases without asking for authority from above. A letter can be withdrawn from its envelope without either cutting it open or unsealing the flap, read and copied and then returned to its envelope. Only a very experienced agent would spot that his letter had been tampered with.

Properly used, letters and postcards are secure for the agent at least, because of the large number of postboxes. Only in a country such as Libya, where practically every student is a spy for Gaddafi, could a watch be kept on every mailing point.

Many an agent is supplied with a quantity of ordinary postcards and when he needs to make contact with his controller (or principal) he selects an appropriate prewritten postcard and drops it into a mailbox. He will do this to send a standard message, perhaps to make an appointment, to give a warning – perhaps that he is under surveillance – to inform his controller that he wishes to return to base or to say that he needs money. His controller responds in the same prearranged way, not necessarily with a postcard but with one of the large and varied collection of advertising leaflets he keeps for just this purpose. A leaflet urging the receiver to take out life insurance could mean that the message has been received but the answer is no. Another leaflet might mean 'message received, make no further operational move until further notice'. Some very important information can be sent on a postcard simply because a postcard looks so innocent.

The Emily*: An exclusively CIA term. It describes a person who is spotted by a KGB recruiter who, though an American citizen, is spying for the Soviet Union. He recognises that somebody he meets has potential as a KGB spy and then conditions, 'pre-recruits' (q.v.) him, and trains him.

There was a genuine Emily, though this is not her real name. As personal assistant to the Assistant Secretary of State in the 1950s she had access to the secrets of a bureau dealing with the Third World. A Soviet agent, posing as an insurance salesman and who was an American citizen, painstakingly, cleverly and patiently cultivated Emily and she served Soviet intelligence for 14 years.

---

* The terms 'Emily', 'Mickey' (q.v.) and 'Philby' were coined by the late Miles Copeland, a senior CIA and MI5 officer, who personally knew the people to whom he applied the labels. Copeland, who claimed to be the CIA's 'first political operative', wrote copiously about intelligence and espionage; his former employers were sometimes startled by what he revealed in his books. I met Copeland from time to time and found him to be one of the few intelligence professionals with a sense of humour and a taste for fun. He irritated some of his colleagues but they could not long sustain their irritation against Copeland's ever youthful charm. He died in 1993, aged 78. I have drawn on Copeland's professional recollections in his own two books on espionage. See Bibliography.

Espionology: This term, new to the language of espionage, was coined by GJA O' Toole in order, as he says, 'to fill a vacuum.' He was alarmed by use of the word 'intelligencer' and he anticipated the even worse 'intelligenceology'. O' Toole was a former Chief of the CIA's Problem Analysis Branch. In 1988 he published the *Encyclopedia of American Intelligence and Espionage*, in which he uses not only espionology but espionologist and espionological. I hope that the terms catch on.

False-flagging: Recruiting a new agent by telling him that he will be working, say, for NATO when in fact he will be operating for Israel. I select this example because Mossad is clever with its false-flagging techniques. Some of its best agents have been Arabs false-flagged to believe that they were being paid by some other country or alliance. If the CIA recruited an agent within the British SIS – which heaven forbid! – it would have to convince him that the Canadian Government was paying him. In this way, and if the operation were smoothly run, the CIA need never come under suspicion. Sometimes a front company is used to give a new agent the impression that he is carrying out some relatively unimportant industrial espionage task. False-flagging is so commonplace that I must conclude that the world is full of gullible people.

The 'Family Jewels': A CIA term given to a list of about 700 CIA activities considered illegal or questionable, following a top-level review in 1973. Among these activities were covert operations to assassinate foreign leaders considered inimical to US interests, such as Fidel Castro of Cuba. Castro survived numerous plots to kill him. A really sinister 'family jewel' activity was the testing of drugs, hypnotism and various methods of applying psychological pressure in covert operations. People were given drugs without their knowledge and one CIA officer is known to have died from an LSD overdose. One objective of this programme, known as MK/ULTRA, was to find ways of reducing the ability of 'enemies' to function adequately. Following press exposure, many of the listed activities were banned, but the term 'family jewel' still exists among CIA personnel. Probably very few outsiders have seen a complete inventory of these 'jewels'.

Giveway information: The term for leaks officially, but not publicly approved. They are a form of misinformation (q.v.).

Heart Attack: A traitor discovered within an intelligence organisation or in an important post in government, may become an awkward embarrassment. At high level and in critical circumstances the decision could be taken that he should have a 'heart attack', and die. In the Soviet Union and countries of the former Eastern Bloc such a person would 'disappear' or be shot. 'Heart attacks' are rare but I personally know of two, both Americans. One case involved a senior member of a key unit which provided intelligence summaries for the President of the United States himself and he knew as much as it is possible for one officer to know. Sometimes, within the CIA at least, a person who is disposed of is said to have 'died of the measles'.

Honorary members: Businessmen, academics and others who can be induced to keep their eyes open when abroad. In their enthusiasm some of these amateurs, such as the British businessman Greville Wynne, find themselves in serious trouble. Others produce information so valuable that it delights their controllers at home.

Human library: A CIA term for its hideaway where defectors are both protected and interrogated. It was in the Allegheny Mountains for many years but is now believed to be in the Adirondack Mountains.

Humint: Human intelligence resulting from espionage and the efforts of individuals.

Lie-detector tests: These should never be regarded, in the intelligence world, as 'invasions of privacy'. When they were first introduced in Western agencies, including the CIA and some SIS offices, they flushed out many obvious security risks including people who then admitted to having passed secret information to journalists, politicians, lobbyists and, in a few cases, to foreign armaments dealers manipulating their way into government contracts. At the time, in the 1960s, these revelations caused great alarm and urgent steps had to be taken to plug the leaks and potential further breaches of security.

Mickey: (The) CIA term for the walk-in spy who, because of special knowledge and experience, is able to get in touch with a foreign intelligence agency and offer his services without being spotted by counter-intelligence controls.

Microdot: The development of the microdot in the 1960s gave espionage a new lease of life and made spies feel much safer. It was simply a matter of photographing objects, plans and papers on small negatives using, among other cameras, the Minox. The equipment to make a microdot is small and readily concealed while the dot itself is so small that it can be used to dot an 'i' or placed under a postage stamp. Probably thousands of microdots, carrying much information, have passed undetected to an intelligence HQ. However there can be slip-ups. A principal sent information to an agent using a dot under an altogether too attractive stamp. An acquisitive Cairo postal clerk steamed it off to steal it and exposed the dot, which he reported to the police. As a result an Israeli agent was caught.

Misinformation: This is different from disinformation. Spies subtly feed false information to enemy spies. Frequently this concerns military strengths or weakness. At times it pays a country to exaggerate its own strength while on other occasions it is better to give an impression of weakness. Some of the great intelligence spy coups, described later, have been masterpieces of misinformation.

Need to know: Intelligence organisations operate on the basis that *nobody* needs to know *everything*. This is a useful security check, though when strictly applied it can lead to duplication of effort and to dangerous confusion. Within the organisation, information is distributed on a 'need to know' basis and the phrase crops up frequently. There have been cases where the need to know principle has been so narrowly applied that key players in a particular operation have been left off the list of those supplied with specific information – with damaging results.

NOC: CIA term for non-official cover. Instead of posing as a diplomat, an operative pretends to be a businessman.

The one-time pad: The one unbreakable code, using a whole new code for each message each time the spy sends his reports. It is repetition that betrays a code or cipher, but with the one-time pad there is no repetition.

Paper mill: A derogatory term referring to the documents produced by 'confidential sources' but which are actually dressed-up rumours disseminated by groups trying to impress a government intelligence service with the quality of their information. Most of it is worthless and wastes valuable time. Every intelligence service in the West is plagued by organisations and groups sending in gratuitous 'intelligence reports'. The groups themselves sometimes interest French, British, American and German intelligence because they are easily penetrated and exploited by agents operating in Russian, Chinese, Arab and Islamic interest. About 25 anti-Saddam Hussein groups are assiduous producers of 'confidential' information – and this in Britain alone.

Penetration: The process of getting an agent into a target and, it is hoped, keeping him there. In popular language this agent is a 'plant' or 'mole'. Kim Philby remains the most infamous mole and one of the most successful.

The Philby: This MI5 and CIA term came into use to describe the long-term agent, recruited in his youth, who at the time of his recruitment was outside his assigned target and took years working into it – as Kim Philby did.

Photint: Intelligence gleaned from the study of photographs, some of them taken from outer space. In the US the National Photographic Intelligence Centre (NPIC) is responsible for photint.

Pieces: A piece is an item of information which, although seemingly unimportant in itself, makes some other piece of information clear. The whereabouts of a particular person at a critical time is a 'piece'. In truth, the fabric of many a large operation is put together from 'pieces' by clever and patient men and women in offices.

Prerecruitment development: Bluntly put, this jargon means softening up a person who has been identified as a potential spy. Frankly, 'softening up' means weakening somebody's resistance to being recruited, by blandishment and praise, gifts and privileges. An officer of the intelligence service working in a foreign country, having spotted a likely recruit, will go to immense lengths of 'prerecruitment development,' perhaps lasting a year or more.

Radint: Radar intelligence.

Resident Director: The KGB term for the chief of a network. For safety, he/she usually has his base in the country bordering the target country.

RPV: Remotely piloted vehicle. The 'vehicle' is actually a remotely controlled small aircraft fitted with cameras and sensors. Its control centre is close behind the battlefront – or border – and though it has a limited range it produces remarkable intelligence results. Popularly known as 'the spy in the sky', the RPV proved its worth when the Israeli Defence Force used it during Operation GALILEE in 1982. Palestinian terrorists had been attacking settlements in Northern Israel for years, using Lebanon as their base. Israel's forces crossed the border and began an offensive not only against the Palestine Liberation Organisation and its many branches, but also against their Syrian backers – Operation GALILEE. Without RPV intelligence Israel would have been at a great disadvantage.

Secret writing: Invisible or secret writing is not obsolete or even old-fashioned, but very much in use and simple in practice. Probably every intelligence service in the world uses it. The sender of a secret message first writes or types an entirely innocent communication, such as a family letter, a business report, a complaint or anything else that seems normal. Dipping a dry ballpoint pen into a colourless ink, he then writes his secret message between the lines of the cover letter, which has itself been chemically treated. The agent steam irons the sheet to smooth away any letterstrokes. He mails the letter to the arranged address, usually at a place receiving thousands of mail items a day. The recipient reads the secret message by heating it or soaking it in a special chemical. Consider the difficulties for security agents if they suspect that a certain person is engaged in espionage. They must seize a suspect letter within seconds before it is swallowed up by the postal system. They do not know what they are looking for and they can hardly go through thousands of letters for a 'suspicious' envelope. There is a million to one chance that they will find the letter, but then they must use the correct chemical agent to bring out the hidden writing. One mistake and they have destroyed the secret message. Occasionally an agent has been caught whilst in the process of bringing the message to light, but this is another chance in a million. To test the efficacy of a simple form of secret writing, use lemon or onion juice in the way that you would use ink. It will vanish when dry, only to reappear when the sheet is heated. But it is a long time since spies used lemon or onion juice!

Specialist chemists employed by the Nazis' espionage machine produced a secret ink 'enhancer' in the form of a white tablet looking like an aspirin. The agent dropped it into the ordinary ink with which he wrote his message, which became invisible. The ink solution would 'take' even on newsprint, which was much less suspect than ordinary writing paper. The secret writing could only be brought to light by a process the Allies did not discover until after the war. Agents kept their tablets in a medicinal bottle, thus disarming suspicion.

Sheepdipping: A strange American term connected with a spy's cover. It applies to any member of the armed forces whose expertise is needed in a covert operation of great importance. As he cannot operate under his military rank of, say, colonel, he is 'sheepdipped'. That is, he ostensibly resigns and is given a completely new civil existence, so that should he be caught the enemy intelligence service could not prove that he is really an army officer. The object of this transformation by 'sheepdipping' is to save the government from any embarrassment. The officer's records are secretly kept up to date.

Sigint: Signals intelligence plucked from radio and satellite transmission.

The Sleeper: The agent sent into a country to lie low until it becomes necessary to activate him, perhaps 20 years later. This is similar to deep cover with the exception that the sleeper will, when 'awakened', operate in the country where he has been sleeping.

Smears: Actions and reports calculated to damage the reputation and credibility of prominent people, organisations and governments. The Soviet Union directs much of its smearing activities against Britain but the US and France have frequently been targeted as well as West Germany (before unification). Russia continues to engage in smearing. Planted reports of traitors in high places, especially in enemy intelligence services, is a form of smearing. It is easily done through journalists, who are always eager to find such a story. They might use the cautious phraseology 'It is alleged that a senior official of MI5 (or the CIA) is a Russian mole', but the damage and alarm can still be considerable. It has been known for the Russians to insert a bogus defector with the sole object of smearing an influential and therefore potentially dangerous opponent of the Soviet regime.

Snatch: (1) The generally illegal arrest of a suspect within an intelligence organisation. (2) The pickup of an agent or spy.

Counter-espionage/security officers go to great lengths to achieve a snatch with minimum fuss and publicity. Between two and four in the morning is the best period, depending on the time of sunrise. The neighbours will be asleep and the suspect in his deepest slumber. The arresting officers do not crash through doors and windows, but operate with stealth and professional expertise.

Sneakies: Technical and scientific devices planted inside a target, such as chemically treated handkerchiefs which pick up factory gasses for later analysis. Miniscule microphone bugs are 'sneakies' – or sometimes 'bugs'.

A Snow-Job: The production of vast amounts of confusing printed reports, and unloading them onto an enemy by devious means. This is done in order to blind or distract the enemy and cause him to use large amounts of manpower to sift the documents.

Static targets: Targets that are always there, such as great industrial concerns.

Station: The place or point at which the report or papers passed by an agent stop after delivery and before they are collected.

Stringer: An intelligence term for a casually employed agent, ready to do odd jobs for a fee, such as acting as a cut-out or a decoy. The term 'stringer' is also used to refer to a reporter paid by the job.

Surveillance: Keeping a spy, supposed spy or other suspect under observation, or even watching a building or some other site. In spy films one or two watchers are generally seen, but serious surveillance of a major target for 24 hours a day, seven days a week can occupy more than 100 observers. This requires a controller of considerable experience. Even a veteran is sometimes faced with a professional dilemma: 'Is it more important not to lose the suspect or not to let him twig that he is being followed?' Many factors come into play here, but in most cases the controller will abort the surveillance if he is certain that to continue it will alarm the suspect. After all, once the chase is resumed he may lead his observers to other members of a ring.

Swallow: The term given to the beautiful women used by the KGB and other Soviet and Russian intelligence organisations to seduce and compromise men from 'enemy' countries who have access to valuable information. Swallows are thoroughly trained for their job. According to one source they are 'callously perverted' so that they have neither shame nor scruple by the time they are called upon to serve the state. Apparently, Russian men sent to seduce Western women in high authority are called 'ravens', but this cannot be confirmed. 'Romeos' would be a better term.

Tradecraft: An American term for the skills of a covert operator whether they be surveillance, lockpicking or computer hacking. It was used briefly in MI5 but did not catch on. The British talk about expertise and professional skills.

Trade missions: A rather cynical term in the intelligence community. The government sometimes arranges a trade mission when an intelligence service wants to insert an agent to collect secret information. Among the members of any large trade mission, of whatever nationality, there will certainly be at least one intelligence agent.

The transfer: Passing of secret documents from one agent to another.

Transmission security check: A secret code that an agent works into his message to assure the receiver that it is genuine and not being sent by somebody with a pistol to the spy's head. Some security checks are simple, such as the deliberate misspelling of the fifth word. An elaborate security check for a message in code might be some reference to the agent which could only be known by the person receiving it. Since counter-espionage agents might at any time capture a spy, some organisations give their people a fake security check. A captured agent 'reluctantly' reveals this to his captors who then order him to use it. Obviously, the receiver at home base on seeing this fake check would suspect the authenticity of the message.

U–2: Code for Utility 2, the American secret spy plane made famous in 1960 when one was shot down by the Soviets.

Vetting: The collection and study of all available information on a person. Some will be public records from the Registry of Births, Deaths and Marriages; some will come from credit agencies, banks and schools. Potential officers who will have access to classified material are put through 'positive vetting' (the British term) or 'full security investigation' (US). In the case of MI5, vetting is carried out by a staff of about 20 officers and the process of vetting just one person takes up to three months. Even then some 'subversives' still slip through the net.

Walk-in: The standard British and American term for a person who approaches an embassy in person and offers to spy for the country represented by the embassy. In recent years the expression has also covered people who telephone, write or otherwise volunteer their services. Maureen Bingham (see pages 59–61) was a classic foolish walk-in. Walk-ins are initially suspect and are given the most rigorous vetting, but many turn out to be excellent agents.

The Willie: A Willie is an agent who does not know that he is an agent. This ignorance may seem to be unlikely, even impossible, but Willies abound in the West and proliferate in Third World countries. Agents who recruit Willies have jobs in an 'advantageous environment', to quote a phrase I have come across in a briefing for agents. This job could be in a private company dealing with electronics, defence equipment or public relations, or even on a newspaper's staff as an investigator for a popular columnist. These agents rarely have access to secret information and they do not seek it. Their mission is to recruit Willies. A desirable Willie is a man or woman with highly developed morality and idealism: such a person is likely to be one who protests about real or perceived injustices. A Willie whose career is known to me worked in the Procurement Department of the British Ministry of Defence and he became indignant about vast sums of money being, he believed, wastefully and corruptly used. He passed on his disquiet to a journalist who was an enemy agent. The journalist sympathised with the employee and encouraged him to report any other incident of 'corruption, inefficiency or wastefulness'. In this way the British Government employee, who would never have voluntarily worked for a foreign power, became a Willie. He was a fruitful source for Warsaw Pact countries. Sometimes the journalist filed a story based on his new friend's information, just enough to keep him happy that he was doing what his conscience demanded.

Sometimes a Willie suspects, in time, that something is amiss; he may even realise that he has been duped. However his idealism does not extend so far as to report himself to his superiors. So he continues with what is now espionage.

Naive Willies exist in their thousands in Third World countries and are easily recruited in exchange for payment of 'expenses'. They think they are providing information for the World Health Organisation, for

UNESCO, for the World Bank, for various religious groups, political parties, even for credit investigators. All the Western nations with political/economic/military interests in the Third World, such as arms sales, use Willies.

In the West, Willies are sometimes discovered but to the best of my knowledge they do not suffer 'heart attacks'. This is because they are seen as unwitting accomplices or innocent victims. However, they are invariably quietly moved sideways in the department in which they worked or they are persuaded to take early retirement.

The difference between a Willie and a false-flag recruit is largely a matter of degree. False-flagging involves much more serious, dangerous and deadly espionage. False-flag recruits are rare, Willies are numerous.

3

THE SPY ORGANISATIONS

Abwehr: Formerly the *Nachrichtendienst*. The German Army Intelligence service, pre-1939 and during the Second World War.

Aman: Israel's Defence Forces Intelligence Branch, responsible in particular for Middle East information of a military and military-economic nature; that is, what armaments the neighbouring countries are acquiring.

ASIO: Australian Security Intelligence organisation. Established in 1949, ASIO is modelled on the British MI5 and was organised with help from MI5 officers. It has a staff of 750.

ASIS: Australian Secret Intelligence Service. This is Australia's foreign intelligence service and is similar in its functions and operations to the British SIS.

BND: Germany's *Bundesnachrichtendienst* (Federal Intelligence Service). With a large staff and massively funded, BND collects information on international developments.

CIA: The US Central Intelligence Agency, the hub of the entire American secret service network. It co-ordinates the intelligence activities of several government departments and agencies in the interest of national security. Its headquarters are at Langley, Virginia. About 12,000 people work in this vast building, and with branches within the US and overseas employees the staff numbers something like 18,000. The number of sub-agents, 'informants' and full-time foreign agents is unobtainable but must run to thousands. Relatively new to intelligence – it was founded in 1947 – the CIA has a mystique comparable to that of the KGB, but less than the British SIS. Its successive chiefs have gone to much trouble to insist that the CIA is not an underground organisation and in a sense it is not. On its establishment, CIA headquarters carried the sign 'Government Printing Office', but the first director, Allen Dulles, realised that this so-called secrecy was futile when he saw Washington sight-seeing bus drivers stopping outside the front gate while the courier explained that this was the most secret and most concealed place in Washington: 'This is where the spies hang out,' they said.

CIAAD: The CIA Administration Directorate, responsible for an array of activities including training, security, supply and finance.

CIAOD: The CIA's Operations Directorate. This innocuous label covers the organisation's 'clandestine' services. Some American intelligence experts refer directly to 'The Clandestine Service'. Its duties include counter-intelligence and covert action..

CIS: Commonwealth of Independent States (formerly of the Soviet Union).

DIA: The United States' Defense Intelligence Agency. This intelligence outfit concentrates on military intelligence relating to foreign countries' activities within the US and abroad. It is responsible for co-ordinating defence intelligence (provided that the other intelligence agencies co-operate). DIA answers to the Joint Chiefs of Staff.

Deuxième Bureau: The organisation responsible for analysing intelligence for the French government. It was once much more active in the field but it was controlled by the traitor Vichy government after 1942 and lost its reputation. Many fiction writers refer to the Deuxième Bureau as if it still exists in its own form. It is actually the intelligence division of the French General Staff.

DGSE: France's *Direction Générale de la Sécurité Extérieur* concentrates on terrorism, human intelligence (HUMINT) and economic intelligence.

Directorate K: Russian Federal Counter-Intelligence Service, an FBI-equivalent with a staff of 75,000, in charge of internal security.

DPSD: France's *Direction du Protection et de la Sécurité de la Defénse.* Military intelligence organisation.

DST: France's *Direction Pour surveillance de la Territoire*. Counter-espionage, counter-intelligence, general high-level surveillance. (Formerly known as the *Deuxième Bureau*.)

FBI: Federal Bureau of Investigation. The detective service of the Department of Justice, the FBI was established in 1908 to investigate violations of US law. It operates over the entire United States. Soon after the beginning of the Second World War President Roosevelt gave the FBI a counter-espionage role, making it comparable to MI5. Its officers have played prominent parts in every major espionage case since 1945. The FBI is roughly similar in function to MI5 except that, unlike MI5, it can make arrests.

FCIB: Soviet Federal Counter-Intelligence Branch. 'Branch' might seem an inappropriate word for an organisation with a staff of 150,000. Counter-intelligence, secret police, border watch.

GCHQ: Britain's Government Communication Headquarters. With a staff of 6,000 (to be reduced to 5,000 by the turn of the century). GCHQ is a listening post of massive proportions. It monitors, decodes (and encodes) radio, fax and telex communications in and out of Britain, in nearly every language, 24 hours a day. GCHQ has a virtual monopoly in Britain in sigint (q.v.). The great complex of GCHQ is a security nightmare and it has been penetrated (see pages 61–65).

GRU: for *Glavnoye Razvedyvatelnoye Upravlenie* or Chief Intelligence Directorate of the General Staff. The GRU is the intelligence arm of the Russian (or Red) Army. In Russia the initials would be pronounced 'Geh Eh Ru', but unlike the initials KGB, which are widely known in Russia, those of the GRU are not because until recently its existence was not officially admitted. During its existence the GRU was known by many other names.

ILD: China's International Liaison Department. It is heavily engaged in covert activities.

INR: The US Bureau of Intelligence and Research. This important bureau is part of the State Department, producing and disseminating intelligence within the many sections of the State Department. One of its critical roles is to help in arranging cover for CIA personnel overseas, though INR has no offices of its own overseas.

KGB: *Komitet Gosuddarstvennoi Bezoopasnnosti.* Russians pronounce its initials as 'Kah Gay Beh'. The KGB was an espionage giant and by some estimates, totally uncheckable, its staff numbered 300,000 to 500,000 at the height of the Cold War. With 20 separate directorates it was undoubtedly the most ruthless espionage organisation ever to exist. As the Soviet Union fell apart in the I990s, so the KGB disintegrated and, says the Russian Government, by 1992 intelligence staff working abroad had been cut by 50 per cent. Certainly the public face of the KGB has changed. Consider, for instance, that a former head of the CIA, Bob Gates, travelled to Moscow to talk in a friendly way with his former enemies. Stella Rimington, head of MI5, also visited KGB headquarters, an amazing event in the intelligence world. It is more correct now to refer to the *former* KGB. Much of its work is now done by the SVR (q.v.).

MBRF: The Russian initials for the Federal Agency for Government Communications and Information. This is another part of the old KGB and is the equivalent of the Americans' NSA.

MGB: The (Soviet) *Ministerstvo Gosudarstvennoy Bezopasnosti,* or Ministry of State Security. The MGB is also known as the FSB, which in Russian stands for Federal Security Service.

MI5: Britain's security Service. An organisation of many branches, MI5 works predominantly on internal security by engaging in counter-espi-

---

* Daniel Defoe, author of *Robinson Crusoe,* was the father of the British Security Service (now MI5) and to a lesser extent of the Secret Intelligence Service (now MI6). It is extraordinary that so little attention has been given to him in his spy role. In 1704, Defoe put forward to Lord Harley, Queen Anne's First Minister, an intelligence scheme to cover the whole of Britain. A natural spy, Defoe built up an amazing network of agents and taught them by methods which are still used all over the world. While travelling around England to set up his network, Defoe's cover was that of merchant or travelling salesman. This is still a good cover. But he changed his story as circumstances dictated, so that when he was in Scotland talking to ministers he told them he was the publisher of a new version of the Psalms. Until Lord Harley was dismissed in 1714, Defoe kept up a stream of intelligence about genuine and perceived enemies of the Crown within Britain and abroad, about 'subversives' (as we would call them today), about people with political aspirations and about the wealthy. Under Harley's successor, Lord Townshend, Defoe secretly gained control of newspapers inimical to the government. He was active for another six years, but he never received adequate reward or recognition for his work. So what's new, cynics at SIS would ask today.

onage and counter-intelligence. It monitors real or perceived 'subversives' including foreign nationals. MI5 is known as the 'Box' in intelligence circles, but the box has been penetrated on several occasions.*

MI6 *or* **SIS** (They are one and the same) Britain's Secret Intelligence Service. SIS recruits agents, engages in counter-intelligence and is responsible for clandestine operations. Its brief also makes it responsible for 'intelligence collection', meaning in this case espionage. Strictly speaking, MI6 means Military Intelligence Department Six, but SIS is the more common form. Not all of MI6's activities are military.

MoD: British Ministry of Defence. Formed in the 1960s through an amalgamation of the old Ministry of Defence, the Admiralty, the War Department and the Air Ministry.

Mossad: Israeli Central Institute for Intelligence and Special Duties. This wide-ranging organisation engages in covert action, counterterrorism and more especially in the acquisition of human intelligence (Humint). In the defence of Israel, it conducts intelligence programmes against Arab nations and organisations.

NCNA: New China News Agency. One of the most successful disinformation organisations and probably China's most professional espionage section.

NIO: The United States' National Imagery Office, a title which reflects its concentration on co-ordinating all US satellite intelligence activities. It is the most security-conscious of all American intelligence bodies.

NSA: The United States' National Security Agency. Dealing with Sigint (signals intelligence) and satellite intelligence, NSA is regarded as more productive for the size of its staff than the CIA itself. It has the best American experts in cryptography. The NSA gets much less publicity than the CIA. The NSA *should* be more productive – it has a larger staff, a matter that irritates CIA chiefs.

PFLP-GC: Popular Front for the Liberation of Palestine – General Command. Commanded by Ahmed Jibril, PFLP-GC has been responsible for some of the world's worst terrorist outrages and was implicated in the Lockerbie disaster.

PLO: Palestine Liberation Organisation. The umbrella organisation for most Palestinian terrorist/resistance groups; they numbered 21 at one time. Led by its Chairman, Yasser Arafat, the PLO has apparently become more 'respectable' since the accord between it and Israel.

SB: Special Branch (of Scotland Yard). MI5 officers have no powers of arrest, so after they have done their work in tracking a spy within Britain they hand over to Special Branch, with which they have probably been working since the beginning of a case. Special Branch carries out the arrests and prepares the case for court. In this way the identity of the MI5 officers is concealed.

The US also has a Special Branch. It is a unit within the Military Intelligence Service and it has functions quite unlike those of British Special Branch. During World War II it was closely involved with communications intelligence.

SHABEK (known as Shin-Bet): Israel's General Security Services, responsible for internal security and counter-espionage. Shin-Bet lost much of its reputation following the assassination of Prime Minister Yitzak Rabin in November 1995.

SMERSH: Many people are surprised when told that there really is – or was – a SMERSH and that it was not invented for television series *The Man from Uncle* or for 'James Bond'. SMERSH is derived from the Russian words *Smert Shpionen* or 'death to spies'. In the 1960s its name was changed to CUKR and it was given a cover as 'the Army's internal security section', but the intelligence world still thinks of it as SMERSH. Its duties are to trace and kidnap or assassinate prominent Russian emigrés considered enemies and traitors to Russia. Leon Trotsky, assassinated in Mexico, was one of its victims. The spread of SMERSH's activities came to light after Nicolai Khakhlov, a SMERSH agent, defected to the West in 1954 when he could not bring himself to obey an order to commit a murder. Bogdan Stashinsky, a SMERSH double killer, defected in 1961 as had Piotyr Deriabin in 1954. These two provided much information about SMERSH's methods. Poison was a principal murder weapon – poison on darts – and in cigarettes, even poison in inhalers intended to relieve asthma. SMERSH was and remains one of the most diabolical organisations ever to function for Russian intelligence.

SVR: *Sluzhba Vneshnie Razvededaki*, Russia's Intelligence Service, and the first part of the old KGB to start up in espionage on its own account in 1991. The SVR took over most of the spies and analysts from the parent organisation and engages in covert and clandestine activities, political 'research' (open research) and economic intelligence.

❹

SPYING – A WORLD SUB-CULTURE

To the average person, and even among journalists and many civil servants, intelligence and espionage are one and the same thing. In the profession they are quite separate, especially in modern times when intelligence has become a term used by management. Intelligence, as valuable information, is sought not only by governments and their military but by corporations, industrialists, fundamentalist religious groups, terrorist gangs and individuals hungry for wealth and power. All of them will go to any lengths to obtain intelligence – and to prevent others from getting their intelligence.

The definition of 'intelligence' most generally accepted by governments was formulated by Sherman Kent, the first chief of the CIA's 'national estimate' group. In his book *Strategic Intelligence for American World Policy*, he said:

Used as an unmodified noun, 'intelligence' can mean (1) knowledge – as in 'What intelligence do we have on Syria?' or (2) an organisation – as in 'Intelligence has not come up with the answer to our question' or (3) an activity – as in 'Espionage is but one of many kinds of intelligence.' Raw information must be processed into finished intelligence. Thus, in the intelligence community it is incorrect to say, 'We have received lots of intelligence from that source.' Intelligence, as knowledge, is produced *only* at headquarters. Even reports from a high-ranking ambassador are, technically speaking, mere raw information until some processor at State or the CIA has sprinkled holy water on it in the form of footnotes, cross references and possibly comments.

This is a fine summary of a complex subject, but not many people will have read Sherman Kent's formulation so intelligence will continue to be seen as virtually synonymous with espionage and not just knowledge but knowledge gained in some covert way.

*　　　　*　　　　*

As a routine, governments used to disavow their spies when they were caught. The diplomatic response came in one of two ways:

- *If you have caught a spy do not expect us to be concerned: he is certainly not operating for us.*
- *We have heard of this man before; he is a maverick out to cause trouble between our two nations.*

Sometimes this line was used: *The person whom your government accuses of being a spy is actually a reputable attaché in our embassy and entitled to diplomatic immunity. Of course he has not been spying.*

When the person arrested is said to have been engaged in espionage activities in a friendly country, the diplomatic response is generally dignified and frosty: *We do not spy on our allies.*

The truth is that allies do spy on one another when information is not being willingly exchanged. Sometimes, after somebody working for a foreign power is discovered in a key position – a Philby, Prime or Lonsdale, a Tyler Kent or a Robert Lee Johnson – a lapse of trust occurs and the Americans and British become wary of exchanging secrets with each other. At such times it becomes necessary to obtain intelligence 'as and how'.

Frequently a government will make no response whatever to charges that its nationals have been spying. The Soviet Union had a policy of nil response, though its special units did their best to rescue their valuable agents. This was in effect an admission that the allegations of spying levelled at certain people were true. In the case of friction between allies over spying charges, there is rarely any public response, on the grounds that accusations and counter-accusations will only further strain relations between the two countries. The difficulties are smoothed over through diplomatic channels or telephone conversations between national leaders.

Much of what is written about 'intelligence' and espionage is fantasy but everybody in the world is affected by it, often without knowing about it. Government decisions are made as a result of secret intelligence and to an even greater degree relationships *between* governments are influenced by the information their 'spooks' turn up.

Since the 1950s the increasing public awareness of spying – a word which covers a wide field of secret activities – has actually influenced espionage/intelligence itself. While the general public remained only vaguely aware that espionage was going on in the world around it, governments were very pleased. Not one of them wanted publicity about their secret activities, and they tolerated and even encouraged the wild stories about so-called spies. Nobody in any government ever sought to scotch the nonsense written about Mata Hari. Some modern researchers say that she was not a spy at all, merely a courtesan who proved to be a useful scapegoat in 1917 to explain the many French military disasters in the First World War. A Dutchwoman named Margarete Zelle, she spent some time in Indonesia from where she returned to Europe with a Javanese name, Mata Hari, or 'Eye of the Morning'. As an exotic dancer she was the toast of Paris and German intelligence recruited her before the war. Promiscuous by nature, she slept with French officers, but there is no evidence that she passed anything of value to the Germans. Nevertheless, in 1917 she was charged with having 'communicated' with the enemy. On orders from French High Command her defence that she was a double agent and had actually spied on the Germans was rejected and she was shot. The execution made her famous and hundreds of writers have tried, in many languages, to turn her into 'the greatest of women spies'. With more justice – and evidence – this could be said of many other women agents. I have learnt to trust very little that emanates from French sources about alleged spies.

While governments used to disavow their spies when they were caught this has changed. Since the 1960s spies have been openly and often publicly traded for one another. Everybody is familiar with the tension-laden exchanges made at the famous Check Point Charlie on the crossing point between West and East Berlin, when two Germanys existed. Sometimes freed and recovered spies are publicly acclaimed and some have been encouraged, even directed, to write their memoirs. This is not done in order to tell the unvarnished truth – far from it – but to expose a conspiracy, to discredit enemy intelligence agencies and, just possibly, to give an edited version of the truth.

Some controversies, such as that which raged about Peter Wright's book *Spycatcher*, further heightened public awareness about what I shall loosely call 'the intelligence business'. Wright, for 25 years a senior British intelligence officer, revealed too many secrets for the British Establishment's liking and from the Prime Minister down they sought to prevent its publication in Britain – thereby ensuring that vast numbers of people would read it when it was published. Wright himself was smeared and vilified but he was an able man with the good of his Service at heart and his warnings about its shortcomings and criticism of its blunders were justified.

The Establishment, that group of powerful men and some women who control a nation's affairs, even though many of them are not in government, has a close relationship with the security services. Indeed, the intelligence service of most nations is an establishment in itself, though this is most noticeable in the West. Intelligence officials tend to come from older families of 'a good background' and 'traditional' education. In Britain the 'old boy network' brought many people into the intelligence service and some of these 'old boys' educated at great public schools and Oxbridge became spies and caused great damage.

When Peter Wright left the intelligence service he sent what he called 'The Dossier' to Mrs Thatcher, in which he said that more than 200 moles and agents were in high places in Britain as well as many minor agents whom they had recruited. In particular, Wright told the Prime Minister, there was an as yet unnamed 'fifth man' who had worked with Philby, Burgess, Maclean and Blunt. This person was a very senior official at MI5.*

Mrs Thatcher should have had Wright's allegations independently investigated but sent his report instead to MI5 for their comments. Not surprisingly, MI5 responded with a report which said, in effect,

---

* Wright made no secret of his conviction that the 'fifth man' was Sir Roger Hollis, who became Director-General of MI5. Other people in the organisation had been suspicious of Hollis even before Wright joined the organisation. Wright explains his reasons for suspecting Hollis in his book *The Spycatcher's Encyclopedia of Espionage*. While circumstantial evidence appears to incriminate Hollis I do not believe that he was the 'fifth man' with Philby, Maclean, Burgess and Blunt.

that Wright's charges had no substance. This was why he wrote *Spycatcher*.

In the US the Establishment is no less powerful than in Britain. The Office of Strategic Services (OSS), the wartime forerunner of the CIA, was cynically known as the 'Oh So Social' because so many of its members came from the privileged wealthy upper classes. The CIA actually came into being at the élite Brook Club in New York.

The link between the Establishment and the CIA was scandalously apparent in 1967 when journalists revealed that the organisation had secretly set up and subsidised a variety of 'foundations' and student groups in order to cover the distribution of money spent on secret intelligence projects. More than this, the directors of the foundations were mostly distinguished members of the Establishment. It was an American version of the British 'old boy' system.

Through publicity given to real-life spying and the enormous popularity of spy fiction and films, the entire world is aware that 'espionage' is going on around them, even if people remain dimly aware of what espionage is. Stores sell 'spy kits' to children, based on invisible inks, simple codes and ciphers, disguises and advice on hide-outs and the concealment of secret messages.

It is not too much to say that spying, in its many manifestations, is a sub-culture. Through industrial espionage, of which economic sabotage is a part, it now spreads its tentacles very widely.

A new openness about security and secret intelligence activities began to appear in both the United States and Britain in the late 1980s and in other Western countries as well. This was the result of agitation in Parliament and the press for the secret organisations to be more accountable not only to Parliament and the US Congress but to the public as well.

These clamant demands became so strong that the Government and Establishment had to give ground and, kicking and screaming, the British intelligence organisations were compelled in the 1990s to submit themselves to 'examination'. Naturally, it was a restricted examination; the security service chiefs are in the business of secrecy and they were not going to reveal more than a prudent minimum. They put into effect a damage limitation policy and made a great show of revealing the whereabouts of MI5's headquarters which, as a new building – Thames House, Millbank, London – could hardly be missed

39

anyway. Even more significantly, the name of the Director, Stella Rimington, was revealed; she was photographed for the press and appeared on television. In a much publicised event, she delivered a lecture on the 'functions' of her service to an invited audience in London. It told specialist journalists nothing that they did not already know, nevertheless it was an amazing event considering that until the 1990s MI5 and MI6 did not officially exist. Now MI5 has an information and public relations officer, as does the CIA. Their main job is to protect their organisations from embarrassment, not to impart information, except that of a wholly innocuous kind. The KGB followed suit in 'public relations' when it saw how successful the new 'openness' was in the West.

However, there has been no real openness, nor would I, for one, expect any. Espionage and counter-espionage have no connection with openness. Stella Rimington (now Dame Stella) and a few other senior officials were named and exposed to public scrutiny in order to concentrate attention on them and lessen the strength of focus on everybody else in the MI5 organisation. Even in Mrs Rimington's case there is a limit to the degree of publicity she may be given. She was justifiably annoyed when a newspaper published her private address. This was an outrageous breach of trust between MI5 and the press. No doubt foreign intelligence organisations knew her address already, but its disclosure made Mrs Rimington vulnerable to the murderers of the IRA and to cranks and fanatics. She was forced to move to another home.

*   *   *

Basically, espionage is simply a matter of obtaining information which somebody else is unwilling to give you. There the simplicity ends. Acquiring that information will almost certainly call for deceit and duplicity and it often demands an intellectual capacity and perseverance of high degree.

Some people spy for money, others for the excitement, many for what they consider a good and righteous cause. For others it is no more than a profession, chosen in preference to accountancy, the law or medicine. A good many spies are driven by patriotism – as are those agents of the counter-espionage services who set out to catch them, who are also patriots.

Overall, espionage and counter-espionage is an intense and

enormous battle of wills in which the penalties for failure can result in disgrace, years in prison or death. People working in the field rarely use the term espionage. The enemy or potential enemy *spy*, while *we* engage in *intelligence*. *We*, the good guys, feel better with this distinction.

The espionage branch of an intelligence organisation has several fields of activity which it considers exclusively its own, though disputes with other branches sometimes occur. The main ones are:

Penetration of targets in other governments Perhaps I should say 'enemy' governments, and naturally they are the most important targets, but 'friendlies' are also penetrated, sometimes with embarrassing repercussions. The ideal is to recruit and employ espionage agents within the policy-making departments of governments hostile or potentially hostile.

Co-operation with foreign security services This is a function of major importance and it amounts to information exchange among friendly countries. The quantity of information that flows through these contacts is vast. Its quality is variable, but sometimes it is of inestimable value.

Third World operations Only the major powers – the US, Britain, France, Russia and China – devote much time, money and energy to this work, and it has decreased since the end of the Cold War. During the Cold War it was imperative for the Western allies to counter or neutralise Soviet activities in such countries as Angola, Mozambique and Afghanistan.

Special Project The espionage branch of the security services is considered the appropriate section to deal with the sensitive matters that sometimes arise. For instance, negotiating with defectors is part of Special Projects, as well as monitoring the activities of emigré groups acting against governments of their former home countries. This is a major task in the US, France, Britain and Germany, though in Britain Special Branch is more closely concerned than any other branch with emigré groups. An emigré organisation can be useful in various ways, for instance it provides information and some of its members are used to penetrate important targets in their native lands. In 1995 I knew of more than 100 Iraqi emigré groups in Britain and France.

Counter-espionage The US Government in particular gives the espionage branch exclusive responsibility for operations intended to penetrate foreign intelligence agencies, to gain 'control' over their espionage agents and pass to them information – or more frequently disinformation – which the US Government wants some foreign/hostile government to have. British counter-espionage also has this function but not exclusively.

*   *   *

In the USA, only one intelligence unit, the espionage branch of the CIA, has the authority to conduct espionage operations. At a lower level, several other agencies are encouraged to become friendly with officials of other countries in order to elicit secret information from them, but if they step into CIA espionage territory they are in trouble. This could happen if the agencies employ permanent or long-term 'agents', though they are sometimes given permission to exploit casual informants, when some special opportunity occurs, and to pay them with money or 'favours'.

In the US in 1995 probably 200,000 people were engaged in 'intelligence', in the very broadest sense. Few of them would have any connection with espionage.

It is often said, mostly by people with no personal experience of it, that espionage is, on the whole, dull, monotonous and tedious. It is true that there is no real 'glamour' in the craft, trade or profession – all these labels fit – but there is often excitement and danger and even more frequently there is satisfaction with a job well done, or so former espionage agents tell me.

For Britain, it is MI6 that carries out espionage abroad and its best operations are those we know nothing about. These are the great successes and if they come to light they do so only many years after they take place. We know more about Soviet successes in penetrating British targets and they have been numerous. This is largely because British security measures against penetration have been remarkably incompetent and careless, even stupidly lax. I am not drawing comparisons. The security of the Warsaw Pact countries – the Soviet Union and its satellites during the Cold War – may have been equally incompetent. However many of their penetration coups were astoundingly successful.

*   *   *

Since espionage *is* penetration it is interesting to look at examples of Soviet successes, even if they embarrass MI5 and Special Branch. One of the best known was Kim Philby, whose name is now applied to the type of Soviet agent who achieves penetration at a high level, as Philby himself did. When working quietly within British Government departments he was deeply effective. Whether he was motivated by powerful ideological motives is unclear, but any 'Philby' is considered to be so driven. Kim Philby was not unique and operators of his type are active in the 1990s, some of them in senior positions in NATO countries. Philby agents did not die out with the collapse of the old Soviet Union; they work for the new Russian Federation because that grouping is still basically communist and will return to communism after the unhappy flirtation with democracy.

Western intelligence had no counterpart to communism in which to find potential agents in the Soviet bloc and develop them. Democratic ideology could not exist behind the Iron Curtain. It does so now and, while the opportunity exists, the Western allies are assiduously seeking agents.

The Russian spymasters had another advantage – in the West communist parties flourished and there were numerous fellow-travellers. British communists assisted Soviet agents, though the Communist Party of Great Britain (CPGB) was successfully infiltrated and bugged by MI5. Peter Wright used to tell diverting stories about bugging British communist targets.

How many young Philby agents are at work in the West is uncertain but, despite more stringent checks and safeguards, I believe that another Philby-Burgess-Maclean-Blunt group could exist in Britain in the 1990s.

In the mid-1960s the KGB recruited several high-ranking West German officers serving in NATO who presented the Brezhnev regime with some of the most valuable information ever passed in the history of espionage. The coup came to light during a random security check in October 1965. Rear Admiral Hermann Ludke, deputy head of NATO's logistic division, was found to have in his possession photographs of many NATO top secret documents taken on a Minox miniature camera. He committed suicide on 8 October, and on the same day his close friend, Major General Horst Wendland, of the West German Intelligence Agency, shot himself. He too had been working for the KGB. Over the next two weeks another eight men in key positions, mostly in the West German Government, committed suicide.

To add to the drama, at least 14 senior scientists and physicists, of East German origin but working in the West, fled back to the East. They had been engaged in scientific and technological espionage. One spy, Dr Harold Gottfried of the Karlsruhe Atomic Centre, tried to ride out the storm and acted as if he were innocent.* He was not careful enough and he was arrested with more than 800 pages of classified documents. The damage done to NATO by the Ludke-Wendland ring was enormous.

West Germany was a constant target for the KGB because of its links with the rest of the West. KGB coups there, when uncovered, were the envy of the British, French and US Intelligence services. East German foreign intelligence operating on behalf of the KGB, recruited Gunther Guillaume, personal aide to Chancellor Willy Brandt in 1970–74. He passed to his Russian chief, the brilliant Markus Wolf, a massive amount of top secret information.

The case of the German senior officers, the scientists and that of Gunther Guillaume showed yet again that people in their position were considered so 'safe' that they did not come under security scrutiny frequently enough. It was the syndrome of the 'old boy' network in a different milieu. These people were assumed not to be security risks – until too late.

The Englishman John Christopher Vassall became a good agent for the Russians for quite another reason: nobody who worked with him in the British foreign service and later in the Admiralty would have considered that he had the gumption or daring to be a spy. A homosexual dandy with good manners, he was referred to slightingly as 'Vera' or sometimes as 'Auntie Vera' and scorned as insignificant. But the KGB did not see him as insignificant, and what they did to suborn him and then run him as an agent is yet another illustration of the ruthlessness which has always characterised Soviet and Russian espionage. His case illustrates something else that is even more alarming –

---

*Perhaps he thought he could brazen his way through any investigation, as Philby had done in 1951. However, he was found guilty of spying. Philby kept his nerve and was completely exonerated in 1955 of any espionage involvement.

that the vetting procedure for people employed in sensitive positions was lamentably inefficient, indeed criminally negligent.

In 1954 Vassall, an effeminate man of 29, had been a junior clerk at the Admiralty for seven years, in a dull and routine job. His evenings were more satisfying because he was a member of the exclusive Bath Club in Mayfair, where he was noted for his fine suits and his velvet-collar tailored overcoats. Probably three times a week he patronised homosexual clubs in the West End, and accepted invitations from the wealthy among his friends there to spend weekends in the country.

His sexual orientation was known at the Admiralty; nevertheless, when he applied for a vacant position as junior attaché at the British Embassy in Moscow he was accepted without a vetting, as if seven years with the Admiralty in London had somehow prepared him for the vastly different life in Moscow. It was very different, since foreign diplomats were confined to certain small areas of Moscow and virtually all of them were required to live in the three great blocks of flats specially built for them – with every flat bugged.

The diplomats lived within a closed society, attending parties practically every night at one embassy or another. The gregarious Vassall went to many of them, sometimes being the only Englishman present. The word went round his own embassy that this junior attaché was living above his status. He was being closely watched by Sigmund Mikhailski, a homosexual Pole, and a KGB agent who had been planted in the embassy. All local staff had to be engaged through a Moscow agency and it had supplied the Pole as a junior interpreter and administrative officer. He reported to his controller that Vassall was weak and lonely and could well be turned into a traitor. The KGB applied the pre-recruiting softening-up process by relaxing restrictions on Vassall's movements and, unusually, when he took photographs no official moved to stop him. Russians now began to invite him to parties where some of the other guests were members of the secret police. They praised him and plied him with vodka, and Vassall lapped up both the praise and the alcohol. Still nobody at the embassy considered him a security risk.

His KGB recruiters arranged for him to meet an attractive, friendly and obviously willing girl in a restaurant, but Vassall was not interested. However, when a man picked him up one day Vassall did show interest. From that moment the Russians knew that they had him hooked. Since Mikhailski had the duty of obtaining theatre tickets and making restaurant reservations for embassy staff, Vassall saw nothing odd in the Pole's subsequent invitation to dinner in a restaurant. They were joined by two Russians who expressed their surprise and delight at this 'chance meeting' with their old friend Mikhailski.

Then Vassall's new friends said that they had enjoyed his company and would he dine with them before Christmas, which was fast approaching. On this occasion they brought with them a third man, an effeminate person, introduced as an actor. Perhaps that was why he wore some make-up. After drinks, the group finished up in a private suite at a large hotel where they feasted and drank. Sodden with vodka, Vassall undressed and lay on a divan with a naked Russian. Another Russian appeared and took photographs but Vassall gave this no thought until, a few days later, at another rendezvous, his 'friends' produced the prints. They suggested that he 'co-operate' with them otherwise the embassy would be told of his indiscretions.

Cold-bloodedly working on Vassall's fears, the KGB men left him to stew in them for three months. In March 1955 they sprang the real trap. Two of the men he already knew insisted that he come to dinner with them, again in a private room, where they met a man who said he was a journalist. All four men drove to a flat for drinks and here Vassall was introduced to a young military officer, who was left alone with the KGB's victim. In the middle of a sex act between Vassall and the officer a group entered the room, one man taking photographs. The journalist now revealed himself as a member of the secret police and he and others fired questions at Vassall. They did not really want answers – they were merely intimidating him. He had two choices, the KGB men told him – to be disgraced and imprisoned, since homosexuality was then a crime in the Soviet Union as it was in Britain, or to co-operate. That sinister-sounding word again.

He collapsed from fear and was taken home but next day, at another forced meeting, the intimidation continued until the last vestige of Vassall's will to resist had crumbled. He did his controller's bidding and produced a lot of relatively unimportant material; he was not to know that the KGB was checking to see if he really was reliable by comparing his information against that they already held. Later that year he developed a system by which he took documents from the office of his direct chief, the Naval Attaché, Captain Bennett. Bennett was not suspicious, for he reported that Vassall's work was generally satisfactory and that he was trying hard to please. He was also socially acceptable, 'despite his handicap of an irritating effeminate personality'.

As Vassall was about to return to London and another Admiralty position, his KGB controller introduced him to Nicolai Korovin, whose cover was that of counsellor at the Soviet Embassy in London. He was actually the senior KGB man there. The Russians were excited because Vassall's new job was in the Naval Intelligence Division, where they expected him to have access to important secrets.

For the first time the Admiralty told Vassall, rather apologetically, that he would have to undergo positive vetting not because he had been assigned to Naval Intelligence but because he had been given the responsibility of handling secret material about atomic weapons.

An inexperienced positive vetting investigating officer merely made 'field inquiries' about Vassall, but he did not question Captain Bennett, even though that officer was now in Britain. Perhaps the investigator was influenced by the general opinion that Vassall was just 'inoffensive Vera'. An efficient security system would have closely re-vetted anybody given a sensitive job on return from Moscow – and Vassall's job was certainly sensitive. He was personal assistant to the deputy director of Naval Intelligence. He found himself in an Aladdin's cave of rich secrets, to the great benefit of his Russian handlers. They were so pleased that they paid him well.

To explain his sudden increase in funds Vassall vaguely mentioned legacies and 'private means'. This, too, should have set alarm bells ringing in the Admiralty's security section but did not. Korovin, an expert at his job, ran Vassall with confidence but caution. Sometimes he set his man unnecessary missions merely to test that he was always obeying orders. One of them was for Vassall to draw a chalk circle three inches in diameter on a tree outside a house in Duchess of Bedford Walk. Another instruction was to telephone Kensington 8955 and ask for 'Miss Mary'. There was no conversation; after Vassall had made his call the line went dead. He was not to know that George Blake had been given this same number to make contact with one of his Russian contacts.

Vassall had two personal interests at this time – his homosexual affairs and decorating his flat; the money given to him by the Russians was helpful in both. Because of the Portland spy case, which broke in January 1961, and the consequent possibility that Vassall's activities might be compromised, his controllers suspended contact with him. They told him not to worry, there would be many more opportunities for him to do valuable work in a great cause. When the Portland spies were in prison, and with Vassall still not under suspicion, his new contact at the Soviet Embassy, Nicolai Karpekov, put his spy back to work. Karpekov showed that he was a master of his trade by giving Vassall a 'little present for loyalty' as he expressed it. It was a black box crammed with bank notes. As the Russian expected, Vassall was flattered and grateful. The extra money enabled him to entertain lavishly, to join expensive clubs and to take several expensive holidays. He did all this quite openly, but still none of his superiors or Naval security considered any inquiries necessary, even though they knew Vassall was being paid only £15 a week at the Admiralty. It was at about this time that he was providing the Russians with details of the latest submarines and sonar detection.

Vassall's luck ran out on 12 September 1962 when he was arrested as he left the Admiralty. His treachery had come to light not through any painstaking detection by the security services, but through the defection of a KGB officer, Anatoli Golitsin. In Helsinki, he revealed to CIA interrogators that high quality British naval intelligence was reaching Moscow in a steady flow. But 18 months before Golitsain's defection the British had known that a spy was at work in the depths of the Admiralty. Had any systematic security check been undertaken, Vassall would have been at the top of a suspects list. Just a visit to his homosexual love nest, with its expensive furnishings, dim lighting, perfumed beds, antiques and all the trappings of a practising homosexual would have suggested a lifestyle out of keeping with that of a dutiful Admiralty secretary. There were secrets, including a secret drawer in a bookcase in which the SB searchers found 14 rolls of exposed, but as yet undeveloped, film. These secrets, at least, the KGB did not get.

Six weeks after his arrest, Vassall appeared at the Old Bailey before the Lord Chief Justice, Lord Parker, who said, 'One cannot shut one's eyes to the fact that almost from the inception, back in 1955, you were accepting large sums of money. I take the view that one of the compelling reasons for what you did was pure, selfish greed.' He sentenced Vassall to 18 years in prison.

The Government took the Vassall case so seriously that it set up a tribunal of two senior judges and a QC to investigate possible breaches of security and 'any neglect of duty' by people responsible for Vassall's employment and conduct, and for his being considered suitable for employment on secret work. The tribunal sat in camera for 22 days and in public for seven and a half days, heard 142 witnesses and considered reports and documents. It also had two Fleet Street reporters gaoled for their refusal to disclose sources of information they obtained and published after Vassall's trial.

In its findings the tribunal stated, 'The selection of Vassall, a weak, vain individual and a practising homosexual can now be seen as the decisive mistake in the history of the case. It exposed him to the attention of the Russian Intelligence Service in conditions in which they were most readily able to identify him for what he was and to compromise him.'

It was revealed to the tribunal that a typist at the British Embassy in Moscow had reported that Mikhailski, the homosexual KGB agent in the embassy, had targeted Vassall and two other staff members. Yet nobody warned or questioned Vassall and when he was returned to London no security service officer followed up the typist's report. The tribunal dealt with this dereliction of duty in a strangely naive way. 'It must remain speculation today whether anything useful would have come out of an interview with Vassall at the time and an insistence on being told all that had passed in his contacts with Mikhailski. Vassall had then been working for the Russians for over six months and he was firmly compromised.'

But given that everybody at the embassy knew that 'Vera' was weak and vain it was very likely that under interrogation by a senior embassy official he would have given himself away; he may even have frankly admitted to have been working for the KGB.

Overall, the tribunal found a few faults with the system, but not with individuals. Of Captain Bennett RN, Vassall's chief, it said, 'There was nothing remiss or careless in Captain Bennett's discharge of his responsibilities by reason of the fact that, knowing what he did, he did not recommend or press for Vassall's recall as a security risk.' Similar comments were made about other senior officials, all of whom were 'in no way remiss'.

Norman Lucas, a senior staff member of the *Sunday Pictorial*, negotiated with Vassall and his solicitors to buy Vassall's personal story. He learnt more about him than possibly any other person. Four years after his conviction, Vassall protested to Lucas that he was an innocent victim of the Soviet blackmailing unit. He denied that his actions were motivated by greed or lust and insisted that everything he did was primarily done because of threats of blackmail. He told Lucas, too, that despite his years of spying and treachery, he was still a loyal patriot. Amazingly, he told Lucas, 'In years to come when people have cause to remember my name no one will be able to deny that I was always a perfect English gentleman.'

This 'perfect English gentleman' was released on parole in 1972 and found sanctuary in a Sussex monastery. People who have cause to remember his name find it synonymous with treachery, deceit, greed and gross behaviour.

While the KGB, GRU and other Soviet espionage agencies, and their 1990s successors, preferred to invest their time, talents, energy and money in big coups, such as suborning John Vassall, creating a ring of British spies within the enemy's diplomatic and intelligence Establishment and penetrating SIS itself with George Blake (see pages 111–115), their operatives have always been alert to relatively minor opportunities to obtain useful information. A classic example of spy opportunitism occurred in 1967 when a KGB officer, Vladislav Slavin, recruited a clerk in the Greater London Council motor licensing department who had access to the registration numbers of all MI5 and SB vehicles and was prepared to sell them.

Slavin's chief, Yuri Voronin, the KGB 'Resident' in London, was delighted. The value of the information was obvious. Neither MI5 nor SB could effectively carry out mobile surveillance because KGB operators could identify their vehicles. In addition, the KGB knew which British vehicles to follow in the expectation that they would lead the followers to certain secret addresses, even those of Soviet defectors. Slavin's work for his Moscow bosses was enterprising and it shows, yet again, how easy it is for an agent to induce ordinary people to part with 'ordinary' information. But how could a list of such sensitive numbers be reposing in a council motor licensing department when it should have been treated as secret? The answer must lie in the sublime innocence of officials who thought that enemy spies were only interested in military secrets. Vladislav Slavin may have found it more difficult to obtain MI5 and SB vehicle registration numbers after 1972 when the IRA became a greater threat to the security of the British realm than the 'Soviet threat'.

The ease with which Slavin obtained important vehicle registration numbers and the relative ease for Russian recruiters in gaining the services of John Vassall illustrate what veteran spymasters have always known – that it is not really difficult to induce people to betray their country. Not that any recruiter ever asks a prospect to do this, not in as many words. He simply wants a little information or confirmation of information. Sometimes he merely asks for 'advice', a request that flatters most people. A former senior French intelligence officer of many years' experience told me, 'Nearly everybody can be induced to part with secrets of his country or of any organisation or commercial company to which he belongs.'

We live in the age of the spy and there are now many branches of the profession. The military and political aspects of spying are those which attract most attention, but there are also technological, commercial, industrial and economic spies. The rewards are great for the spies themselves and immense for the principals for whom they work.

The growth of the security organisations has kept pace with that of the spying profession so that overall we live in the midst of a subculture of espionage and counter-espionage, terror and counter-terror. Civilised societies need the protection of the security services. This can readily be illustrated. The IRA terrorists who planted the massive bomb in London's Docklands in February 1996 could bring off this horrific coup because their intelligence was good. MI5's intelligence and that of Scotland Yard's Anti-Terrorist Branch was not adequate to foresee and prevent the disaster. This is not a criticism of MI5. The IRA is one of the world's most difficult terrorist organisations to penetrate.

5

SOME PENETRATIONS WORK, OTHERS FAIL

The stories so far indicate that the KGB and its agencies are eminently successful in recruiting people to spy for them in foreign intelligence organisations, but the Russians do have their failures. One that appeals to me took place in Australia in the early 1960s. It began in 1959 with the arrival in Australia of Ivan Fedorovich Skripov to re-open the Soviet Embassy in Canberra. It had been closed since 1954 following the famous 'Petrov case'. Petrov and his wife had defected to the West, in Australia.

Skripov held the rank of first secretary, but that was only his cover. He was actually a KGB officer given the job of re-establishing the espionage network. It is a daunting task to rebuild a blown or decayed network and Skripov, who was a man of much personal charm, cast about for recruits.

He was an assiduous worker and within 18 months he had made a thousand contacts in the Canberra community which, given its political and diplomatic intensity, was a rich hunting ground for spies. The Australians, though relatively inexperienced in counter-espionage, were alert and quick to learn. Officers of ASIO (Australian Security Intelligence Organisation) were on to Skripov from the moment of his arrival and they were very suspicious of all kinds of activities around the Soviet Embassy.

Meanwhile, working in Wellington, New Zealand, in the passport office of the British High Commission, was an Englishwomen, Kay Marshall, who had gone to New Zealand to marry a serviceman. The marriage was a failure. Ervily Luttsky, Soviet press attaché in New Zealand, called regularly at the British High Commission to collect visas. Actually Luttsky was a Soviet intelligence officer and this Kay Marshall, as well as British and New Zealand officials, suspected Luttsky took Marshall for country drives, showered her with gifts and with great smoothness began to ask her for immigration and passport forms. This was clever because such forms were freely available over the counter but for Luttsky they were a form of bait so that he could ask for more sensitive material. Marshall was by now working for the New Zealand Security Service, which provided her with a case officer who debriefed her after each of her outings with Luttsky. Soon she was feeding him with dummy documents stamped CONFIDENTIAL.

Luttsky was recalled to Moscow in 1960 for other duties, but by then the KGB was sure it had a useful agent in Marshall. Luttsky's replacement was a very different personality, an objectionable man who treated Marshall as Soviet property. With the approval of her New Zealand security friends, she told the Russian she would no longer work for him and intended to go to Australia. The Russian advised her that he would arrange for a friend in Australia to contact her, a matter of some satisfaction to ASIO. When the Russian informed her that his friend would meet her on the third Saturday of the month at Taronga Park Zoo, Sydney, and that she should hold a copy of *The Age* newspaper to identify herself and use certain passwords, Australian intelligence was even more pleased.

The new Russian, for whom Marshall as yet had no name, failed to keep the first rendezvous. This was almost certainly in order to observe Marshall and then follow her in case she made contact with anybody who could conceivably be an ASIO agent. No contact whatever was made and, following the original instructions, 'Sybil' – the Australians' code-name for Marshall – turned up exactly a month later. This time she was approached by a man calling himself 'John'. The Australians watching the meeting knew him as Ivan Skripov.

'John' began 'Sybil's' recruit development and the Russian, who always met Marshall in public places, taught her how to be a courier. The pair corresponded in invisible ink and gradually the cautious – and courteous – Skripov became confident of his agent's skills. She recovered for him a metal cylinder hidden inside a water meter in a park, drove it to Canberra and handed it to Skripov in an obscure place.

By now ASIO had a list of the many contacts the energetic Skripov had built up and trusted some of them to report his movements. Skripov often went very public indeed – lecturing to Rotary Clubs and other groups. ASIO was filming Skripov every time he met Marshall, though some of the packets she carried for him could not be opened without showing that this had happened. The relationship worked well for nearly three years and served as a form of in-service training for many ASIO operatives.

One package was safely opened and inside was found a Canadian passport, issued in 1960, and therefore still current, to a Czech, Andrew Huba. Carefully resealed, it was passed on to Skripov. In December 1960 Skripov wanted another job done: Marshall was to meet a man in Adelaide and under conditions of extraordinary secrecy was to hand him a package. ASIO agents opened it and found inside a metal container with a lock that needed a brilliant locksmith to pick. Inside the container was an amazing find – a radio transmitter of the 'burst transmission' type, together with advised transmission times. In a few seconds a spy could send a lengthy coded message.

How could this development be handled? Surveillance was set up, with a view to the arrest of the agent expecting to collect the package. Excitement within ASIO and government was intense but nobody kept the first rendezvous with Marshall or even the second fallback one. Possibly the agent was so experienced that he smelt the trap that had been prepared. Marshall had to face the inevitable and tell Skripov that no handover meeting had taken place. She also told him that because she was worried, she had not brought the package back to him but had locked it in her flat. This was the end of her contact with the Russian because she was instructed not to keep arranged meetings with him and not to answer invisible-ink letters. A month later Skripov was declared persona non grata and ordered to leave Australia in seven days.

Kay Marshall, 'Sybil', was an outstandingly successful 'double' agent, though most double agents have been 'turned'. Marshall never did spy or work for the Soviet Union, but she succeeded in convincing the pathologically cautious Russians that she *was* working for them. Cool, clear-headed and brave, it is a pity that she did not experience the coup of capturing the man for whom the burst transmitter was intended. Not that this failure could be blamed on her. Almost certainly, the stake-out using her as the bait was clumsy. Several ASIO operations were fiascos.*

*   *   *

While penetration conveniently refers to an agent inveigling himself into a target objective, to obtain or plant information or disinformation, or to deceive an enemy into believing that he has successfully recruited an agent – a deception that Kay Marshall achieved – there is another kind of penetration. The 'Berlin Tunnel', officially known as Operation GOLD, is perhaps the best and most fascinating example in modern times. It is also a story with a sting in its tail, just as so many spy novels have. The Berlin Tunnel was real.

Operation GOLD was the logical development of Operation SILVER, by which the CIA was able to tap into Soviet wire communications systems in Vienna after the Second World War. Vienna was fruitful but East Berlin, as the hub of communications linking Moscow with not only East Berlin but also with Budapest and other cities, would indeed be 'gold' if the cables passing through East Berlin could be tapped. Carl Nelson of the CIA's Office of Communications found a flaw in the teletype encryption system used by both the Soviets and their Western opponents. Thus it became feasible to make the tap. As it would entail a great deal of expense and labour, the two organisations collaborated. The CIA would dig a tunnel to a spot below the buried cables; the SIS would then take over and dig a vertical tunnel upwards from the end of the horizontal tunnel, tap into the wires and relay the flow of communications to the rear where CIA experts would record the signals. Charts of Berlin, which the SIS had possessed for years, showed that the cables passed a mere 18 inches under a ditch near the Schoenefelder Road, on Berlin's southern edge.

Before the tunnelling could begin the Allied planners erected a large building to conceal the excavation and give their personnel somewhere from which to work. Shrewd minds went to work on a

---

* Kay Marshall's story was published in instalments in *Thursday*, a New Zealand magazine, in 1971. A summary of it appears in David McKnight's *Australia's Spies and Their Secrets*.

deception plan that, in principle, was based on the Trojan Horse used by the Greeks. Soldiers openly put up a 'warehouse' about 500 feet from the border and then placed on the roof an impressive set of antennae. The idea was to convince the ever-suspicious Russians and East Germans that an 'elint' listening post was going into action. The 'warehouse' was ringed with barbed wire, which was patrolled by dogs and guards.

In August 1954 US Army engineers, working in the warehouse, dug down 20 feet and then progressed horizontally eastwards. The 16–man team, working in shifts, laboured around the clock and as the spoil came out, large-diameter steel tubing went in. Noises were muffled while the lookout on the warehouse roof kept an eye on the enemy border guard, who sometimes actually walked over the tunnel. The spotter then warned the diggers by telephone and work would cease.

After removing 31,000 tons of earth the Americans handed over in February 1955 to the SIS team who slowly and painstakingly began the upward shaft. Only 12 feet above they came upon the three rubber-sheathed cables. It was a moment of exhilaration but there were still dangers. Only 52 inches overhead traffic was using the Schoenefelder Road and to prevent a breakthrough the shaft was filled with a reinforced concrete roof.

Technical expertise of high order was needed because each of the cables carried 172 circuits and each circuit had a minimum of 18 separate communication channels. The SIS men intercepted every signal and relayed them by amplifier back to a bank of 150 tape recorders in the warehouse. 'We could not translate the stuff that poured into that great shed,' said an officer who was there at the time, 'but we were sure that the Soviet bloc countries were spilling their guts.'

The voice transmission tapes were flown at once to London where Russians from families who had emigrated to Britain after the 1917 revolution translated them. CIA experts and linguists handled the teletype tapes in Washington.

A Russian maintenance crew discovered the tunnel, apparently by accident, in April 1956, forcing the SIS–CIA teams to evacuate it quickly, sealing the tunnel behind them. 'The haul of intelligence from the great tap was still being processed at the end of 1958. However, the quality of information did not match the quantity and for both the British and American governments there was not enough return for the $30 million invested in it. Everybody involved in Operation GOLD became resigned to the belief that the cables carried only low grade information. It was just bad luck.

In 1961 the real truth came to light with the arrest of George Blake, ostensibly an SIS officer but in fact a Soviet penetration agent. It was then recalled that in 1953 Blake had attended early SIS-CIA meetings at which the tunnel had been planned. He had 'spilled his guts' – to use the tunnel officer's term – to his Moscow masters. The amazing tunnel had penetrated into enemy territory and into the heart of their communications network but Blake had penetrated SIS. Operation GOLD had been fatally tarnished from the beginning and years of translation following the cable flow meant nothing. We now know that the 'accidental' discovery of the tunnel was intentional. The Soviet leadership could no longer be bothered with the inconvenience of sending a stream of low-level information while going to the expense of building a more secure system. One clever agent, Blake, had defeated the massive combined resources of the SIS and CIA.

The Berlin Tunnel, which had promised much and which had seemed such a spectacular success was, after all, a Soviet victory.

*   *   *

An interesting example of yet another kind of penetration was carried out by the British Army in Northern Ireland in the 1970s. The MOD was dissatisfied with the quality and quantity of intelligence being gathered about the IRA terrorists and as a result the Military Reconnaissance Force (MRF) came into being. MRF recruited members and former members of terrorist gangs and induced them to work for the British. In effect, this meant using terrorist tactics against terrorists. MRF was effective but could have been more so if its officers had been more tightly controlled from above. This would have resulted in better reporting of their intelligence gathering to other arms of British security.

A great failing of British Intelligence generally is that its various branches have not been willing enough to share information, but treat it as secret unto themselves alone. It is understandable that MI5 should be reluctant to share some operations with Special Branch: officers of that branch are often too quick to release details of an arrest and the events leading up to it. This prevents MI5 officers concerned in the case from getting clear of the consequent publicity and sometimes they find themselves compromised in the publicity. On the whole, though, former officers agree that greater co-operation among security services would lead to better use of resources, time and effort.

*   *   *

While some agents survive for many years and give good service to their controllers others barely get started on the road to treason. If the recruiters and controllers, who are themselves taught to be patient and cautious, can teach these virtues to their recruits and keep them under a tight rein for about two years the chances are that they will survive for much longer. I am referring here, of course, to homegrown traitors, not the foreign spies who can hardly be guilty of treason since they owed no allegiance to their country of operation in the first place.

People tempted to become spies for a foreign power against their own country need to do a lot of thinking about the complex world which they seek to enter. In Britain, the US, Germany, Sweden and France a disconcertingly large number of men and women succumb to urges to engage in treasonable espionage, perhaps because they expect to make easy money or because they genuinely prefer the policies and ideologies of another country. Excitement lures some people and others have a pathological need for intrigue.

Maureen Bingham, the attractive, sophisticated and spendthrift wife of a Royal Navy sub-lieutenant turned up openly at the Soviet Embassy in London one day early in 1970 and offered the services and knowledge of her husband David. The Binghams had money problems, chiefly because of Maureen's mounting debts. In despair she had left home and put her children into care, but after getting the bright idea of selling information to the Soviet Union she returned home.

The Soviet official who interviewed Maureen, L T Kuzmin, was surprised at the openness of the approach and he and his colleagues suspected that MI5 officers would learn of it. In fact, they knew about it from the moment that it happened because MI5 had a permanent watch on the Soviet Embassy. Had the Binghams possessed any genuine sense of espionage Maureen would have flown to a continental capital to offer her husband's services to a Soviet Embassy or, for even greater security, she could have gone to a Third World country. Even better, she could have visited a Soviet Intourist travel office and asked for a quiet word with somebody there. At the time, any and every

59

Russian could have arranged for an introduction to a government official. However the Binghams had no guile and not much common sense.

MI5 took no direct action against the Binghams. Its chiefs wanted the Soviet controllers to believe that Maureen's first visit had been unnoticed by British security. In the best traditions of espionage cunning, MI5 hoped to make use of this odd couple. David Bingham was fed harmless but impressive-looking information which Maureen duly passed to her Russian handler, sometimes in such careless ways that he must have been horrified. On one occasion, for instance she left information at a city dead-drop long before making arrangements for it to be collected. In sound practice it must be picked up and spirited away within seconds.

Nevertheless, Kuzmin gave Bingham £600 and told him that some of the money was for his wife. He bought a camera, as instructed, and kept a rendezvous with his handler outside Guildford Cathedral. Here he was given further instruction on the use of dead-drops in the Guildford area and the handler advised him how to go about photographing documents. With the camera he went to work taking pictures of secret documents and drawings at Portsmouth naval base.

Despite their suspicions that the Binghams would be under surveillance, the Russians continued to run the couple since some of their information seemed valuable. The connection lasted for two years, but Maureen Bingham's indiscretions and stupidities became so obvious that the GRU men controlling the Binghams had to assume that MI5 knew they were traitors. From that moment the Binghams were 'dead'. Nobody would answer Maureen's calls, nobody met her and her 'expenses' payments ceased.

David, worried and apprehensive and harassed by his wife's creditors, confessed to his commanding officer. This was fortuitous for MI5 and Special Branch because they did not have to reveal, at least not openly, that they had been watching the Binghams all along. The pair had never suspected that they had passed disinformation to the Soviet Union.

Nevertheless, the judge who presided over David Bingham's case at Winchester Crown Court in 1972 made no allowance for this. He said, 'You have been guilty of a monstrous betrayal of your country's secrets. The harm you have done to these interests is incalculable.' And he sentenced Bingham to 21 years in prison.

In truth, the damage had been carefully calculated beforehand by the MI5 team who managed the affair. No great harm had been done because the Russians could have gleaned the same information from specialist publications bought at a bookstall or from Her Majesty's Stationery Office, publishers of government documents and books. Technical intelligence, such as that from sigint, elint and photint, would have furnished the GRU with the same information that had been passed by the Binghams. Among the photographs taken by David there may have been a few gems, but not enough for the British nation to feel itself any more vulnerable to the Soviet Union than it had been before his spying activities. David Bingham's sentence of 21 years was intended to set an example to other serving officers; Maureen Bingham was given a suspended sentence 'for aiding a foreign power in the procurement of information covered by the Official Secrets Act'.

The young Binghams – both were in their twenties – were out of their depth and they were manipulated by both sides. The GRU and British Intelligence regarded them as expendable and no doubt the Binghams, who now live under another name, still rue their venture into the spying world. Their case crops up in coffee-table conversation among intelligence professionals. A veteran of the game told me, 'In a way I am sorry for the Binghams – they were rabbits among wolves.'

He would not have said that in 1972. Truly there is no sentiment in the intelligence business.

*   *   *

Geoffrey Prime was, like the Binghams, a walk-in but the damage he inflicted to British, American, Canadian and Australian interests was immeasurably greater than that caused by the Binghams. Prime, a social misfit and sexual pervert, passed four positive vetting procedures and numerous security checks and was employed in an intelligence holy of holies, the Government Communications Headquarters (GCHQ) in Cheltenham, England.

The importance and scope of GCHQ's work cannot be over-emphasised. From this vast complex, intelligence officers use a massive battery of technological aids to spy on the military, political and commercial life of virtually the entire world, but notably the Russians, the Chinese, the Irish and even the Americans. The centre's work is eavesdropping on a global scale. GGHQ is so efficient that it had details of the Soviet plan to invade Afghanistan three weeks before the invasion took place in 1980. It is the brain of the British contingency plan for dealing with a nuclear attack. Also, it is an important communications channel through which MI6 contacts its informants and agents abroad by transmitting on pre-arranged wavelengths. In the wrong hands these wavelengths could lead to the identification of those agents.

The base is jointly funded by Britain, the USA, Canada and Australia, a further dimension to its significance. At the time of the Prime case, GCHQ was closely linked to the 'Rhyolite programme'. Rhyolite satellites, the first of which was launched in March 1973, intercept microwave communications, usually long-distance telephone calls, radio links and telemetry signals – the streams of high frequency digital information by which a missile reports back to its earth station every aspect of its performance. In the 1970s the Rhyolite was the ultimate bug.

At any one time at GCHQ officers are watching up to 200 'indicators' – military, economic, social and political – to measure a state's warlike intentions. From Cheltenham, GCHQ sends processed information to Whitehall for daily meetings of various 'intelligence groups' to review up-to-date intelligence assessment, medium term prognoses and reports on sudden changes in indicator patterns. In Washington there is a similar daily meeting based on the same information. The four contributor governments refuse to admit it but it was clear by 1980 that their eavesdropping is not aimed solely at obvious enemies; they also eavesdrop on allies, on one another and on domestic citizens.

It was into this highly sensitive world that Geoffrey Prime found his way by a route that started with his first job as a clerk in a copper factory. He left in August 1956 to do his national service with the RAF, with which he spent 12 years. In 1963 he took a course in Russian and German at RAF Leuchars in Fife, Scotland. This six-months' training allowed Prime through the door of signals intelligence (sigint). In June 1964 he was posted to RAF Gatow, West Berlin, where he eavesdropped on Russian pilots and listened to Radio Moscow.

Friendless, sexually inadequate, a misfit in the RAF, Prime decided to 'make something of himself', as he said later. He took the first step as he passed through an East Berlin border checkpoint in January 1968. He palmed a note to a border guard, offering to work for the Soviet Union. The Russians reacted quickly, setting up a meeting at a railway station with two KGB agents, 'Igor' and 'Valya'. With a child-like eagerness to please, Prime poured out secrets and using a miniature camera he photographed the RAF's internal telephone directory. Then he offered to return to London to work in the Joint Technical Language Service, which processed transcripts of material intercepted from around the world. Positively vetted and approved, Prime got the job – and at once returned to Berlin for a KGB course in espionage in East Germany.

Full of confidence in his new spying skills, the traitor began work in his London job in September 1968. When he had information to impart he prepared an invisible ink letter and posted it to an address in East Germany or he left it at a dead drop. He stopped his spying in 1973 but only because he had lost his code pads. Without them he could neither understand his instructions nor encipher his own messages.

He wrote to Igor and Valya to tell them of the problem and possibly they found the letter suspicious for they did not make contact again for a full year. Then a man and a woman, speaking broken English, delivered a suitcase to Prime's sister, Gladys, and asked her to pass it on. Gladys thought this was odd but she mentioned it to nobody. Brother Geoffrey was pleased because the case contained new equipment and some money. It also lifted his spirits which had taken a battering following the end of an unhappy four-year marriage.

He was so mentally unstable at this time that his doctor sent him to consult a psychiatrist. Also, he was behaving oddly at work but his superiors at the Joint Technical Language Service were blind to his behaviour. In 1974 Prime sailed through another positive vetting and soon after he was upgraded to work on even more sensitive material.

His KGB handlers were excited about this development and invited him to Vienna in September 1975 to tell them more about his work; they knew he liked to boast and how much he appreciated praise. He took to Vienna a briefcase of secret material including photocopies of secret material. The KGB men slapped him on the back, toasted him with vodka, told him that he was their most trusted agent and gave him £750.

A sycophant, Prime ingratiated himself with his direct British superiors who, in March 1976, posted him to GCHQ. Prime knew that this would please his KGB friends so off he flew to Vienna again, carrying another case of priceless secret material, though the Russians valued it at £1,000. To obtain the documents he was passing to the Russians, Prime had to remove them from the files, a process which normally required approval from superiors. In November 1976 Prime was himself a superior, nothing less than a section chief. He now attended planning meetings where he acquired ever more sensitive material.

In September 1977 Prime resigned from GCHQ on the grounds of 'excessive strain'. He was not under suspicion, but the resignation of an officer on these grounds should have been investigated, especially as he was only 39 years old and doing well in his career.

The KGB did not permit Prime to resign as easily as GCHQ had done. In April 1981 his controllers called him to Vienna to hand over many reels of photographed documents as well as voluminous notes that he had held since leaving GCHQ. In November they invited him to East Berlin where he was paid the large sum of £4,000 for his services. As a former employee still bound by the Official Secrets Act Prime should not have visited East Berlin at that time.

Prime had passed from one kind of fantasy to another: he was committing sexual offences against young girls in and around Cheltenham. Feeling under pressure as police were looking for the yet unidentified offender, Prime confessed to his second wife, Rhona, about the assaults. Once, when he was absent, she found some of his spying equipment under the bed and he also confessed his espionage activities to her. Rhona wrestled with her loyalty to this twisted man and with her conscience, and reported him to the police. She later told the Old Bailey that he had lived a triple life – that of ordinary man, Soviet spy and sex offender.

The court sat in camera while the Attorney General, Sir Michael Havers, gave details of the secret and vital information which Prime had passed to the Soviets. He was sentenced to 35 years in prison on seven charges of spying and an additional three years for his indecent assaults on young girls.

The Americans were profoundly angry that they had not been given full information about the spy's activities until seven months after his arrest. By coincidence, an American spy had recently been seriously involved in espionage for the Russians. But for this there may have been irrevocable damage to joint British–US intelligence operations.

The CIA estimated that Prime had done one billion dollars' worth of damage to combined British–US intelligence, not to mention the loss of agents caught and executed by the Russian as a result of Prime's treachery. The Prime Minister, Margaret Thatcher, instructed the Security Commission to inquire into the case and it reported in a White Paper in May 1993. It found that Prime had been positively vetted four times, that he had successfully lied and named referees who either knew little about him or were not prepared to reveal what they knew. During one week when the positive vetting team was carrying out inquiries which cleared him for access to Top Secret information, Prime was in a flat in East Berlin being trained by KGB specialists in espionage techniques. At various times Prime removed secret documents to photograph them at home but not once was a spot check carried out at the GCHQ gates. Nobody sought to inquire into Prime's many foreign holidays, not only in Vienna and Berlin but also in Rome, Cyprus and Eire, where he met KGB controllers.

In all, GCHQ had not much more security than a public hospital. Security has improved immeasurably since Prime helped himself to its secrets but if he, a not very intelligent man, could inflict such damage, what havoc might be caused by a much cleverer spy without Prime's weaknesses?

*   *   *

One of the few publicly-known Western penetrations of the KGB was carried out by a brave Frenchman, Colonel Bernard Nut, a staff officer of the *Direction de la Surveillance du Territoire* (DST). Just how he got into the KGB's Directorate S and how he managed to fool the Russians for so long is still unknown. Nut had to be brilliant to penetrate Directorate S, because it was the KGB branch that placed Soviet-born agents, using assumed identities, into Western societies. Konon Molody (alias 'Gordon Lonsdale') was one of the best known.

Colonel Nut had convinced the KGB spymasters that he had turned against France and wanted to work for the Soviets. He fed them some impressive-looking information and in time they trusted him completely. For some time he operated under diplomatic cover in the Soviet Embassy in Paris. His cover was all the more effective because Nut spoke fluent Russian.

His espionage coups for France were outstanding and led to the exposure of perhaps 20 KGB agents and staff operatives in France. One of the agents was Patrick Guerrier, whose cover job was as archivist/librarian at Charbonages, the giant state-owned coal company. Guerrier had access to secrets other than those connected with coal and he was arrested while passing documents to a Soviet Embassy attaché.

It was Nut who reported to the French Government that the French naval base at Toulon had been penetrated by not one but several agents; this was serious because the nuclear hunterkiller submarine *Rubis* was based at Toulon. The KGB, in association with the Bulgarian secret service, was involved in the attempted assassination of Pope John Paul and it was Nut who found out that the key Russian implicated was Viktor Pronin, working as an Aeroflot official in Rome. He was arrested on 12 February 1983.

Three days later, Bernard Nut's body was found in the French Alps. He had been shot through the head. President Mitterand was angry, in common with every minister and senior official who knew of Nut's work. Mitterand was already irritated by the Soviet theft of French technology and he was further exasperated by the unwarranted increase in staff at the Soviet Embassy in Paris and at the consulates elsewhere. In ten years the Paris personnel had increased from 200 to 700. DST chiefs reported to Mitterand that the vast majority of the extra Russians were spies or case officers and that the French counter-espionage service could not cope with the problems that the Russian activity posed for them. For Mitterand, the murder of Bernard Nut was the final provocation. On 31 March 1983, 47 Soviet citizens were expelled from France for espionage. They included the KGB station chief Nikolai Chetverikov, whose cover as 'information officer' had not deceived DST officers. As insurance against reprisal expulsions of French embassy staff from Moscow, Prime Minister Pierre Mauroy handed the Soviet ambassador a list of another 40 Russians who would be thrown out if the Soviet Government engaged in tit-for-tat expulsions. The blackmail worked.

The French example gave many other countries the courage to expel Soviet spies. They included West Germany, Belgium, Switzerland, Canada, Australia, Thailand, Bangladesh, Spain and Iran. Following the Russians' lead, other Warsaw Pact embassies were ordered to send staff home; at the time NATO estimated that fully 70 per cent of the embassy staff of the Soviet Union and its satellites were connected with espionage activity.

In life, Colonel Bernard Nut had achieved much; his death had accomplished much more – a great body blow against KGB and GRU activities.

6

A COUNTRY DEDICATED TO PREVENTIVE INTELLIGENCE

No nation this century has needed an efficient intelligence service more than Israel, a tiny country within a sea of vengeful Arab and Islamic enemies. The nation's intelligence services and their successes excite the admiration and respect of other countries' security and espionage agencies. Some of Israel's spy missions have ended in disaster, but not before they have produced information that gave the government and defence forces time to prepare themselves for attack. Israel, unlike other countries, has lived with a very small margin of error. If one small piece of information failed to get through to intelligence headquarters or if it was incorrectly assessed there, Israel faced destruction. It came close to this fate in 1948 when five Arab armies attacked it simultaneously and in 1973 when the invading Egyptian army crossed the Suez Canal and established a bridgehead in Israeli-held territory while the Syrians invaded from the Golan Heights. The government of any country would claim that intelligence services form its first line of defence, but most of them have time and space in which to react to a foreign threat. Israel never did have this luxury – the enemy was there, just across the river or over the hill.

*   *   *

The original intelligence organisation operated by the Jews of Palestine – before the creation of the State of Israel – was Shai. It was effective against the British, who controlled Palestine under a mandate from the League of Nations after the First World War, because the British political administration and its military support needed Jewish manpower.

Jewish men and women were employed in almost every British office in Palestine. They had no psychological hang-ups about any conflict of loyalties – they served their own people first, even though they accepted British salaries.

During the latter years of the British Mandate, 1945–48, the Jews saw themselves as a resistance movement in the way that the *Maquis* was the French resistance against Nazi occupation. To them, the British were occupiers by force and the factual legality that Britain was governing by decree of the League of Nations did not convince them otherwise.

Information came to Shai, then led by Israel Amir, in a torrent from volunteer spies, postal workers, telephonists, waiters, motel chambermaids, journalists, departmental secretaries – all passed on whatever seemed to be important. Few confidential telephone conversations escaped monitoring. Codes and ciphers were little protection. Shai's agents stole or photographed most of them – sometimes in the headquarters of the British Criminal Investigation Department. Those they could not steal, they broke.

When no Jewish employee was to hand to tip off a kibbutz or a Hagana base about a British military raid, then the Jewish leaders could usually depend on a warning from some British officer.

Shai worked from Jabotinsky Street, Tel Aviv, only 200 yards from a major British headquarters, and often broadcast the contents of confidential reports before they reached their addressees. Shai's own radio station, Kol Israel, was probably the greatest irritant to the British administration. Its announcers broadcast the substance of top-level communications, thus rendering useless any action they proposed against Hagana, the underground army. In effect, Shai was Hagana's eyes and ears, its intelligence service. No army, underground or otherwise, ever had more rapid, reliable and detailed information about its opponents.

The frustrated British never did plug the security leak, although they transferred some Jewish employees and fired others. The British moved out one Jewish clerk whom they rightly suspected of being a

Shai informer and replaced him with another Shai agent who never did come under suspicion.

Few 'surprise raids' were in fact a surprise. The British troops who arrived to arrest Hagana men or to seize contraband arms usually found nothing. Even when one of its men was caught red-handed, Hagana had ways and means of saving him. One night in 1946 a Hagana official was arrested in a spot check and had no time to get rid of a notebook containing the names and addresses of many of his colleagues. It was a dangerous loss but the British made the mistake of delaying their investigation until the following morning; in the meantime the notebook was locked in a safe at CID. One of Shai's master forgers obtained a notebook identical in appearance and filled it with fictitious names and non-existent addresses in the same handwriting as the original. Then a brilliant lockpick switched notebooks. The job was so neat that the British never did suspect that they had been fooled.

In the summer of 1946 all three Jewish underground organisations – Hagana, Irgun and Stern – decided to co-operate as it became clear that the British authorities were determined to crack any Jewish resistance. The Jewish Revolt Movement blew up ten bridges on roads leading out of Palestine – a symbolic gesture rather than an act of practical warfare.

The British Army and CID replied by preparing BROADSIDE, an operation to round up key Hagana men and cripple it by leaving it without leadership. BROADSIDE also aimed at finding proof that the Jewish Agency was actively involved in illegal operations. A British officer lent Shai a priceless file, from a CID safe, containing 5,000 names and addresses of Hagana and Palmach officers and maps showing training areas and arms depots.* Each piece of paper was quickly photographed and the file was returned. Before the British could act, most addresses in the file were useless. When the operation was launched, on 29 June 1946, thousands of Jewish homes were raided and several hundred people were arrested. Superficially it seemed to have been a successful raid, but no military leader of Hagana was picked up because the political chiefs stayed at home and 'offered' themselves for arrest, thus giving the Hagana officers time to get away or to conceal themselves in *sliks* (secure hiding places). Despite the

* Palmach was the élite commando or 'storming force' of Hagana.

71

British cordon, Hagana's chief-of-staff, Moshe Sneh, slipped out of Israel and went to Paris. The British did find a few incriminating documents but the arms haul was poor and the training camps had vanished.

Understandably, acute tension existed between the British and the Jews, especially after Irgun blew up the wing of the King David Hotel, Jerusalem, where the Government Secretary had his offices. Irgun's intelligence was good, and its terrorists planted a great deal of explosive in just the 'right' places. The blast killed 90 people and injured many others, and did the Jewish cause much harm. The King David Hotel affair was tragic proof that the Jews' military and political intelligence were not in harmony. Chaim Weizmann, the Zionist leader in London, had sent a messenger with orders countermanding the attack but the violent men of Irgun disregarded him. (In 1948, Weizman became Israel's first President.)

In those days very few Jews spoke openly on the telephone. Everything was in code, so that 'I'm telephoning for my brother, David, who wants to know if you can let him have three dozen cases of oranges' meant that an emergency meeting had been called at a particular address. The Jews also had the advantage of being able to speak Hebrew, in itself almost an unbreakable code for the British.

In Jerusalem, too, Shai's activities were breathtaking in their audacity. Every Friday at noon a staff officer carried to the office of the Chaplain General of the British Army in Palestine one of the 20 numbered copies of a top secret document called 'Order of Battle and Location Statement'. Its half dozen pages gave the exact location and the movements anticipated for the coming week of every British unit in the Middle East. The chaplain, having read the document, would lock it in his safe before going to lunch at the King David Hotel. Before his return an hour later a photocopy of the document was on its way to Hagana intelligence – by courtesy of a Jewish secretary.

Head of Shai in Jerusalem in 1946 was Shalhevet Freir, a German-born physicist aged 26. As a sergeant in the British Eighth Army he had learned British military methods and later, posing as a British major or colonel, he had run illegal immigrants into Palestine past British posts in Italy. From an office in an establishment called 'The Institute for the Study of Social Affairs' he directed 20 agents who had penetrated every level of Britain's military and civil administration; Freir even had an agent in the office of the High Commissioner.

Another key figure in Hagana's intelligence, as its organisation became more sophisticated, was Vivian (later Chaim) Hertzog. Born in Dublin and educated at Oxford, with war service as an officer in the Guards, Hertzog had spent 18 months with British military intelligence. His assignment for Hagana was to establish a network of pro-Jewish officers inside the British Army.

David Shaltiel succeeded Amir as another competent head of Shai but in 1948, at the time of independence, Shai's chief was Iser Be'eri and under him were district chiefs. Isser Harel, with Tel Aviv District, had the most difficult job since he came closer to the intense hatred between Hagana and Palmach on the one side and the dissident extremist groups, such as Irgun and Stern on the other. In those turbulent, pre-State days every group was striving for domination and resentful of anything that looked like poaching. Hagana took to tracking down Irgun and Stern men, beating them up and betraying them to the British. The rough and ready rationalisation behind this policy was that when independence came there could be only one Jewish force and authority or chaos would be inevitable.

*   *   *

Six weeks after the commencement of the War of Independence in May 1948, with their Arab neighbours threatening endless conflict, the Israeli leaders quickly expanded their secret services, replacing Shai with five distinct departments, three of them undercover. These were Aman, the Bureau of Military Intelligence; Ran, the Department of Counter Espionage; and Shin Bet, the Department of Internal Security; the other two were the Political Department and the Research Division of the Foreign Ministry. This branch engaged in 'legitimate espionage' – information culled from newspapers and magazines, many of them printed in Arabic.

Right from the start the over-riding priority was for Israel to develop 'preventive intelligence'. The country was too small in size, population and resources to allow enemies to take advantage of these weaknesses; hence intelligence must aim at stopping an incursion or war, rather than winning it after it had commenced. Similarly, if some country or foreign organisation planned a diplomatic or economic assault that, too, must be foreseen and forestalled. The Israelis were confident that they could surmount such difficulties, but it would be better to try and stop them from developing.

Israel's intelligence community had special advantages. It could draw agents from a population whose members came from different countries with various languages and cultures. When the Arab nations expelled their Jews or forced them to leave by subjecting them to humiliation, poverty and brutality Israel acquired people who could, if necessary, be sent back to the Arab countries as agents. An Iraqi Jew would not need to pose as an Arab – he was an Arab until deprived of his original nationality.

In October 1948, following Isser Harel's breaking of the Stern Gang, David Ben-Gurion, Israel's first Prime Minister, took a further step towards controlling those Jews who might want to operate outside the law. He instructed Yaa'cov Shapiro, the Government's chief legal adviser, to formulate a law against Jewish internal terrorism and very quickly the Provisional National Council – operating as a makeshift Legislative Assembly until elections could be held – approved regulations which prohibited membership of terrorist gangs and imposed heavy prison sentences for terrorist offences.

Principles, procedures and rules had to be established for the secret services, quickly and without outside help. Israel's leaders would have welcomed some expert help and a few Englishmen and Americans, formerly employed by the secret services of their own countries, gave technical advice on the structure necessary for an intelligence department. However no country offered any official help except the Soviet Union, whose motives were so patently obvious that its emissaries were turned down. The Israelis had no wish to have their secret services penetrated in infancy by the communists.

By 1950 the men and women employed by the secret services had conditions of employment which were the same as those for all other government employees. The great Ben-Gurion and his colleagues were insistent that intelligence agents would not be regarded as 'special'. They could foresee that, since Israel's enemies had declared eternal war, secret service work would be as essential a part of life in Israel as the postal service. It was just as well, then, to establish the fact that as a career the secret services were different only in their secrecy. Also, the leaders hoped that by this matter-of-fact acceptance of the normalcy of intelligence work the risk of any secret service leader taking too much power to himself could be obviated.

The secret services were the first of Israel's administrative departments to cross political barriers and to hire former members of Hagana, Palmach, the Stern Gang and Irgun. The secret services asked only that its members put loyalty to the state of Israel before loyalty to party. Still, from the beginning it was decided that, unlike many foreign secret services, Israel would not recruit criminals, no matter what skills they might have. People convicted of criminal offences after they joined Aman, Ran, Shin-Bet or Mossad were fired.

From about 1951, too, the government finance controller audited secret service accounts just as he did those of other departments. The details were not made public, but as the accounts were presented to the Knesset, the Israeli parliament, and open for politicians' inspection, there was little risk of corruption or of money being used for irregular purposes. No other country's secret services were subjected to such stringent accountability.

In the early years Shin-Bet was busier than any other department and to streamline its work and prevent duplication the Department of Counter-Espionage, Ran, was incorporated into Shin-Bet.

When any new state is formed foreign powers try to plant their agents in the country during the initial confusion. Israel was no exception: British, American, Russian, French, German, Italian, Greek and Japanese agents were discovered and ordered out of the country. Numerically, the Arabs were the worst menace, but as they were also the most inefficient they were easily spotted. Then, in the first half of 1950, the Arab nations employed Western agents. Many UN army officers, officially posted to the region as impartial observers, took Arab money to spy on Israeli defences and report to Cairo, Damascus or Beirut. Since they had diplomatic immunity they could operate with impunity and take their reports openly to the Arab capitals.

Exasperated, Shin-Bet struck back by planting microphones in the rooms of the UN observers when they stayed at Israeli hotels, and since most of them used the Hotel Kete Dan in Tel Aviv the task of radio surveillance was relatively simple. The Israeli technicians were still learning their job and some of their microphones were inadequately secreted and were discovered, leading to a clamorous diplomatic row. The Government apologised – and quietly told Shin-Bet to be more careful in future about where they put their microphones. With substantial reason the UN officers earned a very

bad name in Israel at that period. The only consolation was that most
of them were as incompetent at spying as the Arabs. Many were
attracted to the 'hostesses' at the Melody Bar, Haifa, all of whom were
Shin-Bet informers. The girls easily managed to get the UN officers talking and through them Shin-Bet fed misinformation and disinformation
to the UN men, who passed it on to the Arabs. Another of Shin-Bet's
functions, taken over from Shai, was recruitment of Arab informers.

Shin-Bet might have been outwardly the busiest of the secret services in the early years but the Political Department was becoming
well established under Boris Guriel, who had much experience as
head of the pre-State Department spying on the British. For his new
group Guriel sought young, highly intelligent and enthusiastic men
and women.

Successor to Be'eri as head of Aman was Vivian Hertzog, one of the
few intelligence professionals. His experience enabled him to give
Aman a ready-made expertise that the other branches at first lacked.
He was not only head of Aman but also its chief instructor.

Hertzog, influenced by his British experience, suggested that for the
sake of efficiency secret services should be linked and co-ordinated. A
'board of directors' under Reuven Shiloach was set up to organise this
co-ordination. This board, whose members included the heads of every
security agency, soon proved its worth in exchange of information.

The Political Department was most criticised, inevitably so because of
its necessarily experimental nature. The Israelis did not know how to
run a foreign service and needed to feel their way. In Israel, allegations
were made that the spies overseas were spending too much money, that
they were being 'un-Israeli' in manner and dress, and that they were
inefficient. Probably the charges were true to an extent, but the Israelis
at home were being less than fair. Their spies were forced to be un-Israeli
while abroad – a pose as a French businessman or a Swiss banker had to
be supported by the appropriate display of dress and affluence.

In the beginning, too, the Israeli spies could not be sure what information was important and what was trivial. Were they to concentrate
on military or political intelligence? What foreigners should they cultivate? Only experience could tell. But dissatisfaction was so rife that
in mid-1951 a supreme-level select committee under Ben-Gurion himself met to consider the future of the Political Department. They

decided to close it and enclose it within the Foreign Ministry. It would have no independent authority and it could take on only tasks set for it by the Ministry. The new 'Political Department' would study and analyse foreign political developments but it would have no spying or espionage role.

The momentous decision was taken to create an entirely new service, the Central Institute for Intelligence and Special Missions, almost at once known simply as 'The Mossad' or 'Mossad' – meaning Institution – with Reuven Shiloach as its head. The consequences of this decision were alarming and potentially catastrophic because the men and women of the now defunct Political Department rebelled and most of those who were abroad abandoned their posts and rushed home to take part in mutinous meetings. The flow of foreign information naturally dried up – Mossad was still barely more than an organisation on paper – and had the Arab nations decided to wage war at that moment Israel would have been naked. The Political Department staff were so angry about losing their role that they even refused to hand over current operations information to the Mossad chief and his assistants. And though the Political Department was dissolved the men continued to hold meetings to plan further discord. Strict measures were necessary. The rebels were dismissed from the Foreign Ministry and barred from employment in any government department.

Mossad took over all work abroad and under Shiloach's experienced and capable leadership it prospered. The cold-eyed, unemotional Shiloach was a lifelong student of intelligence, another genuine professional. In the 1930s he had spent three undercover years in Baghdad, posing as a teacher and journalist; he had been a counsellor to Weizmann at the Round Table Conference in London in 1939; and during the Second World War he was responsible for special operations. One of these was the formation of the 'Arab Battalion', whose members – all Jews, speaking flawless Arabic and dressing as Arabs – undertook special missions in Arab territory.

Intelligence is a competitive industry and Shiloach's ability and success invited disparagement. Even Isser Harel of Shin Bet was guilty of petty-mindedness about Shiloach, perhaps because he subconsciously resented the man's legendary reputation. The truth is that Shiloach had great self-discipline, a remarkable memory, a fertile mind capable of imaginative ideas, a cool, probing brain that saw to the roots of a problem and to the weaknesses of a man. He was one of the great spymasters of the century but he had two weaknesses – he lacked capacity for detail and ability to organise. He should have delegated to an assistant the organisation of some Mossad schemes.

When Shiloach left the Mossad early in 1953 and Isser Harel was appointed its chief executive the organisation of the intelligence community was firmly established. In addition to Mossad, Aman, Shin-Bet and the Research Division of the Foreign Ministry there was now the Special Branch of the Police Department, whose duties were to track down and bring before the courts undesirable aliens, to keep watch on foreign visitors who might possibly be engaging in illicit activities and to take over suspects from Mossad and Shin-Bet and interrogate them. Israel's Special Branch was closely modelled on Britain's SB.

In four years Israel had developed a system of secret service which suffered from one defect, lack of experience outside the country. That defect would soon be remedied. In all other respects Israeli intelligence was equal to any in the world and man for man its members were more versatile, with a greater command of languages and skills than those of other countries. They needed every skill as well as much enterprise and courage and never more so than when operating in Arab capitals.

*   *   *

During 1964 a Syrian businessman and noted patriot named Kamal Amin Tabas, aged 40, several times visited the Golan Heights on the Israel–Syria border. A close friend of several senior Syrian army officers, on intimate terms with Brigadier Amin El-Hafez (who later became President of Syria) and other leaders of the Ba'ath regime, Tabas had easy access to this top secret area, and nobody dared ask him not to use his camera. He and his officer escort would call at some army mess for lunch and Tabas was always welcome for he was known for his charm, wit and generous hospitality. He was in line for a cabinet post so the Syrian officers realised that he was a useful man to cultivate. They showed him plans of the complex project to divert the water of the Jordan River, which rises in the Golan Heights region, and thus bring Israel to ruin by thirst; they took him to see the great guns which would destroy the Israeli armed forces.

Back in Damascus Tabas sent coded messages of this and such other information to Tel Aviv, using a transmitter concealed in the ceiling of his bedroom in his luxury apartment across the street from army headquarters. The quantity and accuracy of his information astonished the Mossad men who assessed it in Tel Aviv and frequently they would say 'Eli Cohen has done it again!'

Eli Cohen, alias Kamal Tabas, has been called Israel's greatest spy and certainly qualifies as outstanding in international company. In Israel his courage and daring have made him a legend.

Born in Alexandria, Egypt, in 1924, Eli was the second eldest of a poor but large and happy Jewish family. Educated at Rabbi Ventura's school, he was alert, intelligent and interested in everything. One game in particular, played with his schoolmates, helped to develop his sense of observation. It consisted of studying an object for a certain limited time and then drawing it from memory in the greatest possible detail. This exercise was a pictorial version of one of the main activities of Jewish schools, where the children are required to learn by heart whole chapters of the Bible and long prayers.

Eli Cohen might well have stayed in Egypt as a loyal Egyptian Jew had not the Egyptian government so brutally maltreated its Jews that most of them fled to Israel. When Eli's family emigrated he stayed on and, in a minor way, served Israeli intelligence. He went to Israel where he became a bookkeeper before joining the Defence Ministry in 1957. He had all the characteristics of what Jews jokingly call the 'typical Israeli' – he was mildly irreligious, he spoke the country's language badly, he was born elsewhere and while not patriotic in any formal sense he was determined to defend the country he had adopted. He also had the qualities which make a competent actor and at parties he was popular for his mimicry; he could imitate anybody from Gamal Nasser to Charles de Gaulle. It was at a party that he met Nadia, a Jewish refugee from Iraq, whom he married in 1959.

He knew a few people in intelligence and offered his own services, but Mossad was disinclined to accept 'walk-ins', the spy trade term for volunteers. Still, the institution's recruiters kept their eye on this confident, calm man who spoke five languages and assessed him as intelligent, courageous and observant. He was not an exhibitionist, they reported, and he was no mere adventurer; he wanted to do something to ensure Israel's future. Mossad tested him. Given a French passport, Cohen was told to go to Jerusalem and entirely by his own efforts to meet and talk with as many influential people as possible, to throw off those agents who would be tracking him and to report any surveillance that he noticed. With his charm, persistence and photographic memory he achieved a great deal and handed over information that any genuine enemy spy would have been pleased to possess.

At this time, early in 1960, the greatest of Israel's troubles was Syria's belligerency. From the dominating Golan Heights, Syrian artillery constantly shelled Israeli kibbutzim in the fertile valleys below. From these same heights came the water which fed the Jordan and Israel's irrigation system. Israel had proposed a joint irrigation scheme with its Arab neighbours but they had rejected the idea, preferring to try to sabotage Israel's own water system.

The anxiety over Syria became a nightmare when Syria invited into the country thousands of Soviet Red Army technicians who arrived with enough military equipment to arm the Syrian forces three times over. Israel's leaders badly needed a man in Damascus and to Mossad Eli Cohen seemed ideal. Instructors set out to make him Syrian in language, appearance, manner and outlook. His cover was explained to him by his Mossad mentor, whose code-name was Dervish.

From now on Eli Cohen was Kamal Tabas,* born in Beirut to Amin and Saida Tabas, who had been forced to leave Syria for the Lebanon because of money troubles. His parents retained Syrian citizenship and they had imbued Kamal with deep feeling for Syria. When Kamal was three his parents had gone to Alexandria, Egypt, where Mr Tabas had established a small textile business. Since Cohen had grown up in Alexandria he could easily answer questions about the place. In 1947 the Tabas family, apart from Kamal, emigrated to Argentina, where the parents had died. Kamal had lived in Europe for 17 years; he had worked for a while in a travel agency and then started an import-export business which he had successfully developed.

Mossad even provided Cohen with a Tabas family album, a masterpiece of forgery containing faked photographs of the Tabas family, including some of Kamal (Eli) taken in a Buenos Aires setting with his supposed father, mother and uncle.

---

* In various reports the name has been spelled Taabs, Tabes, Tabas, Tabet, Tabat. Cohen's documents were made out in the name of Tabas and the Syrians also use this spelling.

To prepare for his job, Cohen pored over the files on every important military and political figure in Syria. He sharpened his perception and memory with daily mental exercises and he improved his espionage skills. He mastered his Morse transmitter keyboard in only two weeks and after six months' training he was ready. He told his wife that he had to travel abroad and would be away 'indefinitely'. Nadia, whose only certain knowledge of her husband's job was that he worked in 'defence', guessed the nature of his travels but she never discussed his work with him. In Munich, Cohen met his contact and was equipped with clothing made in Argentina and arrived in that country in February 1961. After a rapid course in Spanish, the language of Argentina, he confidently entered the thriving Arab community of Buenos Aires.

Gregarious and friendly, he was accepted by the expatriate Syrians and was soon attending parties and diplomatic receptions. He was introduced to Brigadier Amin El-Hafez, the Syrian military attaché, who liked this businessman who was so well informed about the need for revolutionary changes in Syria. After nearly a year in Argentina, Cohen's cover was well established and he could move on. He told his Syrian friends that his sense of duty to country was taking him back to Syria for he believed that he could develop the country's foreign trade. Impressed by his character and patriotism, several influential Syrians gave him letters of recommendation and introduction to people in Damascus.

Cohen applied for and was at once granted an Argentine passport – a genuine passport to replace his forged Syrian one with its record of long residence in Europe.

Changing planes several times, Cohen returned to Tel Aviv for further briefing and to see Nadia and their two small daughters, the second born during his absence. Mossad instructors further improved his knowledge of codes, secret broadcasting and smuggling of documents. In January 1962, by way of Zurich, Genoa and Beirut the spy reached Syria. He had a transmitter and other espionage equipment concealed in a food mixer but the customs man at the border did not even open his cases, since the visitor was vouched for by Sheikh Magid El-Ard, a wealthy Syrian whom Cohen had met and cultivated on the ship from Genoa to Beirut.

After a few weeks residence in a hotel he found, with the help of Sheikh El-Ard and other new friends, just the apartment he was looking for – a luxury flat on the fourth floor of a building in the Abu-Rumana district. He transmitted to Tel Aviv his identity code number – 88. This also meant, on the first sending, 'Apartment found, am starting work'. Then he added the most important fact – 'Opposite Army Staff Headquarters'.

The Israeli spy felt his way carefully and did not commit himself to political affiliations until after the take-over by the Ba'ath Party, when, of course, he became a Ba'athist sympathiser. The new regime was increasingly hostile to Israel and Cohen sent back many warning reports – some by radio, others concealed in backgammon boards which he sent as 'gifts' to a contact in Germany who forwarded them to Tel Aviv.

Soon after his arrival in Damascus, Kamal Tabas, the gay, gregarious bachelor, began to give dinners and parties; nothing was too good for his guests – caviar, French liqueurs, Scotch whisky. Later, for certain important friends he wished to cultivate, Tabas arranged parties of a special kind – the type where the guests were entertained by Damascus's best bellydancers, a small troupe of Oriental ballerinas or the most expensive of Syria's prostitutes. He was so discreet about all this that his important Syrian friends trusted him still further.

Among these friends were Colonel Selim Hatoum, who commanded the army's élite parachute commandos, Colonel Salah Dali, a senior staff officer, Colonel Ahmed Sweidany, the Syrian army's intelligence chief, and, above all, General Amin El-Hafez, now president of the Syrian republic, whom Cohen had first met in Buenos Aires. Another important contact was the businessman Kamal Alheshan, son of the editor of Buenos Aires's Arab newspaper; through Alheshan Cohen met and became friendly with Lieutenant Maazi El-Din, nephew of the Syrian Army's Chief-of-Staff, General Abdul El-Din.

'Dervish' wanted to talk with him personally, so Cohen told his friends that he was going to visit Argentina to rally support for the Ba'ath and to induce rich Syrians to establish an organisation to market Syrian products in South America. His Ba'ath friends were delighted with his idea of setting up a Ba'ath fund in South America.

He called first at Tel Aviv, where his controller, Dervish, was anxious for his safety; he was too valuable to be unduly risked but Israel did need information on two vital matters and he was the only person who could get it. 'I'm quite secure,' Cohen said, 'What do you need to know?'

Dervish told him that another Israeli spy, working in the Soviet Union, had reported that the Soviets were about to give Syria a great quantity of arms, including the latest MiG-21 fighters and *Komar* class missile boats. The Israeli defence forces needed to know everything about this new weapons situation. Also, the Syrian plan to divert Israel's water supply was known to be nearing completion; detailed information was now vital.

In the spy trade it is not enough to pretend to travel to a certain place – cover stories must be carried through. So Eli Cohen went on to Buenos Aires where he raised from among the Syrian community $9,000 for a Ba'ath fund. For this purpose Mossad had authorised him to draw up to $10,000 from its South American funds, so in arranging a genuine fund Cohen had saved a lot of the Israeli taxpayers' money, but he did add $1,000 of Israeli money to the fund. Just as importantly he bought a fur coat worth $1,000 as a gift for President El-Hafez's wife, a sound investment.

Cohen took his cover further by encouraging Syrian merchants to import goods from Syria. 'You will find it helpful to use my name when you contact the Ministry of Trade in Damascus' he told them and they did. In this way he strengthened his credentials with the government.

In Damascus Cohen gained access to the frontier fortifications by the simple expedient of criticising their inadequacy. The Israelis could break the Golan frontier in hours, he complained. In the summer of 1964 he told President El-Hafez himself that he was shocked by the poor state of the border defences. This was too much for El-Hafez. Not only was Tabas ignorant, but by his criticisms he was putting the Army in a bad light. He must be given a detailed tour of the front. Cohen confessed himself impressed by all that he saw but he silently noted that while the field of fire enjoyed by the Syrian guns was excellent a few sheltered ravines were not covered; Israeli attackers could move along these undetected and protected. He sent to Tel Aviv professional sketches of the entire defence system. From two friendly colonels, Dali and Hatoum, he gained a list of Soviet arms shipments and told Tel Aviv that 200 heavy Russian tanks were to be deployed in the Golan region. When war came the Syrians planned to use them to cut Upper Galilee from the rest of Israel. As for the MiG-21 jet fighter, Cohen sent photographs and specifications. Tel Aviv was delighted.

According to Damascus sources, Tabas was so impressed by the Syrian army's activities and so contrite for having been critical that he wrote out a cheque 'to the army' for $35,000. In Arab lands, where the army is the only effective power, such donations are a common kind of insurance against the effects of political upheavals. Eli Cohen was investing in army support for himself. The money of course, found its way into the pockets of his officer friends.

Cohen tapped Hatoum and Dali for information about the water diversion scheme. Through Hatoum he met the chief engineer, Saab, who was pleased to be able to talk in detail to such an intelligent and interested man as Kamal Tabas. Before long Cohen sent Tel Aviv a diagram of the scheme, which would be completed in 18 months. Installations included a large pumping station on the banks of the Baniyas River.

When the Syrians shelled Jewish border settlements it was easy enough for the Israeli gunners, in retaliating, to bring accurate fire to bear on the diversion installations without making it appear that they were making a special attack on them. It became impossible for the Syrians to continue with their diversion work – no sooner did they complete some part of it than Israeli guns blew it to pieces. The frustrated Syrians put it down to 'Jewish luck'.

Cohen did not restrict his dupes to senior army officers. One of his best friends was George Seif who, at the age of 33, controlled Syrian radio's information and propaganda programmes. Through Seif, Cohen gained the type of supercover which most spies can only dream about – the Government offered him the job of chief of programmes for Spain and Latin America. While making weekly anti-Israel broadcasts in Spanish, Cohen was able to send Mossad information through a code worked out in Tel Aviv.

Seif had a special reason to be grateful to Cohen, for the spy lent him and Colonel Hatoum the key to his apartment during the lunch hour or between five and seven in the evening. Here, in complete privacy and security – for Tabas was regarded as the only man in Damascus who never revealed another man's secrets – the Syrians developed their extra-marital affairs. One of Hatoum's more tempestuous mistresses was Loudi Shamania, a popular television singer.

Sometimes the parties in Cohen's apartment were more public. About the middle of May 1963 some of his friends organised a party that two years later was described as 'the Orgy of the Revolution'. Senior Syrian officers and diplomats and their high-class prostitutes lusted and drank the night through. At times like this, Eli Cohen, who could not always manage to be 'absent on business', needed all his self-discipline to stay sober and listen to the state secrets so frequently disclosed.

Cohen never used a motor car in Damascus; he had realised that a spy sees so much more by walking. One day he came across a small shop specialising in Syrian Army uniforms and regimental insignia. Posing as the owner of a souvenir shop from the northern town of Aleppo, Cohen bought an illustrated catalogue of insignia from the shop's owner. This later reached Tel Aviv where various branches of Israel's intelligence community considered it priceless. Its acquisition illustrates Eli Cohen's perception and observation.

He made new and important contacts, such as Eliya El-Maaz, co-ordinator of civil and military traffic at Damascus International Airport. At that time, between March and July 1963, Syria was sending four MiG-19s in reconnaissance sorties over the Israeli frontier each day. Then the flights ceased. Israel's Staff HQ was still pondering over the reason for the sudden break in pattern when a message arrived from Eli Cohen: 'Four MiG-19s based Damascus grounded. One pilot transferred for political instability, second pilot ill, third injured car accident.' Staff HQ drew the obvious – and correct – conclusion. If Syria could not replace three MiG reconnaissance pilots it was desperately short of trained airmen. It was a case of 'Eli Cohen has done it again' – in this case through casual information learned through Eliya El-Maaz.

Several reports have alleged that while in Damascus Cohen was given the job of tracking down the Nazi war criminal, Franz Raedemacher, an aide of Adolf Eichmann hiding in Syria under the name of John Rosallie, and of then eliminating him. Cohen certainly located Raedemacher and may well have felt like killing him but by temperament he was not a killer and Mossad did not ask him to dispose of Raedemacher. Mossad has never risked its most valuable agents by hazarding their cover in attempts to kill war criminals. A message from Tel Aviv told Cohen to forget about Raedemacher and concentrate on his special task, but in 1965, as a result of Cohen's information, passed on through diplomatic channels, West Germany had Raedemacher extradited.

Reports about the setting up and training of new terrorist squads reached Cohen and he signalled Tel Aviv: 'You can expect terrorist raids. Sweidany is training groups to destroy water pumping stations and to raid kibbutzim.' Because of this advance warning the pumping stations were better protected and the infiltrating terrorists could not destroy them, but they committed many terrorist acts and caused much border tension.

In November 1964 Cohen again visited Israel, taking with him a photograph of himself shaking hands with President El-Hafez and another with George Seif and the head of Syrian TV and Radio, Al'-goundi. He was home for further discussions and to meet his third child, a son, but he could stay no more than a few weeks before returning once more to Damascus to resume his vital work.

The only puzzling aspect of Mossad's handling of Cohen's activities in Damascus is that he was not provided with cutouts. Any regularly reporting espionage operation is worth at least three men – the information source, a radio operator removed from the information source and a courier to liaise between the two. Cohen was so confident in himself and Mossad had so much confidence in him that cutouts were not considered necessary.

The inevitable happened. The Syrian counter-intelligence radio room at last picked up some of his broadcasts. They lasted only a few seconds as they were now transmitted on ultra high-speed equipment, but all that is required to locate an illegally operating transmitter is patience. Time schedules, no matter how varied, repeat themselves and the transmitter can be plotted.

In mid-January 1965 Cohen had just completed a transmission to Tel Aviv when Colonel Sweidany and a group of secret police smashed into his apartment. Cohen could insist that he was Kamal Amin Tabas, a Syrian from Argentina, but in the face of the discovery of a reserve transmitter, several cameras and a code book his name was largely academic. Whatever he called himself, he was obviously a spy.

The Syrians say that they first became suspicious of Cohen after one of his visits to the Syrian-Israel border. According to this story, another visitor at the time was General Amer, the Egyptian chief-of-staff, and a photograph was taken of him for publicity purposes. 'Kamal Tabas happened to be included in the shot. In Cairo, Egyptian intelligence men who saw the photograph recognised Tabas as a Jew who had lived in Egypt. They alerted Damascus and Colonel Sweidany was able to catch Cohen in the act of transmission. Since this story shows Cohen's capture as more a matter of luck than counter-intelligence skill it appears to have some substance, for the Syrians would obviously prefer to be regarded as clever rather than lucky.

Sweidany forced Cohen to transmit a false message to Tel Aviv but he did so with a pre-arranged security check (q.v.) to indicate capture. Tel Aviv recognised the alarm and, playing for time, replied next day 'Yesterday's message unclear. Please repeat.' Thinking he was tricking the Israelis, Sweidany compelled Cohen to send another message and this time, to emphasise his capture the Israeli transmitted at a slower tempo. President El-Hafez was impatient with this intelligence battle of wits and told Sweidany to finish with it. Cohen's final forced transmission read: 'To Prime Minister Levy Eshkol and the head of the Secret Service in Tel Aviv, Kamal and his friends are our guests in Damascus. We are waiting for you to send us all his colleagues. We shall give you news of his fate. The Syrian Counter-Espionage Service. End.'

El-Hafez, having been duped by an Israeli spy, sensed the likelihood of a major political scandal. He was right. The governments of Egypt, Lebanon, Jordan and Iraq condemned El-Hafez and the Ba'athist regime. The anti-Ba'ath press in the Arab world erupted with criticism. Sweidany's police arrested hundreds of innocent people who had known Cohen – and many others who knew nothing more than the close connection between the spy and Colonels Dali and Hatoum; the colonels wanted to keep their involvement quiet.

Israel and friendly nations tried to rescue Eli Cohen or at least guarantee him a fair trial. The Pope, the King of Greece, the Queen Mother of Belgium and many famous people appealed on his behalf. Damascus ignored all. The French sent leading lawyers including the internationally famous Jacques Mercier to appear on Cohen's behalf but El-Hafez would not permit them in court. A wealthy Frenchman, Colonel Lezanne, flew to Syria to offer vast 'economic aid' in return for Cohen's life. According to the *Sunday Times* in London the offer was for $28m, plus army lorries, tractors and a large quantity of pharmaceuticals. El-Hafez knew Lezanne personally but refused to see him.

Israel offered to exchange five Syrian spies for Cohen but that trade, too, was turned down. Through diplomatic channels Israel then pointed out that Israel had never passed sentence of death on an Arab spy. This left El-Hafez unmoved; his personal pride had been wounded, an affront few Arabs can forgive. Cohen's death could be the only real consolation, but presumably the Syrians gained some satisfaction from the appalling tortures they inflicted on Cohen, which are better not described here.

No fewer than 37 others were accused with Cohen; the names were never announced but it is now known that 20 were junior officials and officers nominated to take the rap for their superiors; the other 17 were Kamal Tabas' party girls. Syrian officialdom had decided that it would be all too damaging to give the impression that the whole Syrian heirarchy had been outwitted by one man, so a 'Tabas ring' and 'Jewish conspiracy' were invented.

Cohen's trial by a military tribunal under the direction of Colonel Dali, with Colonel Hatoum as a member of the tribunal, began on 27 February and ended on 19 March; the sentence of death was reached on 1 May and announced a week later. The Israeli was convicted of 'infiltrating a restricted military area for the purpose of obtaining secret information that would weaken the security of the state of Syria. For this reason we sentence the accused to death by hanging.'

Eli Cohen was hanged before a crowd of many thousands in the main square of Damascus on the night of 18 May. Those who could not make the trip to see the 'performance' watched it live on television. The body was left dangling for more than a day, and all efforts to have it returned to Israel for burial were ignored.

Colonel Hatoum was executed in June 1967 by Ba'athist ultra-leftists after a coup; Colonel Dali was sentenced to life imprisonment with hard labour. Colonel Sweidany, who had risen to Chief-of-Staff, was removed after Syria's defeat by Israel in the Six-Day War and is thought to have been murdered.

In Israel Eli Cohen's memory has been honoured in many ways but probably he himself would have been pleased enough to know that his work as a spy was largely the cause of Syria's rapid and devastating defeat in the Six-Day War three years later. A sentence from Mossad's first report on his work sums up the man and his accomplishments – 'He always aimed higher'.

By the standards of any nation's intelligence service, Eli Cohen was outstandingly successful, but like many other brave and dedicated spies he was kept in the field for too long.

The traitor Kim Philby, perhaps the most effective spy to have worked for the KGB against Britain.

Guy Burgess – drunkard, homosexual and spy. He escaped justice but died a lonely man in Russia in 1963.

Donald Maclean, after his exposure as a traitor to his country. Was he experiencing remorse when this photograph was taken in Russia?

Anthony Blunt, whose knighthood was withdrawn by the Queen when it was revealed that he had spied in collusion with Philby, Burgess and Maclean.

John Vassall during his service days. Known to his colleagues as 'Vera', he was a homosexual and an easy blackmail victim for the KGB.

Greville Wynne, a British businessman who spent several years in a Soviet prison for spying; he had been a courier for Oleg Penkovsky, an officer of the GRU and one of the most important spies known to have worked for the West in the USSR. *(Hulton Getty)*

Oleg Penkovsky arriving for his trial in Moscow.

Greville Wynne (left) and Oleg Penkovsky stand trial in Moscow. Wynne was later exchanged for the Soviet spy 'Gordon Lonsdale', but Penkovsky is believed to have been executed or to have committed suicide in prison. *(Hulton Deutsch)*

After the uncovering of the Berlin Tunnel in 1956, Russian officers show journalists where communications cables in East Berlin had been tapped from the Tunnel. *(Hulton Getty)*

The Press in front of the exit to the Berlin Tunnel, 24 April 1956. *(AKG/Gert Schütz)*

East German guards in the Berlin Tunnel after its discovery in April 1956. The notice reads: 'You are now entering the American sector.' *(AKG/Gert Schütz)*

Sub-Lieutenant David Bingham who, with his wife Maureen, betrayed naval secrets to the USSR.

Geoffrey Prime, a spy for the USSR at the heart of GCHQ. He has been called the 'Two million pound spy'.

Isser Harel, an early head of the Israeli Mossad.

Jonathan Pollard, a dreamer who wore himself out spying for Israel in the USA.

7

THREE WOMEN IN INTELLIGENCE AND ONE WHO WAS SEDUCED

Some women have been involved in intelligence as prostitutes (Rahab, the harlot of Jerico), as double agents (Kay Marshall) and as couriers (Maureen Bingham) among others. They are representative of a large number of women who have spied for their own country or for a foreign power, while others have seduced men into turning traitor. While it is true that some nations have expected women career intelligence officers to entice 'enemy' officials into bed they are the exception, not the rule. When Western intelligence agencies want a woman for sexual entrapment operations they recruit an intelligent prostitute to do the job. They are better than 'ordinary' women at cold-blooded seduction because they are not acting an unpleasant role. For them it is a job.

The Soviet Union and its satellite countries also use prostitutes for entrapment purposes, but apparently the spymasters there have less confidence in them than the British and American had in their prostitutes because for really important missions women KGB and GRU officers were expected to lie back and think of Russia in the course of worming secrets from the target diplomat, services officer or foreign service official. Most embassies employ local people as domestic and personal servants so it is simple, in Moscow, for the Russians to insert a KGB operative into an embassy as an ordinary worker. One British ambassador, Sir Geoffrey Harrison had a jolly time and a wild relationship with a KGB woman officer in the embassy linen room. The liaison was discovered, and the ambassador was recalled and given early retirement – as well as his nation's highest decoration. Another European ambassador to Moscow was so infatuated with his Russian *enamorata* that he tried to correspond with her even after he had been called home to explain his conduct. He too was given a coveted decoration on the understanding that the relationship with the KGB major had ended. Not that he had any say in the matter; the KGB saw that there was no more mileage in him and released the major from duties which, I am told, she had found distasteful. In the new climate of openness many tit-bits of information are filtering out.

*   *   *

Some women were spymasters long before the leaders of the revolution in equality for women would have insisted that they be called spymistresses. Perhaps the greatest of women espionage instructors was Dr Elspeth Schragmuller – better known as *Fräulein Doktor* – who was a lieutenant in the German Army of the First World War. She was then in her mid-twenties and according to somebody who knew her then she was 'a slim blonde with steel-blue eyes with sharp intelligence'. She so impressed her superiors that she was transferred from censorship duties to the Special Intelligence Corps, and in an army school at Baden Baden she was trained in basic espionage. On graduation she was far too intelligent and innovative to be used in the field, and instead she was posted to the staff of a specialist school in espionage at 10 rue de la Pepiniéres in occupied Antwerp.

As the first women instructor in German espionage she had to overcome male chauvinism and resentment; she mastered the first by being much better than the men and the second by ignoring it. She was so dominant and so thorough that the school became 'The Fräulein Doktor's School', even though she was outranked by a major. She spent much time with each trainee, mainly to instill in him or her the absolute readiness to die for the Fatherland. Some of her espionage precepts are practised to this day, though most people in the business probably do not know their source.

Young though she was, Shragmuller knew human nature and she understood that most spies experience the temptation to want to appear 'mysterious'. Consequently, they then speak or behave in a give-away manner. Shragmuller told her learner-spies that in just one situation they might, with advantage, act a little mysteriously. It could happen that, as a spy, they would be working on a person who obviously had secrets to tell but could not reach the point of disclosure. Then, she said, you may tell this person a 'secret' of your own, a wholly spurious one, as if confiding in him. The implicit flattery would probably soften him to the stage where he would talk. In all other situations agents should be casual and relaxed.

'You are no use to the Fatherland if you get yourselves caught or if you have to abandon your mission because you are suspected. Your own security is everything.' She then went went on to list ways of ensuring, or at least enhancing, personal security. Here are some of her security points, translated from an instruction card which has survived. The *Fräulein Doktor* would be angry about its survival; such things were to read, memorise and destroy.

- Do not bargain with an informant on his ground;
- Make him travel as far as possible and by night so that he is tired, then he will be less cautious and suspicious. Do not meet him on your own immediate ground;
- Assume that you cannot trust your memory and therefore record information but in innocent appearing terms. For instance, remember statistics and sizes as items of personal expenditure;
- Conceal your knowledge of languages or at least appear poor in them. This encourages other people to speak more freely in your presence;
- The only safe way of destroying a document or letter is to burn it, crush the ashes to powder and throw it to the winds.

The phrase 'throw it to the winds' is significant in Shragmuller's career because she sacrificed or threw away some of her agents in order to distract the enemy's attention from spies carrying out more important missions. Not surprisingly, considering her reputation and male prejudice, she was variously called the Terrible Doctor Elspeth, the Beautiful blonde (or Beast) of Antwerp, or Tiger Eyes. We know very little about Shragmuller following the war, which is surely how she would like it.

*　　　*　　　*

We know much more about Sarah Aaronsohn, who spied for the British, also during the First World War. The daughter of Rumanian Jews, Sarah grew up in Palestine and became a linguist, a fine horse woman, a dead shot and ready for any adventure. The Arab marauders were raiding Jewish settlements and destroying what they could not steal, especially the grape harvest. In 1914, at the age of 23, Sarah showed her selfless character by marrying a merchant from Constantinople (later Istanbul) to give her younger sister Rivka an opportunity to marry the man she loved. In Jewish society at that time a younger daughter (Rivka) could not marry before her elder sister.

When war broke out and Turkey sided with Germany, Sarah watched with dread as the Turkish Army greatly strengthened its forces in Palestine in order to hold it against the British. She sent her family military information by writing under the stamps she put on her letters, an elementary form of getting a message through. Sometimes she wrote in French and Hebrew using words ambiguously to pass on information, a safer way than writing under stamps.

When the Turks invaded they ordered the Jews to hand over their weapons but through Sarah's letters many Jews, especially those around the town of Zichron Yaakov, now knew that the Turks had disarmed the Armenians as a preliminary to massacre. They handed over some weapons but kept most. Betrayed by Arab informers, some of the Jewish men were tortured by *bastinado* – beating on the soles of the feet – but they did not reveal the weapons caches until the Turks threatened to hand over the young girls of Zichron Yaakov to the officers 'for their amusement'. The treasured weapons were then distributed among the Arabs.

Into 1915, the Jews waited for the British to invade Palestine. There was nothing to stop a landing on the coast and Jews, Christians, Druze and even some Muslims were ready to welcome and help them. They were appalled when the British landed instead at Gallipoli – and certain defeat. They also lost confidence in British Intelligence which they had long considered to be supreme.

Nevertheless, they set up an espionage network to inform the British in Cairo about Turkish movements and weaknesses. At this time 'spy' was a vile word among the Jews of Palestine for to them it meant someone who had betrayed them to the authorities in the countries they had come from. They rationalised their own spying by seeing it as acting in their own cause. It was a principle that was to actuate all Jewish and later Israeli spying.

A Jewish pro-British spy ring was operating from Athlit, Palestine, including members of the Aaronsohn family and their friends. Sarah, sick of a loveless marriage, joined them after a terrible month's journey through Turkey. In the absence of her brother Aaron, the ring's leader, Sarah and her sweetheart, Absalom Feinberg, kept the anti-Turk movement going, building up the Jews to the pitch of armed rebellion, which they were convinced the British would finance and arm. Absalom set off through the desert to evade the Turks and reach the British in Cairo. Sarah became leader at Athlit while Aaron tried to convince the British of what his spy ring could do. The British kept him waiting for a month and then asked him for his qualifications for service with British Intelligence. Had he attended a British public school, for instance.

Irritated by what he regarded as a frivolous interrogation, Aaron remained patient and pressed on. The Athlit spies got going at the end of 1916 under the code-name Nili (prounced 'nee-lee').* Aaron gave orders from Cairo while Sarah was leader in the field, gathering accurate and comprehensive information, encouraging the Jews of Palestine and providing help for those in desperate need.

Wise, energetic and determined, Sarah not only directed Nili's activities but took part in them, travelling to Jerusalem, Haifa and Tiberias, paying bribes when necessary to get travel permits.

Crossing the Jordan River, she induced an old friend of the family to act as spy at Afula railway junction. It was his medical duty to inspect all soldiers passing through the junction so it was easy for him to find out all troop movements and report to Sarah. In Jerusalem, Sarah stayed at the Hotel Fast, the rendezvous of many German officers working with the Turks. She left it with copious information, much of it written down in the dining room. Back to brother Aaron in Cairo went maps, numbers, and troop dispositions passed on by a few trusted men who crossed the Red Sea in a small boat.

---

* 'Nili' was formed from the initial letters of Netzach Israel lo Ishakara, taken from 1 Samuel XV. The New English Bible 1961 renders the sentence as 'God who is the Splendour of Israel does not deceive or change his mind.'

Because Sarah and her lieutenants were constantly bringing more people into Nili's work, rumours about a dangerous gang began to circulate in the Jewish community. Aaron and Sarah realised that Nili's activities were as much political as military. After the war, if Nili were recognised as having acted in the name of the Jewish community, Aaron Aaronsohn could demand international recognition for himself and the Palestinian Jews. However, now Nili's work was leading to conflict with other Jews, not so far-sighted, who were trying to prove to the Turks that the Jewish community was loyal to them. This faction decided to end Nili's existence.

In March 1917 the British captured Baghdad and made a three-day attack on Turkish lines in the south. In reprisal the Turkish commander, Djemal Pasha, expelled all Jews from Jaffa and Tel Aviv. Refugees fled to Jewish settlements all over the country as the Turks prepared to massacre them. Sarah sent a message to her brother Aaron in Cairo and within hours Reuters news agency in London was circulating the hot news of 'an impending massacre of Jews in Palestine'. Played up by British and American propaganda, the affair quickly became so sensitive that the Germans urged their barbarous Turkish allies to desist. Sarah Aaronsohn had saved many lives.

Aaron called Sarah to Egypt where the British offered her sanctuary. She insisted on returning, but war emergencies and enemy activity prevented her from getting through for two months. When she did return – with 50,000 francs in gold coins for the relief of refugees – she found her Nili organisation in chaos. The Jewish elders had demanded that espionage against the Turks must stop. Zvi Aaronsohn, less dynamic than his brothers and sisters, assured them that rumours of espionage centred on Athlit were untrue.

Sarah's predicament was a lesson in the need for continuous control of a spy ring. Now she had to renew contact with her agents, many of whom had disappeared. Some had stopped collecting information about Turkish activities and others had been transferred in their ordinary jobs. Before long, through her ceaseless activity, vital information was again going to Egypt and British attacks against the Turks were more successful. Some Nili spies were able to get information directly from Turkish officers – that is, freely given or bought and not wormed out by cunning. The Germans, who also had their spies, warned the Turks that pro-British spies were operating in their midst.

In Cairo, Nili's reputation impressed General Sir Edmund Allenby, who had taken over Middle East Command. He asked for certain precise information, to be sent by carrier pigeons provided by the army. Could Nili indicate the weakest point in the Turkish defences in the Beersheba centre? Sarah replied that she could. When Allenby wanted pictures of rock formations to help his engineers find water in the desert, Sarah supplied them from Aaron's files at the Agriculture Experiment Station the family ran. But Nili's advice about a landing from the sea was still ignored; the main British interest was an Arab desert revolt.

Unknown to Sarah, her Jewish enemies, motivated by panic or malice, had prepared a list of 100 names, those of the chief spies and 'troublemakers', to give to the Turks should it be necessary to save the rest of the community. Her name headed the list. Money was a problem too. At a time when T E Lawrence was spending a huge £500,000 a month on the Bedouin, Nili was receiving a paltry £400 a month for work of an infinitely more complex nature.

Some of Sarah's carrier pigeons were getting through and the British were able to shell Turkish troop concentrations through the information she provided. Then, through a pigeon, came danger. On 3 September 1917 Sarah sent off several pigeons but later found one of them near the Experiment Station. She frightened the bird into flying and next afternoon received word that it had alighted at Caesarea, just along the coast, right into the hands of the local Turkish chief of police who was feeding his own pigeons. He had found the coded message.

The other pigeons were destroyed and anything incriminating was buried. The police had not yet deciphered the code, but they were investigating and on 6 September they arrived in Zichron Yaakov. Sarah had yet another serious problem. At a safe distance from Athlit and Zichron Yaakov she was hiding an intelligent, well-informed Turkish officer who had defected. She desperately wanted to move him out to her brother in Cairo, but night after night her men waited in vain for the British ship that was to collect him.

The Turkish search net was tightening, with a focus on Athlit. Sarah reduced her immense problems to the simple question of whether the British intended to go on sitting in Egypt. If not, Nili work could stop for a few months until the alarm over the pigeon had subsided. Meanwhile, without any pigeons the spies' information was building up into a mass. Still the ship failed to arrive. Sarah was not to know that the key swimmer between shore and ship wanted more money for the risks he ran and the British would not pay the few extra pounds involved. Incredibly, as Allenby's plans for a major campaign drew to a climax, penny-pinching economy was depriving him of his most valuable intelligence.

Sarah, still not 27 years of age, must have felt that the world was against her. And then the danger heightened. The Turks picked up a key Nili spy, Naaman Belkind, after he had been trapped by some Bedouin. The Turks proposed to hang him but the Germans, more astute, advised them to flatter and feast the captive, to give him drink and hashish. Under this treatment Belkind talked frequently – as many spies before him had done. When the Turks by fake friendship had extracted all they could from Belkind they took him to Beersheba in chains. The German commander, von Kressenstein, had him tortured for more information and then hanged.

The British ship arrived, bringing money for the refugees and for Nili. It would return the following night for the Turkish defector and the painfully acquired reports, including information about the weakest points in the Turkish lines. As the Nili leaders made arrangements to flee Palestine the Turks drew ever closer, for Belkind had revealed everything. Sarah, who planned to be the last to leave, was still sending information on replacement pigeons. One of her most daring colleagues, Absalom Fine, had brought her a rough map showing most of the machine gun emplacements on the Gaza-Beersheba front. The British officer in Cairo who received this piece of priceless paper telegraphed the information to GHQ.

With this vital information Sarah sent a message insisting that the ship come again on 27 September to collect at least six people who must not fall into Turkish hands. But spies are often sacrificed for 'higher reasons' and in Cairo it was decided that Nili had to be sacrificed in order to save the entire Jewish community of Palestine. If the leaders of Nili were to slip through their fingers the Turks would certainly begin a vengeful massacre. Sarah's plea for rescue was ignored.

On 2 October the brutal Turkish Brigadier Hassan Bey led the troops who surrounded Zichron Yaakov into the town. The searches and tortures began at once. The Turks beat Ephraim Aaronsohn, father of Sarah, Aaron, Alex, Zvi and Rivka but he told them nothing about his children. They started on Sarah next day, tying her to a gatepost and beating her until she was unconscious. Hassan Bey, having captured several Nili members, told the people of Zichron Yaakov that he would obliterate the place within three days if a key Nili member, Yusuf Lishansky, was not produced. Sarah had given the Zichron Committee £500 in gold for use as bribes – any Turk could be bought – but the men were frightened and dared not approach any of the Turks.

Sarah Aaronsohn did not lose her head. Taken in chains along the street she managed to ask a friend to close a particular window. This was a warning of danger to the British ship. The Turks tortured their prisoners diabolically, Sarah worst of all, pulling out her hair and fingernails and burning her. Hearing that the group was to be taken to Nazareth for more expert torture, Sarah asked permission – a request aided by a bribe – to return home and change her clothes. Here she wrote a remarkably coherent letter in which she gave directions for the welfare of the Experiment Station workers, revealed the names of four women who had informed on Nili, called for vengeance on the Turks and instructed that Yosef Lishansky should kill himself rather than be caught. Then she retrieved a hidden revolver and shot herself through the mouth. She lived through three days of agony before she died.

Lishansky, though wounded, made a valiant effort to reach the sea for an arranged rendezvous with a British ship on 12 October. He eluded the Turks but an Arab recognised him, knew he was worth money and sold him to the Turks who hanged him in Damascus. Because of Belkind's betrayal every Nili member in Palestine was tracked down and tortured, some so viciously that they were invalids for life. But the Turks never did find out how the Nili organisation worked.

With information provided by Sarah Aaronsohn, Allenby's troops won the third battle of Gaza on 9 December 1917 and soon after this he took Jerusalem. Some of the Nili members who had remained free, including Alex Aaronsohn, were given British decorations. All that Aaron Aaronsohn received was vilification from the Jews of Palestine. They blamed him for the Turks' violence and tried to stop him entering the country. Nevertheless, Aaron attended the Peace Conference in Paris where he was considered great among the great. In London, he prepared a report in Palestine's boundaries – one of the most vexatious matters ever to plague history. On the way back to Paris on 15 May 1919 his plane was lost over the English Channel and the Nili saga ended.

Some Jewish mothers named their daughters Nili, thus paying a sentimental compliment to Sarah Aaronsohn. Aaron credited Sarah with having won Palestine for the British. Allenby did *not* do so but spies are rarely credited with work that helps generals to achieve victories.

In retrospect, the entire Nili project was flawed from the beginning if only because too many people knew too much about too many other people. But the Nili intelligence network was run by amateurs not by trained, hard-nosed professionals. On the other hand, it is doubtful if professionals could have achieved more than the dedicated Sarah Aaronsohn and her band of patriots.

*   *   *

Cairo has always been a city of intrigue and a generation after the activities of the Nili spies it was again the strategic nerve centre for Allied operations around the Mediterranean and in Asia Minor. The teeming city had a large British intelligence and military population as well as German, Italian and Arab spies and Greek, Jewish and Arab profiteers. Interlaced with foreign military plotting was domestic political intrigue – King Farouk's court and the Egyptian administration were both notorious for their scheming. In the middle of this intricate web of mystery lived Yolande Gabay, a wealthy Spanish-Italian Jew, part-educated in France and long resident in Egypt.

In the annals of Jewish/Israeli intelligence, Yolande's story has an unusual place because the Jewish intelligence chiefs had decided that she had neither the wit nor aptitude for spying work. She not only proved them wrong, she became one of the greatest women spies of history, though her story is little known in Europe and the US.

Before she became involved in espionage Yolande had only the chance of her birth to make her Jewish; she had little feeling for Judaism and she knew nothing of Jewish history. She deserves her special place if only because of her ability to make friends with so many Arabs in high places. Few Israeli spies can claim to have had an influential Arab fall in love with them.

She was certainly attractive, petite, with laughing brown eyes and lips which smiled readily, a smooth olive skin, wavy hair and a vivacity which appealed to everybody who met her. When the Second World War broke out in 1939 Yolande was 28 years old, divorced, and with a six-year-old son, Gilbert. She had been married to a man

98

chosen by her Orthodox Jewish parents and not surprisingly this love-less union broke up. The experience made Yolande cautious with men, but as she was by nature romantic, adventurous and gregarious she began to meet Palestinian Jews serving in the British Army, though almost without exception they were also members of the underground Hagana. These direct, dynamic men impressed Yolande, more accus-tomed until then to mixing with softer, equivocating Arabs, commercially minded Levantine Jews and British officers seeking sexual conquests.

Her first opportunity to take part in intelligence work was indirect. In 1943 the British began dropping Hagana volunteers behind German and Italian lines in Europe to rouse Jewish resistance against the Nazis and Fascists. Enizo Sereni, a Palestinian Jew of Italian back-ground and an impressive leader, was a natural choice for work in Italy. While under training in Cairo, Sereni also broadcast propaganda programmes to encourage the anti-Fascist civilian population of Italy. Then he disappeared. British intelligence and military police searched vainly for him and decided that Egyptian Fascists – Cairo had many Arab pro-Nazi supporters – must have kidnapped or killed him.

Hagana wanted to be sure and asked Yolande to use her contacts for a more thorough search than the British could make. She coaxed her Egyptian police friends into searching Cairo's many prisons – and Sereni was found in solitary confinement in a dungeon cell. He had been kidnapped by Fascist agents and imprisoned by bribed prison officials on false charges under another name. The Fascists wanted to stop his broadcasts. The British authorities extracted Sereni from prison and Yolande was invited by Hagana to visit Palestine. She did not know it, but Sereni had told Hagana leaders that she was utterly reliable, intelligent and enterprising.

Hagana leaders followed Yolande everywhere, hoping to find in her the makings of a spy, but they concluded that this attractive women of 'only average intelligence' was too frivolous and they were surprised that Sereni had been so mistaken about her. Still, early in 1944 when Yaacov Tzur was ordered to open a Jewish Agency office in Cairo – ostensibly a social club for Palestinian Jewish soldiers – he was told to employ Yolande when dealing with the Egyptian authorities. Tsur, too, quickly decided that Yolande was too frivolous to be a successful spy.

Then Yolande came under the shrewd eye of Levi Abrahami, a

Hagana agent sent to Cairo disguised as a British Army officer. In his forties, self-contained and cautious, Abrahami was to be chief of Hagana's intelligence in Egypt and he had the particular mission of organising the collection of much of the debris of war which littered the North African deserts. By now the war had moved away from the deserts of North Africa to the northern Mediterranean and the British Commonwealth armies, the Germans and the Italians had left behind masses of weapons and other equipment. It had not exactly been abandoned and much of it was in stores, but it seemed to Hagana that the combatant armies had no further use for it. Abrahami needed local help but he dared not contact his many friends among Palestinian Jewish officers in Cairo for fear that they might unwittingly give him away.

He contacted Yolande, and they spent a long evening together at her home. Abrahami asked this pretty women many direct and sometimes personal questions and he decided after several hours of conversational interrogation that her frivolity was only superficial. He concluded that she was responsible, discreet and most intelligent and that his mission would be safe with her. His colleagues, he believed, could never have looked *behind* Yolande's 'frivolous' eyes.

Yolande was delighted to help and not far from Alexandria she found a large secluded, tree-surrounded villa which Abrahami could use as an arms collection depot. Yolande rented it in her name and disguised it as a convalescent home for Allied soldiers. Occasionally she posed as the 'matron' and now and then, to add depth to the cover, soldiers in British Army uniform could be seen lounging in the grounds.

Abrahami found that Yolande had an impressively large circle of friends, including Egyptian and foreign journalists, Egyptian and other Arab politicians, and senior British and Egyptian service officers. He considered that her talents were under-used and suggested that Yolande become a journalist. She quickly built up a connection with several French newspapers, which gave her accreditation as a correspondent. She was then able to interview important people and ask them questions which might seem suspicious had they come from anybody other than a journalist. One of her first important interviews was with Azam Pasha, secretary of the Arab League, who saw the possibility of good foreign publicity through the attractive correspondent. Characteristically for an Arab, he gave her much confidential information in order to ingratiate himself with her.

On 6 November 1944 two Stern Gang terrorists assassinated the British Minister of State in the Middle East, Lord Moyne, at his home in Cairo. The long trial and execution of the two young Palestinian Jews, Eliahu Bet-Tsoury and Eliahu Hakim, inspired Egypt's own independence movement and Egyptian public opinion was strongly in sympathy with the Zionists in their anti-British struggle. Most Egyptians at that time were not anti-Jewish. Yolande disliked the Stern Gang but the terrorists' execution brought home to her the eternal Jewish tragedy and made her approach to intelligence even more serious. For the first time she was conscious of fighting for a Jewish nation.

She now helped Abrahami smuggle into Palestine thousands of Egyptian, North African and European Jews and she constantly recruited assistants for the jobs involving bribery, forgery and transport. Then a much more important mission cropped up. Jewish leaders, such as Ben-Gurion, wanted to make contact with Arab leaders, for they saw the opportunity of working with them against the British, so that Arabs and Jews between them could develop a 'free' Middle East. Such liaison was impossible in Palestine where extremist Arabs led by the Mufti of Jerusalem, Haj Amin El Husseini, killed or terrorised any Arabs suspected of wishing to live in peace with the Jews. Yolande was asked to lay the groundwork for a direct approach by Jewish leaders to Arab leaders in Cairo. The instructions given to her and the way she fulfilled them are an example of the thoroughness of preparation in Jewish intelligence projects.

Yolande supplied Ben-Gurion and his assistants with reports based on direct interviews with key figures and gradually she employed assistants who supplied other accounts founded on contacts with Egyptian editors, politicians and foreign diplomats. Yolande developed her personal friendship with Mohi Bey, secretary to Azam Pasha, chief of the Arab League. An idealist and in love with Yolande, Mohi wanted Jews and Muslims to live in unity and he regarded his relationship with Yolande as symbolic of his religious-political dream.

Yolande also expanded her journalistic dragnet by having herself appointed Cairo correspondent for Jerusalem's English language newspaper, the *Palestine Post*. She needed all the information she could get to satisfy Hagana's demands.

Arab League activity was intense, for its members were now evolving a policy and programme should the Anglo-American Commission on Palestine recommend the establishment of a Jewish state. Yolande was able to provide much information, even when the Arabs held their conference in seclusion in the Lebanon, but she was dissatisfied with her pieced-together deductions of Arab plans. This led to what was her greatest coup. One hot morning in late August 1946, Yolande telephoned Abrahami and invited him to spend a few days at her summer cottage on the Nile, in company with Mohi Bey.

While Mohi busied himself with files that afternoon Yolande, her young son Gilbert and Abrahami swam and sailed. That night Abrahami and Mohi had what Abrahami later called a fantastic conversation about Arab ambitions and plans. As he was going to bed Yolande squeezed his hand and whispered '*au revoir*'.

This puzzled the Hagana man – and he was even more bewildered when before dawn he was awakened by the noise of a car and looked out to see Yolande driving off with Mohi and Gilbert. On the living room table he found a note from Yolande: 'In case you are upset I have left you a consolation present in the cupboard.'

The present was nothing less than Mohi's briefcase, stuffed with documents carefully divided into files labelled CLASSIFIED, SECRET and TOP SECRET. Abrahami, who understood Arabic perfectly, found that he was reading private correspondence between Arab rulers, plans for frustrating any Anglo-American solution about Palestine, estimates of Hagana's strength and much other valuable material. Hurrying back to Cairo, he had the documents copied by a Jewish photographer friend and hastened to return the briefcase to Yolande.

It was then that he found that Mohi Bey had risked his neck because of his love for Yolande and because he still believed that Arabs and Jews could resolve their differences without fighting. The documents, he hoped, would give the Jews a better understanding of the Arabs.

For Hagana the photographed documents were priceless intelligence and the organisation's experts on Arab affairs were inclined to agree with Mohi that peace was possible for the papers showed that important Arab personalities were not anti-Jewish. On the strength of this information, the Jewish High Command now instructed Yolande to arrange an interview between the Egyptian premier Ali Maher and Eliahu Sassoon, a Syrian Jew who could represent the Jewish Agency.

It was a delicate assignment. Yolande sought a newspaper interview with Maher and gradually brought the conversation round to the

Palestine question. Well briefed, she recollected that years before Maher had met Chaim Weizmann and had admired him. Maher proudly told her that he, Ali Maher, had suggested the St James Conference on Palestine in 1939, when Arab and Jewish representatives had met in London to discuss the issue. Eventually, Yolande, speaking as an international correspondent, suggested that Maher might achieve something of world importance by meeting Eliahu Sassoon, who 'happened' to be arriving soon in Cairo. At that time nothing prevented Jews from travelling to and from Egypt. Maher was understandably cautious for Cairo was alive with political and public tensions between the Egyptians and the British. The persuasive Yolande convinced Maher that such a meeting was of great historical importance and that through it Arabs and Jews might come together as oppressed peoples and make the Middle East a prosperous, peaceful region.

Yolande's success was complete. Sassoon met not only Ali Maher, but several other important Egyptians and Syrians. The meetings were friendly and Sassoon asked if he could arrange for Ben-Gurion and other important Palestinian Jews to talk to Maher. The Egyptian leader thought this might well be possible.

Delighted and impressed by Yolande's efforts, Ben-Gurion sent other leading Zionists to Cairo to make contact with moderate Egyptian leaders and the possibility of a negotiated agreement on a Jewish state seemed bright. But Arab politics are volatile and Ali Maher lost the leadership to extremist Egyptians who wanted no collaboration with the Palestinian Jews – though at that time the Egyptian public still had no particular feeling about Palestine.

Yolande continued her work, running a large spy ring with remarkable efficiency, and her links with Hagana remained unsuspected. Ben-Gurion and others, sensitive to political shifts of wind, advised her to be ready to leave at a moment's notice.

Yolande's personal life had now got in the way of her spying. Early in 1947 she had met Major Albert Hermor of the South African Army, stationed in Libya, and they had fallen in love. Before Hermor left for the airport to return to duty they were engaged. His plane crashed on take-off and for a month Yolande was Hermor's principal nurse in a Cairo hospital as the doctors fought, none too optimistically, for his life. When he had recovered sufficiently the couple went to Ramat David, a settlement in the Jezreel Valley of Palestine, where Hermor, who was Jewish, had friends. From here Yolande drove her fiancé to see many parts of Palestine. By permission, she also disclosed her secret activities for Hagana, and Hermor offered to help with them. After a week in Alexandria, Hermor and Yolande travelled to Tripoli, Libya, where Yolande was to wait while the South African flew off to his unit to arrange for his discharge from the Army. Again his plane crashed. Yolande, taken to a British army hospital, saw her lover die without regaining consciousness.

As much for her own sake as for the Jewish nation, Levi Abrahami put Yolande back to work. The Mufti of Jerusalem and other fanatics were in Cairo stirring up trouble, the moderates were losing ground and King Farouk was being influenced by ranting anti-Jewish Arabs. Yolande and her friends worked incessantly at cultivating the Arab leaders who might still avert conflict. Again and again she saw Azam Pasha, but pressure for armed opposition to the Jews mounted, and large supplies of arms were sent to the Palestinian Arabs. British Intelligence as well as Yolande knew about these shipments, but made no effort to stop them.

Yolande, still able to acquire reports of the deliberations of Arab summit conferences, informed Tel Aviv that the moderates had lost. She warned that the Arab nations would violate the United Nations' resolution on Palestine and oppose the major powers which had voted for the establishment of a Jewish state. The Jewish leaders were reluctant to believe her.

With her spy ring under strain but still holding together, Yolande refused to leave Egypt and in May 1948, after Egypt and four other Arab nations launched a war against the Jews in Palestine, she and thousands of other Egyptian Jews were rounded up and imprisoned. She had been unwell and while in prison, despite favoured treatment from the bribed guards, she became very ill. The faithful and gallant Mohi Bey, again risking his life, smuggled her from the prison and flew her to Paris. After a long illness and several operations, Yolande, her aged mother and Gilbert emigrated to Israel. She soaked herself in Israeli life and was given a minor job in the Foreign Ministry. One day, visiting the Knesset, she met Premier Ben-Gurion, who embraced her lovingly in front of the assembly. It was Yolande's last great moment. She died in hospital in Jerusalem in 1957.

Yolande's great comrade-in-espionage, Levi Abrahami, had a distinguished post-State career and ended it as director of the Israel Numismatical Society. He once said that it was a pity that Yolande's work was not commemorated numismatically. She had the features and the character worthy of her bust on a coin. But then, he had seen her merit from the beginning.

Yolande Gabay's success as a spy might not be unparalleled among women in intelligence, but it was remarkable. Along the way she proved that even shrewd men can make mistakes when they are recruiting spies. The example of Yolande certainly influenced Mossad's leaders, who have probably employed more women in foreign intelligence activities than any other country, proportionate to the size of the organisation.

*   *   *

It is popularly considered that women in intelligence are frequently used to seduce enemy men into betraying secrets and certainly KGB women saw this as part of their duty. However many women involved with espionage have neither condoned nor practised seduction. Elspeth Shragmuller would not have expected a female operative to bed an enemy officer; Sarah Aarohnson would have been horrified at any suggestion that she could get what she wanted by seduction; and Yolande Gabay was not promiscuous.

The annals of espionage are punctuated by cases in which women diplomats or intelligence officers have succumbed to the blandishments of a foreign male career intelligence officer. Such a fate befel a Scotswoman, Rhona Ritchie, who on first analysis of her career might have been labelled 'least likely to betray secrets to a foreign power'. She was the product of a strict Scottish middle-class upbringing, head girl at school, a brilliant law student at university and a talented university lecturer. Somebody who had followed her progress reported: 'Highly intelligent, honest, reliable, loyal, a cultured young woman of elegance and style.' An experienced security official might have said that all this was irrelevant should Ritchie be exposed to the outside world: she knew nothing about it.

Ritchie graduated in law with a second class honours degree at Glasgow University in July 1973 and went back into university life, taking up a post as lecturer in the Department of Jurisprudence at Glasgow and remaining there for 12 months. She had ten years of protected university life before deciding to join the Foreign Office.

At a party in London's Mayfair the petite and elegant Rhona first set eyes on Rifaat El-Ansary, a divorcee and Second Secretary at the Egyptian Embassy. El-Ansary was known in diplomatic circles as the Cairo Casanova, though this label could have applied to many Egyptian men of his type. The handsome, smooth El-Ansary found Rhona Ritchie to be an easy conquest.

In September 1981 Ritchie was posted to the British Embassy in Tel Aviv as Second Secretary and quickly learned Hebrew to add to her good French and German. After the Camp David peace agreement between Israel and Egypt a new Egyptian Embassy was opened in Israel, and who should turn up there on the staff but Rifaat El-Ansary. If Rhona Ritchie thought that this was a happy coincidence, she was being naive.

Before long the Egyptian roué and the British diplomat were so often seen together that fellow diplomats referred to them them as 'R and R', a play on their initials and the army term for rest and recreation for tired troops. The more cynical staff at the British Embassy reckoned that Ritchie was getting little rest while El-Ansary was getting his recreation, but nobody at the embassy thought it necessary to check on possible breaches of security that might take place in Ritchie's luxury flat at Herzliya or in El-Ansary's apartment. In fact, she leaked the contents of official telegrams to him. One telegram she passed to her lover contained the text of a letter from the Foreign Secretary, Lord Carrington, to Alexander Haig, US Secretary of State. Another telegram, sent on 26 November, again contained a message from Carrington to Haig, and it was this one over which she was charged. She appeared in Number One Court at the Old Bailey in November 1982.

She claimed that she told El-Ansary only about messages that would be made public next day. El-Ansary had told her that he wanted to know the contents of the telegrams for his own background knowledge so that he could 'fully understand' them. She was defended by George Carman QC who said, 'In the current climate which prevails in this country may I make it plain that this young lady has never been a spy. She quite innocently brought her own conduct to light and on advice she has had the courage to plead guilty to the indictment.'

Much of Carman's argument hinged on the extent to which Ritchie was authorised to handle the information which came into her possession. He said there were innumerable cases in the diplomatic service where there was an implied authorisation to disclose information.

Even the Attorney General, Sir Michael Havers, said that Ritchie's behaviour was more foolish than wicked. Her tragedy was that she had fallen under the spell of an Arab envoy who abused her trust. And he added, 'Egypt is a friendly power and most of the information she disclosed would have become public in due course anyway.'

Ritchie had faced only a single charge under Section 2 of the Official Secrets Act of 'wrongful combination of information'. She was given a nine-month suspended prison sentence. A greater punishment was that her career had been cut short by ignominy and disgrace. El-Ansary was promoted for his 'coup', being posted to Vienna as First Secretary where, the SIS says, he continued his seductions 'in the interests of his career'.

Two matters arise from the Ritchie case. One is that the Foreign and Commonwealth Office does not give its women staff any formal instruction about foreign male diplomats with whom they will certainly come into contact when posted abroad. Educated Arabs are charming, courteous and generous when in pursuit of European women and Rhona Ritchie was only one of thousands left to rue their betrayal by such a man. I am told that any training given to Foreign Office women diplomats about their conduct abroad is superficial.

The other matter, as disquieting in the 1990s as it was in 1982, is Sir Michael Havers' assertion that Egypt is a friendly country and that – by his implication – it did not matter if the Egyptian Government got hold of Ritchie's information. Shrewd intelligence chiefs know that there is no such thing as a 'friendly power' in matters of intelligence. In any case, the Egyptian Government almost certainly passed El-Ansary's information from Ritchie to the Soviet Union and other nations with which Egypt wanted to ingratiate itself in 1981.

Intelligence is a commodity, to be traded and bartered. It would be disturbing if a British Attorney General did not understand this, but his use of the term 'friendly power' might have been cautious diplomatic language.

8

SPYING AS PART OF FOREIGN POLICY: TWO GREAT KGB TRIUMPHS

Successive British, American and other Western governments appear never to have understood that imperial Russia, post-revolutionary Russia and then the Soviet Union – of which Russia was the powerhouse – looked upon spying as a normal part of foreign policy. The leaders of the 'new' Russia have the same outlook. Even more clearly, the Western general public has no understanding of this simple truth if only because, in innumerable films, they see agents from the KGB, GRU and SMERSH as underhand, devious, treacherous, dishonourable and ruthless. Probably, by Western standards, they are, but down the years from 20 December 1917, when the Cheka (see below) was founded, leaders of Russian governments and intelligence organisations have never sought to justify their unbridled espionage activities. They would not consider justification necessary, unlike their Western counterparts who have often felt that they need to explain why the CIA, SIS, MI5 and the DST, among other agencies, exist.

The Russians have never clarified the functions of any of their secret organisations other than in the titles of some of them. Cheka, for instance, was the short form of *Chrezvychaubaya Komissiya po Borbe a Kontr-revolutisei i Sabotazhem,* meaning the Extraordinary Commission for Combating Counter-revolution and Sabotage. The tenor of the

109

Cheka's work was set by its first chief, Felix Dzerzhinsky, a fanatic driven by a perverted religious romanticism. In defence of the state, Dzerzhinsky killed, tortured and terrorised. No political leader tried to check his excesses because, as I have indicated, they were tools of government. It is significant that up to the end of the Cold War in the early 1990s KGB men were called *Chekists,* and this may still apply. That they were commonly known by this name shows to what extent Dzerzhinsky's methods were accepted by Soviet society into the 1990s, even though he died in 1925.

Under a succession of men directing intelligence, espionage and counter-revolutionary activities, torture and terrorism became growth industries and the organisations needed to manage them proliferated. There were so many of them that a book would be needed to describe them. Their leaders were public figures and senior members of the Communist Party, and they remain so today. This is in stark contrast to Western nations and indeed to most democratic countries where intelligence or security chiefs could not possibly be open supporters of a political party and where their say in government is nil. They are merely professional providers of information and security and when government ministers ask for their advice they give it.

The great bulk of the Russian public has always accepted without demur the all-pervasive role of the security services. Until recently, if anybody demurred in the hearing of an informer, then that was the end of him. If he was not summarily dispatched he was sent to a gulag to live out his life in misery. About 50,000,000 people are believed to have perished in Stalin's purges, including many who had turned informer in the hope that this would protect them.

Taught for generations to live in fear of foreign invasions, Russian citizens could readily accept every action carried out by its spies and assassins abroad, just as Bulgarians, East Germans, Poles and others would have applauded the deceptions and killings carried out by their agents. It was all part of a defence against 'Western imperialism' which, they knew from their schooldays, was intent on either wiping out or enslaving the population of the communist countries.

Officers of the security services themselves fell foul of their masters and were executed or sent to gulags. The infamous and powerful Lavrenti Beria, Director of Soviet Intelligence, was safe only while Stalin was alive. When the dictator died and Malenkov took his place

Beria was arrested, accused of conspiracy to overthrow the new regime, secretly tried and executed. No employee of the enormous Russian/Soviet security apparatus has ever been truly safe. What could happen to traitors was demonstrated in film to Russian intelligence men early in their career. They were shown a traitor being slowly fed into a fire, feet first, to die in an agony that could last for hours.

A KGB or GRU man who betrays his country does not warrant even a footnote in Russian history: he 'disappears'. In contrast though, espionage agents who serve the Soviet well are awarded such decorations as Hero of the Soviet Union and Order of Lenin.

This chapter tells the story of two Soviet successes in getting agents into the highest levels of Western intelligence and maintaining them there for years with consequent immense damage to the West. The preparation needed to give a spy the necessary cover is immense and the professionalism of such enterprise can only be ruefully admired. Again, it needs to be said that the British and American secret services have suborned a few Russians and turned them into spies to operate in senior echelons of the Soviet Government. The most famous was Oleg Penkovsky, whose real value to the West is controversial and is still being assessed.* I have heard of one Russian who has been working for the West within the Soviet intelligence system since the early 1980s, a very long period of time for an agent to remain active, but I am unable to confirm the report.

The Soviet successes in this chapter do not include Philby, Burgess, Maclean and Blunt, for so much has already been written about their treason.

*   *   *

By any yardstick, George Blake was one of the Soviet Union's greatest agents. Former KGB officers themselves say so. 'What a triumph the Blake operation was!' one of them exulted to me, and he was speaking more of the Russians' handling of Blake than of what Blake himself achieved – and that was a great deal. His career is difficult to analyse with accuracy because the British and Soviet intelligence ser-

---

* We do know, however, that he passed to the West more than 5,000 valuable documents providing new or confirmatory information. In addition he provided the entire syllabus for the Dzerzhinsky Artillery & Engineering Academy.

vices have woven disinformation into the fabric, to protect sources
and agents in place and, in the case of the British, to minimise the
immense damage done by Blake and thus also to minimise the culpa-
bility of the SIS.

Blake, born in Holland in 1922, was a curious racial and religious
mixture. His father was an Egyptian born in Constantinople (later
Istanbul), Turkey, and his mother was a Dutch Lutheran. His father
possessed a British passport and during the First World War he had
served both Britain and France in their armies. George, then using the
family name of Behar, was visiting his mother in Holland when the
Second World War broke out and the occupying Nazis interned him.
The Dutch Resistance helped him to escape and after working with
them for a time he reached Britain. Here he changed his name to
Blake and joined the Royal Navy.

The war over, the Navy sent Blake to Hamburg in command of a
small intelligence unit to seize and interrogate U-boat commanders.
He did an efficient job, by sometimes ruthless methods. On demobili-
sation, he went to Cambridge to learn Russian, ready for a job with
SIS, though ostensibly he was merely an official of the diplomatic service. Blake was posted to Seoul, Korea, as vice-consul. In 1950 the
Korean War broke out and Blake, with the rest of the embassy staff,
was interned.

This was against all the conventions of war, which declared that
embassy staff of each belligerent country is entitled to safe passage
home. When a ceasefire was arranged in 1953 the British survivors
were set free. The Foreign Office considered that Blake had acted with
dignity and courage, but it was later discovered that he had met two
Soviet intelligence men while interned, probably following an offer to
work for the KGB. He had certainly been the subject of much Communist indoctrination – or brainwashing as it was then called. This may
have changed his ideological orientation, but some researchers say
that communism had interested him since his youth.

Whatever the truth, Blake returned to Britain as a Soviet agent. In
London his contact was Nicholei Korovin, whose cover at the Soviet
Embassy was as first secretary. MI5 knew him to be the KGB's man in
London and teams of watchers followed him. Despite their undoubted
skill, Korovin lost them and always met Blake punctually at the
arranged rendezvous. He did this by leaving home at 8am for an

appointment at, say, 8pm and stayed mobile all day, dodging into a few safe houses from time to time. Because of this remarkable thoroughness Korovin and Blake were never seen together.

SIS now improved Blake's value to the KGB by moving him to Section Y, a top secret scientific department dedicated to infiltrating Soviet military and diplomatic communications. The SIS and CIA were worried by signs that the Russians were learning about their secret projects, but Blake was not suspected. While on post in Berlin he made trips into East Berlin to talk to a double agent and through the information he gained Blake was able to pass to SIS the names of a number of petty Soviet spies. The KGB thought that these 'sacrifices' were justified to strengthen Blake's position with the SIS.

Meanwhile Blake betrayed to the Soviet Union the CIA–SIS Operation SILVER (or PRIME) which for three years ran a tap on the main cable from Soviet military headquarters in Vienna. He was also in on the CIA–SIS Operation GOLD (see page 56) to tap similar cables in East Berlin. In fact, Blake was secretary to the intelligence committee that planned and operated the operation. He told the KGB about that too.

Systematically, Blake was photographing every document, plan and photograph that he could lay his hands on and passing them to Korovin and other contacts. Blake had married Gillian Allen, a secretary in Section Y – and not a spy – and they were posted back to London in 1959. Here Blake worked in 'Production Research', a cover for a unit recruiting contacts among British businessmen travelling abroad, such as the ill-fated Greville Wynne.

This was dull work for Blake and when in 1960 he was offered a posting to Beirut, Lebanon, he accepted at once, first attending the Middle East College for Arabic Studies, run by the Foreign Office for special training of its staff going to the Middle and Near East. In 1961 SIS officers heard from the CIA that a communist intelligence officer, actually an American agent, had sent an interesting report. It was that the KGB had got hold of a list of 16 Polish officials whom the SIS believed could be recruited for Western intelligence. This list, the SIS, believed, could have come only from George Blake's safe.

Blake was called home for some plausible reason in March 1961 and soon afterwards he was arrested and charged under the Official Secrets Act. He soon confessed and as a result his trial was very short – just one day, 3 May 1961. He was sentenced to 42 years in prison – 'one year for every person he had betrayed', as it was so colourfully put at the time. It has never been possible accurately to measure the damage Blake had done in his seven years of spying but Lord Chief Justice Parker said, 'It would clearly be contrary to the public interest for me to refer to the full contents of your confession. I have listened to all that has been said on your behalf and I fully recognise that it is unfortunate for you that many matters urged in mitigation cannot be divulged.'

Blake had served less than five and a half years in Wormwood Scrubs, London, when three former prisoners who had known Blake in prison, Sean Bourke, Pat Pottle and Michael Randle (with his wife) engineered his escape, on 22 October 1966.* Many scenarios have been suggested for this audacious escape, especially when Blake turned up in Moscow a year later, to be decorated with the Order of Lenin, a measure of the high respect the Russians had for him.

The most popular story concerning the escape is that Bourke, Pottle and Randle were paid by the KGB experts. One author suggests that the escape was the result of a deal between SIS and the KGB. Another says that both SIS and the KGB were eager to find out how Blake had left the country and with whose help. Phillip Knightley offers what is, to me, the most convincing argument: that 'Blake played a brilliant triple game in which the SIS came off second best to the Russians'. Knightley argues that Blake reported to SIS that the Russians had recruited him and asked how this could be put to good use for Britain. SIS then authorised Blake to pass certain selected material to the KGB. Then, says Knightley, Blake reported back to the Russians for whom he was really working all the time. To explain Blake's confession, Knightley suggests that SIS offered him a great deal of money to confess together with a light sentence and later a secure haven abroad. SIS, like everybody else, was amazed by the massive 42-year sentence, Knightley says.

Like Knightley, I believe that the KGB organised the sensational escape. Its chiefs had to do so if they were going to get spies of Blake's calibre in the future. I do not agree with Knightley that the KGB made use of the IRA. IRA folklore is massive and detailed among the Roman Catholic community in Northern Ireland, but the Blake escape is

---

* The role of Pottle and the Randles is discussed by Sean Bourke in his *The Springing of George Blake.*

never mentioned. Sean Bourke died in mysterious circumstances, at the age of 47, in County Clare in 1982. The inquest found that he had died from alcoholic poisoning, a form of death which – by coincidence ? – has befallen other people exploited by the KGB.

Two interconnected matters interest me. One is Lord Parker's comment about the 'many matters in mitigation' that had been presented to him. Among these matters, perhaps, was coded information that Blake had been a loyal SIS servant. Apart from that, 30 years after Blake's trial no retired SIS officer will say a word about Blake's escape even though they will talk fairly freely about other affairs of the period.

*   *   *

The case of Aldrich 'Rick' Ames will haunt all levels of American intelligence for generations, if only because it showed up glaring deficiencies in the CIA's internal security system. Ames operated deep within the CIA itself and for nine years he sold the KGB and its successor agency, the MBRF, priceless information about many aspects of 'United States' defence secrets.

Ames was an unlikely spy, which is why he made such an effective one. But the sheer improbability of his being a spy should have been reason enough for CIA or FBI security to subject him and his affairs to a thorough vetting. Born in 1941, Ames was part of a respected family in River Falls, Wisconsin. Aldrich's initial interest in spycatching probably stemmed from his father, Carleton, who was a member of the CIA's counter-intelligence staff. He made no special impact on the organisation and after he died in 1960 he was quickly forgotten. Two years later his son Aldrich signed on as a trainee.

He wanted to become a case officer, but first he needed a college degree and this necessitated five years' work at George Washington University, which awarded him a degree in history. Ames could then begin his training as a case officer basically learning the business of detecting spies and trying to recruit them as American agents.

In 1969 Ames and his wife Nancy, also a CIA employee, were sent to Ankara, Turkey, an important post because of the possibility of recruiting Russians among the large detachments of Soviet Embassy, press and trade staffs. He seems to have done his job in a routine way and in 1972 he was returned to CIA's headquarters at Langley, where he spent a full five years on intelligence analysis, an intellectually demanding job – too demanding for Ames – which also gave him access to much top secret material.

His next posting was to New York City and the key job of 'talent spotting', that is, looking for potential 'human assets' in the United Nations. The great building teemed with officials from every country in the world and has always been a happy hunting ground for recruiters. The Ameses lived in Manhattan and enjoyed its social life.

Posted to Mexico City in 1981, but without Nancy, Ames again sought out potential agents, though his former friends say that he was unsuccessful. This might have been recorded as a blackmark failure because President Reagan had put the CIA and the FBI on notice that he wanted recruitment results in his campaign against the 'Evil Empire', as he dubbed the Soviet Union and its satellites. The FBI did indeed land two big KGB fish in Washington, Colonel Valeri Martynov and Major Sergei Motorin.

Ames made a catch too, though of a different kind. He fell for Maria del Rosario Casas Dupuy, a cultural attaché at the Colombian embassy. The CIA was interested in her, too, because agents were needed in Colombia, one of the world's major suppliers of narcotic drugs. Rosario was not only highly intelligent, she had connections everywhere and in April 1983 the CIA put her on its payroll. Meanwhile, she and Ames lived together.

Rosario lost her CIA income in December of that year and at the same time Ames was transferred back to Langley and promoted chief of the Soviet counter-intelligence branch in the South-East Europe Division. Between March 1984 and July 1986, when he was transferred to Rome, Ames had authorisation to hold frequent telephone conversations with Soviet embassy officials. Under CIA rules, every such contact had to be approved beforehand or reported afterwards. There could be no exceptions. Ames, however, began to have unauthorised and unreported conversations. This was a dangerous breach of security that should have been noticed by security staff making 'spot taps', but apparently Ames was now considered too important to be checked in this way.

By now Ames and Nancy had been divorced and he had married Rosario. The pair of them had expensive tastes, which KGB recruiters had taken notice of years before anybody in the CIA thought of finding out how the couple could afford to indulge these tastes. Exactly when Ames had his first face to face meeting with a Russian is not clear but he certainly met a KGB man on 14 February 1986. It can hardly be a coincidence that the very next day Aldrich and Rosario Ames deposited $24,000 in an account in the Dominion Bank of Virginia.

The entire US security apparatus had been tense with apprehension at the end of 1985 for during the year many Americans had been caught spying for Moscow. The fact that they had been exposed might seem like a triumph for security but with each case came the fear 'How many more moles are there in the system?' Those caught included Edward Lee Howard, Ronald Pelton and John Walker. The latter two were named by Vitali Yurchenko, a senior KGB officer who had been debriefed by Aldrich Ames and others, only to re-defect three months later. Howard evaded arrest and fled to Moscow for sanctuary. Somebody had tipped him off that security agents were on his tail.

Also in 1985, Motorin and Martynov, the CIA's recruits from 1981 – now acting as double agents – were instructed to return to Moscow for 'routine re-posting'. In fact, they had been betrayed and soon after they arrived home they were executed. It was natural for the CIA and FBI to suspect that a mole had sent them to their deaths. No wonder that the American media dubbed 1985 'the year of the spy'.

Almost certainly Ames was the mole concerned but the following year he passed the lie-detector (polygraph) test to which all intelligence officials must submit every five years. It is difficult to have faith in polygraph testing after its 'acquittal' of Aldrich Ames, but perhaps the officials who did the testing asked him the wrong questions.

There was so much wrong about the life that Aldrich and Rosario were living that they might as well have been waving red flags to attract attention. He drove an expensive Jaguar XJ6, sported an equally costly Gucci watch and wore suits that only the wealthy could afford. In his office he had taken to sitting with his feet on the desk, smoking heavily and reading old intelligence files. He was drinking to excess and he and Rosario were going dancing. While he was in Italy, after 1986, Ames's name was even mentioned in Milan's daily newspaper *Corriere della Sera* because of his many appearances at the best night clubs. What was less public was that he and his wife were banking large amounts of money in Switzerland, Italy and Colombia.

What they spent when they returned to Washington in 1989 was much more open than their banking transactions. They paid $540,000 for a house in Arlington, $7,000 for furniture and $19,500 for a Honda to add to the Jaguar. Also, they paid $275 each week for care of their son Paul and they were having frequent foreign holidays, mostly to South America. Everybody accepted Ames's explanation for his lavish spending on his frequent assertion that 'Yep, I'm a lucky guy with a rich wife'. He used to tell younger colleagues that the key to happiness was to marry a wealthy woman.

In the whole of the CIA only one member of staff, a woman who worked in covert operations, was truly suspicious of Ames. In November 1989 she formally notified her supervisors that Ames's lifestyle was incompatible with his CIA salary. Furthermore, she did not believe his rich wife story. Indeed, it was easily proved that Rosario was not wealthy in her own right and that she really missed the money that the CIA had paid her during her brief time as an agent. The CIA woman officer was so insistent that internal security began a financial check on the Ames couple, but just one junior officer was detailed to the investigation. Given no co-operation from his seniors, he asked the Treasury for information and was told that Aldrich Ames had many foreign transactions totalling a 'surprisingly large amount' of dollars. The young investigator reported his findings but still no action was taken and, almost as if in reprimand, he was sent off on a training course.

In 1990 one of the CIA's most important agents, code-named 'Prologue', disappeared. This man was a counter-intelligence officer within KGB headquarters and his loss was alarming. Ames had access to information on Prologue, so here was another finger as big as a signpost pointing towards him.

That year Paul Redmond was promoted to the post of deputy chief of counter-intelligence and it was he, listening to the continuing shrill voice of the lady from covert operations, who ordered that the hunt for a mole be stepped up. Ames came under direct suspicion, but, incredibly, the CIA once again did not inform the FBI. Ames was slipped into an agency backwater, the anti-narcotics centre, where he had no access to real secrets and from 1991 he was watched. Rather than alert him, no special polygraph test was given so that it was April of that year and the time of his routine test before he next faced the lie detector. Here another security blunder occurred: nobody warned the polygraph operators that Ames was under suspicion. Had this hapened, the operators might well have asked him 'Have you received any money from a foreign power?' and other questions bearing on his wealth and lifestyle. As it happened, Ames was asked only anodyne questions. We must speculate that he was terrified when he faced the polygraph because he had become a millionaire from spying. The only possibly difficult question asked was 'Are you concealing any financial difficulties from the agency?' 'No' he said, perfectly truthfully. He had no financial difficulties whatsoever – naturally!

Nevertheless, other investigators were doing a thorough and painstaking job. They bugged the Ameses' phone and home, conducted electronic surveillance on Aldrich's personal computer, retrieved papers and typewriter and printing ribbons from the garbage can. This went on for two years and among other information that surfaced was proof from Ames's computer that he had really been responsible for the betrayal of agent Prologue.

On 6 October, 1993 the hunters retrieved a damning message from the pile of garbage. It had been written 12 months earlier and said, in part, 'You have probably heard a bit about me by this time from your (and now my) colleagues in the MBRF.' And later, 'My wife has accommodated herself to understanding what I am doing in a very supportive way.'

In fact, Rosario was as supportive a wife as any traitor ever had. His carelessness worried her and she often urged him to be punctual in sending messages and in handling the money they were receiving. The listeners on the wire tap heard all this and much more.

The bugging of the Ameses' home was sophisticated. Working from a vehicle parked down the street, officers picked up the electromagnetic waves that flitted across Ames's PC screen and converted them back into letters and words on a monitor. When the FBI was finally notified about Ames and joined in the investigation, they planted a devict in his computer that broadcast every keystroke, though they may have used an even more advanced technique. It is possible to plant a bug enabling the crew to turn on the computer from another location, to call up the internally stored files and transmit them by radio or telephone modem to FBI's machines. Then a remote signal turns off the computer and modem.

On 22 February 1994 Ames was due to fly to Moscow, a trip cleared by his superiors so as not to alarm him that the security services were onto him. It seems very likely that he intended to defect, and despite all the care taken by his watchers he must surely have suspected that something was going on.

On 21 February the FBI sprung their trap. When Ames left his house and backed his Jaguar from the garage, at least 20 agents were in various key positions. At the street corner the Jaguar was blocked in front and behind and he was arrested. Minutes later Rosario, back at the house, was also picked up. At FBI headquarters they were separately shown into a fake 'operations centre', the walls of which were lined with giant photographs of the Ames's house and, even more telling, of the dead drops they had used in Washington when passing packets to the Russians. And there was much else on the walls, including enlarged print-outs of conversations Ames had thought were secret. The entire display was intended to show the couple that they could never hope to deny their crimes – and it succeeded.

A separate raid on Ames's office at Langley turned up 144 secret documents and 10 files that he should never have even known about. It was a shocking indictment of CIA internal security. Panic swept through the upper echelons of the CIA, and though these professionals managed to look relaxed about the matter, as if Ames were small fry, the fact was that he was the most senior known source ever recruited by the KGB in the United States. The results of his treachery are profound, for the CIA was left without any 'assets' in Russia and most of what it had achieved in the previous nine years had been neutralised. No wonder the Russians paid Ames more money than they are known to have paid to any other agent. They paid him too much: he could not discreetly handle the wealth they thrust upon him.

Some of the techniques that Aldrich and Rosario Ames used came to light in FBI documents. Listed chronologically, the various moves made by the Ameses make interesting reading. To what extent the FBI had knowledge of all these moves at the time is impossible to say: they may have reconstructed them in chronological order as the FBI investigation neared conclusion. The period covered is that from 8 September to 4 November 1993:

8 September: Ames deposits a message at a dead-drop known as 'Pipe': 'I am ready to meet at B 1 October.' (B meant Bogota, Bolivia.)
9 September: Aldrich and Rosario, returning from a function at their son's school, drive past one of their signal site's mailbox. On it is a

chalked cross to show that the KGB contact has picked up the message.

19 September: Ames makes an airline reservation to fly to Bogota.

29 September: Ames sees a signal at another mailbox, which he and his Russian friends know as 'North'. Following this he telephones Rosario to say, 'There's news – no travel.' [The FBI tapes the conversation.]

3 October: Ames collects a note from 'Pipe'. The KGB notifies him that their people will meet him 'in a city well known to you on 1 November'. From his office in Langley, Ames tells Rosario, 'All is well'. (This too is taped.)

13 October: Ames acknowledges the Russian note. He makes a chalk mark on mailbox 'Smile', which is on the road that the Russians drive to their embassy. The mark means that he will keep the rendezvous.

28 October: Two days before Aldrich's departure, Rosario asks him, 'You get the money in dollars, right?' (This is a reference to an earlier difficulty in which the Russians wanted to pay Ames in some other currency. The FBI tapes this conversation, too.)

30 October: Without telling his CIA superiors, Ames flies to Bogota, having told Rosario, 'If anybody from the office calls, you tell them I went up to Annapolis'. (The FBI picked up this instruction from a bug in the Ames's house.)

1 November: Ames meets KGB officers in Bogota, a meeting observed by US security agents. From his hotel room (which has been bugged) he tells Rosario that everything is going to plan. His voice is relaxed and cheerful.

3 November: On Aldrich's return home, Rosario asks him, 'When do you go back to Bogota? In a year or what?' His response: 'Yeah, well, not Bogota, either Caracas or Quito.' This puzzles Rosario, who asks 'Why those places? Oh well, at least it's not Lima. You could get murdered in Lima.'

4 November: Beginning on this day and spread out over a week Aldrich and Rosario make bank deposits in cash totalling $21,600. The FBI knew of three deposits at the time but they had missed a few others which came to light later.

Ames was often absent from his office for a day or so without telling his superiors or having told them that he needed to make inquiries at some stated place, which he did not then visit. It seems incredible that no check was ever made, as a matter of routine, before the official inquiry at last began.

The KGB, like their agent Ames, seems to have become overconfident, otherwise they would have insisted that he and Rosario handle their finances more discreetly. Some of the Soviet payments were paid into an account run by Rosario and her mother in Colombia, but this appears to have been one of the few precautions the Ameses took. Aldrich must have known that the US Treasury had ways of knowing about large sums of money being sent overseas.

The Ames affair caused great damage to the CIA's reputation. Every associated intelligence service was appalled and remains so, for many of their own secrets were compromised. More than this, it is difficult for the British, French, the Australians and others to have confidence in the CIA. 'Personally, I wouldn't tell the CIA anything beyond what they can read in open sources,' an Australian intelligence officer said. 'How can we know that there isn't another and brighter Rick Ames?'

It is true that Ames was not highly intelligent; he just happened to be in the right place to pick up secrets and he was protected by an incredibly inefficient internal security system. MI5 had earlier been defeated by its own complacent 'Old Boy' network; the CIA was now by its own simplistic and naive 'I trust you, you trust me' culture. It is significant that the young investigator who reported Ames's massive financial transactions to his superiors is no longer with the CIA. He should have persevered until he had their attention, he was told. By not having done so he had shown that he was not CIA material. The lone lady whistleblower who had gone on insisting that Ames was a Soviet mole also suffered. It could hardly have been said of her that she had not persevered, but she took 'early retirement'. I believe that she was pressured to retire so as to save the embarrassment of her superiors every time they passed her in a Langley corridor.

Rosario Ames was sentenced to five years in prison, but Aldrich will never be released. He may get some satisfaction in his cell from knowing that his Russian friends regard him as the equal to Philby and 'the greatest agent we ever had in America'. What a pity he will never receive the Order of Lenin. Then again, if the American prison system is as lax in security as the CIA, it might get through to him.

At the beginning of this chapter I stressed that revolutionary Russia, then the Soviet Union and, since the early 1990s, Russia, have seen espionage as simply part of foreign policy. This applies in reverse – the Russian government made no fuss when it arrested 20 foreign spies in

1993, including a Russian who had caused major damage to national security. The Russians, especially those in key positions in the great intelligence organisations, could not understand why the Americans made such a fuss about the Ames case. In March 1994 Yuri Kobaledze, press spokesman for the SVR, said, 'The incident does not concern relations between our two countries. We will not stop gathering information on you or you on us. Right? There are friendly states but no friendly intelligence services.' This is a succint and pithy explanation of the position on espionage from the Russian point of view.

*　　　*　　　*

One of the Soviet Union's most interesting spies was Stanislav Levchenko. Born in Moscow in 1941, the son of a major-general, he grew up in an army-political background, so it was no surprise that he found a career with the 'International Department', which was responsible for thinking up 'active-measures operations' for the ruling Politburo. When the Politburo approved a plan the innocuous sounding International Department put it into practice. 'Active-measures' comprise every possible method of penetration and manipulation, deception, coercion, blackmail, forgery and subversion. One of the departments main roles was to recruit and run 'agents of influence', such as foreign jounalists, political leaders and people in high society.

Levchenko specialised in the Japanese luguage, but he underwent wide training. For instance, in 1966 he was training to infiltrate into Britain in time of emergency to report on the state of readiness of Britain's nuclear strike force. In that year, too, he was sent to Japan, ostensibly as an interpreter for the Soviet Trade Delegation. His real mission was to become 'friendly' with the leaders of the Japanese 'peace' movement.

In 1971, the KGB's First Directorate enrolled Levchenko – a promotion in espionage terms – and he spent a year at the Intelligence School before assignment to the Japanese desk in the First Directorate's Moscow HQ. For his mission he was attached to the journalistic staff of the *New Times Magazine*, a Soviet-owned 'international' magazine published in Russian, English, German, Spanish, Polish, Czech, Arabic and Japanese. A quick learner, Levchenko absorbed his lessons in journalism, though it is doubtful whether the many articles that appeared under his name in the *New Times* were

123

written by him. They were certainly adequate cover for his posting in Tokyo, in 1975, as a *New Times* correspondent. Actually, he was only one of 12 Soviet spies posing as journalists for the *New Times*.

Levchenko's KGB brief was 'active-measures operations' and his targets were people connected with the media – editors, writers, commentators and producers. He developed genuine friendships and came to detest the work of deception.

While in Japan in 1979, Levchenko defected to the USA. The CIA and the State Department arranged the escape of Levchenko and his wife but they had no way of getting their son out of Moscow. Levchenko was to say later that Marxism-Leninism was a perverted type of religion. For a time, Levchenko's defection disrupted the KGB's activities in Japan. Also, officers being considered for foreign postings were then required to obtain personal recommendations from five of their colleagues, not the three required before the Levchenko defection.

The American security agencies put Levchenko through an extraordinarily rigorous screening to ensure that he was not a plant. Even though he must have expected this, there were times when he was desperate at his early failure to convince them of his sincerity. Once he was accepted, he become the West's single most important source of information from within the KGB.

He reported that the foreign journalistic community in any country of the free world was continuously targeted by the KGB. Once under control, the jounalists were used to plant pro-Soviet forgeries and other disinformation, to acquire stationery, letterheads and signatures for use by the forgery factory, and to pass money to Communist publications and front organisations.

According to Britain, American and German intelligence sources, Levchenko's information has been invaluable because it reveals how the Soviet spy system works. They say, too, that most of his information is as relevant now to Russia as it was to the Soviet Union in 1979. There is still an 'International Department'.

The Soviet Union sentenced Levchenko to death and he was hunted by KGB killer teams. Even into the 1990s he was disguised and living in hiding, and his family in Russia is persecuted. Russia might have, to a point, embraced democracy, but for its leaders some 'crimes' can never be forgiven and the SVR has as long an arm as the KGB.

9

MODEL OPERATIONS BASED ON INTELLIGENCE

Espionage operations concerning men and women who have turned traitor to act as agents for foreign powers gain widespread publicity and lasting story-value when they are found out. Philby vanished from Beirut in January 1963, but his activities as a spy for the Soviet Union are described in virtually every book about intelligence. In the US the name Tyler Kent, a code clerk in the American Embassy in London in 1939–40, is well remembered. He stole 1,500 documents from the embassy's code room and sold them to the Germans. Similarly, the 'atom bomb' spies – Allan Nunn May and Klaus Fuchs, among others – were described as infamous and their infamy has echoed down the years since the 1940s.

Not nearly so public were a clutch of intriguing operations carried out by Israel's Mossad in collaboration with Aman, Israel's military intelligence branch, together with small parties of army, navy and air force 'special units.' Most took place in what Israel regards as its 'War of Attrition', 1968–7I, when the nation's survival was at stake as its Arab enemies improved their military capability.

A Soviet air force officer who visited Cairo immediately after the Six-Day War of June 1967 paid Israel's intelligence services an unintended compliment. He was attempting to discover the reasons for

Egypt's rapid and humiliating defeat and he conceded that not even the experienced and gigantic Soviet intelligence apparatus had been able to gather such exact and precise information on the Egyptian defence forces as Israel had done.

Since at that time the Russians were advising, training and equipping the Egyptian forces, the officer's admission was significant. But the Russians' relative ignorance of Egypt's military capabilities would not have surprised the Israelis. Soviet Intelligence in Egypt, as in all the Arab countries, was inept because the Russians had only a superficial knowledge of the Arab mind. The Israelis knew the Arab mind-set thoroughly – many of them had grown up in Arab countries. Recognising that the Egyptian is basically lazy, they exploited this weakness in some daring intelligence-based operations.

*   *   *

During the War of Attrition, Israeli and Egyptian troops were constantly raiding each other's positions across the narrow Suez Canal. Sometimes the Israeli commando raids, based on sound intelligence, were long-range and destructive. For example, on the night of 29 June 1969 a commando team in helicopters raided Suhaj, deep in Egypt and about 90 miles from the Red Sea, to cut power cables. The purpose of the raid was psychological – to cause the Egyptians anxiety over the obvious vulnerability of the Upper Nile Valley. The commandos could not have cut the cables without precise local knowledge.

On 2 July Israeli commandos crossed the Canal in three separate landings and killed 13 Egyptian soldiers. That day the Egyptians announced that an Israeli spy ring had been discovered in Cairo, headed by Yusef Hamdan, 'a German of Egyptian origin'. One of his ring, it was said, possessed a classified map of the Egyptian canal defences stolen from a Cairo office. The Israelis had many such enemy maps, but they had been photographed and then returned during raids on Egyptian posts. Yusef Hamdan, whoever he was, had no connection with Israeli intelligence. The Egyptians, exasperated by the Israeli attacks, were constantly claiming to have uncovered spy rings – a dangerous tactic in itself. The Israelis, knowing the truth about the existence of such rings, then also knew that the Egyptians were acting in desperation when they invented one.

On the night of 19 July, 40 naval commandos attacked Green Island, a fortified rock at the north end of the Gulf of Suez, where 70 Egyptian soldiers manned and protected a radar site. The Israelis, helped by a meticulously drawn map of the defences, scaled the walls, killed the sentries, destroyed equipment and withdrew after an hour. By sending fake and uncoded radio messages to their own headquarters they convinced Egyptian officers listening to the radio reports on the mainland that they were still there. Egyptian guns then bombarded their own installations for hours and caused more damage and casualties to their own men.

When the Israeli High Command planned air strikes against the Egyptian guns along the Canal Aman, aware of the advantages of fine-timing, suggested the afternoon of 20 July. On that day the Americans were making a moon-landing, and air attacks in the Middle East would therefore attract minimum publicity overseas.

But there was no way of avoiding publicity about the 'Cherbourg gunboats'. The Israelis had ordered 12 250-ton gunboats from the French and seven had been delivered before President de Gaulle, in an effort to be more neutral on the Middle East, ordered that no others were to be handed over. The last of the remaining five were launched on 19 December 1969 and all were impounded at Cherbourg. But on Christmas Day all five boats, manned by skeleton Israeli crews, gave the French the slip and sped at full speed for Haifa. Two French generals were suspended and disciplinary action was taken against other officers for suspected complicity.

The Israelis had tricked the French officers at Cherbourg. The crews, such as they were, were smuggled aboard the gunboats by night. A few Israeli officers then arrived openly, though in mufti, 'to inspect' the boats. Some dispute had arisen, they said, and until they had certified the boats as having been built to the correct specifications their government would not pay for them. In particular, they told the dockyard officials, they had to test the engines.

On Christmas Day the French officials on the spot did not want their festivities disturbed and no senior officials were available in Paris. The whole business of government had come to a standstill, which the Mossad planners knew. Snatching the gunboats was a relatively simple operation and they were soon in action defending Israel's coasts from Egyptian attacks.

The year 1969 ended on a triumphant note for Israeli intelligence. Working to a Mossad-Aman plan, the Air Force made a diversionary three-hour raid on Egyptian canal positions while naval commandos crossed the 18-mile wide Gulf of Suez to raid the Egyptian naval base at Ras Ghaleb, 115 miles south of Suez. Circling in from the west – the 'safe' side for the Egyptians – the commandos occupied the base. Israeli helicopters at once flew in and took away the new Soviet P-12 mobile anti-aircraft radar system that was used in conjunction with SAM missiles. It weighed about seven tons, had a range of 200 miles and just been placed to plug a gap in the Egyptian early warning system. Nobody other than the Russians had seen this particular radar, one of the most modern in service anywhere. The raid's daring and initiative caught the world's imagination, but it could not have been made without good intelligence.

When Israeli commandos raided Shadwan Island at the entrance to the Gulf of Suez on 22 January 1970 they left with an entire British Decca radar unit.

With limited manpower against the Egyptians' enormous reserves, the Israelis have always relied whenever possible on their wits and preventive intelligence rather than on their strength. Not long before the Yom Kippur War in 1973, Aman put forward a scheme for execution by the Air Force and Army. The idea was to capture other radar stations intact and, it was hoped, without loss of life or aircraft. At dusk one evening Egyptian radar control saw four 'blips' as Israeli helicopters crossed the Canal, but before officers could even give the order to their pilots to scramble the enemy 'blips' turned away, back into Israeli territory. The Egyptians relaxed, as the Israelis had anticipated, and took no action. In fact, *eight* Israeli helicopters had crossed the Canal, but flying in dangerously tight pairs, they produced only four 'blips' on the radar screen. The second aircraft in each pair landed, waited for a while and then took off again. Egyptian radar controllers, naturally enough, now assumed that the 'blips' represented Egyptian aircraft in home territory, so they were not suspect. To complete the deception, these helicopters wore Egyptian markings.

At the pre-planned points where the helicopters had landed their commando crews captured radar stations by surprise and the Israeli Defence Forces were soon presented with undamaged radar equipment. The same technique was used several times to capture Egyptian officers for interrogation. Several of these officers were then returned to their own side of the Suez Canal and most did not report their capture, such is the strength of Arab shame.

*   *   *

At this period, too, Mossad had succeeded in planting an agent within Cairo Radio. This was a considerable feat, because applicants for positions on Egyptian newspapers and on radio and television are screened as thoroughly as officer applicants for the armed forces. Cairo Radio has always been a collecting point and filter for secret or confidential information, much of which is considered too sensitive to broadcast and is censored on the spot.

The Mossad chiefs had long pondered the relative merits of having spies in various walks of Egyptian life, but each seemed limited in scope for espionage. It would be possible to insinuate a spy into a job in some government ministry, but for safety he would need to confine his interests to that ministry. If he asked questions about another ministry he would arouse suspicion in Egypt's spy-sensitive society.

Much the same limitations would apply to a spy posing as a foreign businessman, an archaeologist, an irrigation engineer or a travel agent. But within Cairo Radio a man could express a natural professional interest about everything. Three years of careful preparation were necessary before the Mossad agent was ready to apply for a post and by then he had an impeccable record as an Egyptian who had been living abroad since boyhood, several years having been spent as an adviser on Middle East affairs to a European broadcasting company. This claim would stand up to investigation. Details of what this spy accomplished are among Mossad's most closely guarded secrets and the Egyptians, who never did break the agent's cover, do not talk about him. An unofficial Egyptian source concedes that on at least two occasions the Israeli agent was a member of a party which toured Egyptian defences. He had certainly learnt something from the experiences of Wolfgang Lotz (see pages 173 and 175) for he did not attempt to ingratiate himself with high-ranking Egyptians and his subsequent report to Mossad stressed the risks of making contact with important Arabs. Every Arab in a position of rank or authority has enemies constantly striving to cause his downfall and when this happens his friends also fall.

The Cairo Radio spy believed that he could find out more and run fewer risks by restricting his social activities to the people of his own class and professional group. He proved his theory correct and after his experiences Mossad seems to have decided that having a friend in high places in an Arab country has only one advantage – his name can be used as a form of insurance in a dangerous situation. But it can be used only once with safety; after that, suspicion is aroused.

The agent in Cairo Radio carried out what all intelligence services recognise as a most difficult feat. He brought in a second agent, whose expert technical assistance he needed, and recommended him for an appointment in Cairo Radio. Because by now the first spy was wholly accepted as a loyal Egyptian, his recommendation concerning his friend was good enough for him to be taken onto the staff without the usual screening. The friend was a skilful radio engineer whose foreign experience and obvious knowledge made him welcome to the Egyptians. His importance as a spy was that he knew how to send out reports at ultra high frequency under cover of a normal broadcast. These messages were picked up in Israel, unscrambled and read with ease and interest. The agent was active until the Yom Kippur War and gave warnings of President Sadat's top-level meetings and mysterious absences from Cairo. The spy did not uncover any details of war preparations, but his knowledge of the president's more than usually busy life led him to suspect that Sadat was planning war. His warnings, it seemed, were not taken seriously enough. Israel was taken by surprise in October 1973.

*   *   *

Because of the advantages gained by the Israelis during the period 1967–73 the Egyptians developed a pronounced inferiority complex, this being the principal reason they refused to meet Israeli diplomats to discuss Middle East problems. Even Russian help and advice did nothing to ease this sense of inferiority. In fact, the Israeli superiority was sometimes nothing more than painstaking attention to detail. For instance, Abba Eban, when Israeli Foreign Minister, had demonstrated the value of keeping records.

Before leaving Jerusalem for the USA late in May 1967– not long before the Six-Day War – Eban had stuffed a large briefcase with papers and memoranda from his own archives. Among them was a document which would turn out to be vital. It contained the minutes of a conversation he had had with Secretary of State John Foster Dulles in the Dulles home on 24 February 1957, in which the Secretary of State had spelled out the American commitment to Israel on freedom of passage in the Gulf of Aqaba. A few corrections had been made in Dulles' handwriting. As soon as Eban arrived in Washington he sent a photocopy of the document to the State Department. No copy of the vitally important *aide-mémoire* could be found in the White House or State Department files, but Douglas Dillon, who had served in the State Department under Eisenhower, confirmed its authenticity from memory. Faced with the promise made by the Eisenhower Government, now confirmed by the document, the USA agreed to live up to it.

In contrast, most Arab documents do not survive the life of a particular government. Many an Arab leader destroys all records when he thinks he is about to be deposed, to prevent his political enemies making capital from them. Israeli spies who have secured administrative jobs in Arab countries have reported that files they wished to inspect no longer existed.

Several lessons can be adduced from these Israeli intelligence episodes, not least of them being that Mossad and Aman were efficient. The success of these ventures, whether to steal an enemy radar unit or to plant a spy in a radio station, required sound information meticulously analysed and acted upon with nerve and judgment.

131

10

A PLETHORA OF AMERICAN SPIES

Soldier Spies – NOC Agents – Psychic Imagers – Spy Planes and Satellites – Espionage in the Cyberspace Age

Since the mid-1980s the CIA has had competition in its field, often without knowing about it, and when its chiefs found out they did not like it. The competitors are Army, Navy and Air Force personnel operating as spies, and that is a giant step from traditional 'scouting'. The CIA is not happy about what its directors call 'this duplication of effort', but it was an inevitable development in a hyper-complex defence system that is always hungry for information. In 1989 the Joint Chiefs of Staff, working on plans to invade Panama and depose the dictator Manuel Noriega, asked the CIA for certain assistance. It was not forthcoming because, astonishingly, the CIA had no agents in place in Panama.

But the Pentagon had an army sergeant willing and able to pass himself off as an international merchant who wanted to do business with the Noriega regime. He presented a bust of Napoleon to the vain Noriega, who fancied himself as Napoleonic in stature. He frequently invited the sergeant to his home and confided in him. The sergeant was able to provide the invasion planners with all the information they needed.

The sergeant was a founding member of a clandestine armed forces spy unit of about 1,000 members. It was some time before even the

Secretary of Defence and other very senior figures learned about the unit and its sections, which were operating outside the normal chain of command.* From where these spies drew their money is unclear, but they had plenty of it. At one time they bought a hot-air balloon and a Rolls Royce for 'special surveillance duties'.

In 1991 a Treasury audit found that a single military intelligence 'programme' had cost $25,000,000. The amount might not have worried the auditors unduly – they are used to dealing with massive amounts of money – but they were disturbed to find that while the programme was in progress only one foreign agent had been signed on. The audit details were never made public.

Generals in command of operations prefer briefings from their soldier spies rather than from the CIA. General Norman Schwarzkopf received a detailed briefing from the CIA station chief in Riyadh as Gulf War planning neared completion, but it did not provide Schwarzkopf with one of his most vital information needs. He wanted to know if Allied tanks could travel on the sand west of Kuwait. If not, what was a better route? The CIA had to admit ignorance so Schwarzkopf's staff sent in army spies who provided the information.

Army, Navy and Air Force spies reporting directly to their own commanders were successful in several different kinds of missions in the 1990s:

- The capture in 1993 of a lieutenant on the staff of the Somali warlord, Muhammad Farrah Aidid;
- The discovery of a division of the North Korean Army that spy satellites had missed;
- The revelation that Iraq and China were working together on a nuclear reactor;
- Information that the Navy's ships, loaded with military transports, would get stuck in the mud just short of the docks in Haiti, when the US was sending in a peace-enforcement army;
- Procurement of the major parts of a former Soviet SA-1O air-defence system. The spies 'found' these treasures in Belarus, one of the former Soviet republics.

---

* The Pentagon, headquarters of the armed forces, has 13,000 intelligence analysts compared to the CIA's 1,500.

Other successes by the military spies remain top secret. By October 1995 CIA protests, backed by some powerful senators, could no longer tolerate the free-wheeling existence of the military spy units, though all reluctantly agreed that they were useful. In that month all the Pentagon's 'irregular' units were centralised under the existing Defense Intelligence Agency and given the title the Defense Humint Service (DHS). The CIA insisted that it must approve the DHs's targets and President Clinton agreed to this. Considering that the soldier spies kept their activities hidden for so many years it is doubtful whether the CIA will know of all their operations.

*   *   *

Since 1991 the CIA has been expanding what it calls its 'NOC programme' (NOC stands for 'non-official cover'): the placing of undercover officers in American businesses operating overseas. This new development came about as a result of the end of the Cold War. While that strange conflict was in progress CIA men and women could pick up much intelligence while visiting foreign embassies and attending cocktail parties. With the end of the Cold war and the easing of tensions between nations, as well as a new international openness, other threats manifested themselves through terrorists, nuclear smugglers, regional warlords, drug traffickers and big-time money launderers. These people are not to be found on the diplomatic circuit.

NOC operatives were at work for decades before the new dangers appeared, but only on a small scale. They always ran risks because they had no diplomatic immunity. One operative, posing as a businessman, passed through several Mediterranean police roadblocks while transporting signal-interception equipment to a CIA boat ready to take post off the coast of Lebanon to eavesdrop on terrorists' communications.

By 1995 several hundred NOCs were in the field and the number was increasing. The system works through senior officers based in what is called the CIA's 'National Collections Branch', a cover name in itself. These people discreetly approach the executives of companies doing business overseas to ask if they will provide cover for CIA case officers. The USA has many suitable companies, such as banks, travel agencies, high-tech corporations and giant import-export firms. Generally the company president and its senior legal officer are the only people to know of any arrangement with the CIA.

For the cover to be plausible the CIA operatives must be business-school graduates who really can work normally for the company while carrying out their intelligence work. Since the CIA does not have a large number of staff members who can be seconded to carry out NOC work, it advertises for them through phony front companies. In effect, these advertisements call for 'young business-school graduates who want to live overseas'. Sometimes the front company retains head-hunting firms, though they are nearly always unaware that they are in effect recruiting for the CIA. Applicants are required to report to a business address and here the vetting process begins. There comes a time when the recruit is told the truth about his new job and if he/she likes the idea they are put through a training course at a secret location. It really is secret and nowhere near Camp Peary, Virginia, where other career CIA officers are trained in what the CIA knows as 'the farm'. NOCs are given new names and trained in groups of only three, for better security.

The CIA began to experiment in 1993–94 with the recruitment of mid-level corporate executives with a longing for adventure. The preliminaries over, they are then placed in overseas firms with the mission of the long-term penetration of a special target. This often takes the form of developing a 'friendship' with some individual regarded as important in the CIA's planning. Later, the executives return to their normal business activities.

The cost of the NOC operation is immense. Placing just one NOC operative overseas is said to be four times as expensive as posting a CIA person under embassy cover. Setting up a NOC officer in Tokyo as a corporate executive cost the CIA $3 million. Part of this expense lies in the necessity to assign a staff member to handle a NOC officer's personal affairs while he is operating under cover. Also, the company providing the cover, while not requiring a fee for doing so, does expect certain security safeguards to be put in place, because should a major company be exposed as having a CIA officer in its top management it could be seriously embarrassed.

The CIA believes that NOCs are the best way to carry out many clandestine activities, but the risks to the individuals can be immense, partly because they cannot turn to the nearest US embassy or consulate for open assistance. In Beirut, a NOC man was seized by the vicious killers of the *Hezbollah* faction, which has kidnapped many

Westerners and killed some of them. *Hezbollah* accused the officer of being from the CIA but he managed to convince them that he was an anti-narcotics agent fighting drugs. *Hezbollah* too condemns drugs, so it released the American.

Colombia is a dangerous posting. Here NOC officers, through companies they have set up as cover, manage to bribe drugs couriers to gain intelligence. Several NOC men have been wounded in gunfights with traffickers and in 1994 two were killed.

In some countries where the US has no embassy in which to place a CIA member, such as Iran, Iraq and North Korea, NOCs are especially effective. Some senior CIA directors prefer NOCs to CIA staff under embassy cover. A few of these senior men say that there is virtually no such thing as embassy cover, since sooner or later everybody in the diplomatic community in any capital city comes to know the identity of the CIA person.

*   *   *

NOCs will be a permanent part of the American intelligence system but another experiment came to an end in 1996 after a 10-year experiment that had cost $20,000,000. It involved psychic spies, first employed by the Pentagon, some of whose chiefs were confident that paranormal imagery could be a great advantage in military intelligence. In 1981 the Pentagon engaged a psychic to tell them where to find American General James Dozier, who had been kidnapped in Italy. The psychic reported that Dozier was being held in a stone house with a red roof, but since this description applied to 2,000,000 Italian homes the information was useless.

The Defense Intelligence Agency credited psychics with creating accurate pictures of Soviet submarine construction hidden from US spy satellites and later with correctly drawing 20 tunnels being built in North Korea near the demilitarised zone. But a psychic team operating from Fort Meade, Maryland, could not pinpoint where Colonel Gaddafi was staying before US aircraft attacked Tripoli in 1986.

The CIA had examined the possibilities of psychic spying. between 1972 and 1977 and after spending $750,000 abandoned its research. In 1994 US Congress ordered the CIA to take over 'Star Gate', as the Pentagon was then called, and report in its psychic programme effectiveness. In turn, the CIA hired the American Institute of Research, which stated that the psychics, predictions were correct in about 25 per cent of cases but that even when they were on target the reports they made were vague and general. The CIA recommended that 'Star Gate' come to an end and this happened early in 1996.

The psychics did well out of the programme while it lasted. Some military intelligence officers retired from the armed forces to become psychics and earned more money than in their former profession. They knew how to present a report with precise military embellishments and some of them made fortunes presenting 'intelligence' that was already known.

*   *   *

If the psychic spying programme was an expensive intelligence self-indulgence, spying from space via high-altitude, high-performance aircraft and from satellites is critical to the defence of Western nations, and is remarkably successful. Spy-planes have been operational from the 1960s and in May 1988 the US government announced that the USA was beginning to retire the SR-71 spy planes that were still in service. A spokesman said that they remained the best in the world but were expensive to maintain, a single flight cost $120,000 and satellites were doing the work that the planes had been doing.

However, this was a form of misinformation, for at the time 'Project Aurora' was in progress to build a new spy-plane with a speed of up to 4,500mph, or Mach 6, and an operational height of 100,000 feet. At Mach 6 the temperature on an aircraft's outer skin would be 2,500 degrees Fahrenheit, but this is countered by new plastics and other unspecified materials. Enormous amounts of normal fuel cannot be carried, but the Aurora uses methylcycolexhane, which at ultra-high speeds breaks down into toluene and hydrogen, which drive the aircraft.

The principal enemy of the 1980s, the Soviet Union and its Warsaw Pact allies, knew nearly everything they needed to know about US satellites – perhaps *everything*. This came about through the activities of traitor Americans. William Kampiles, a former CIA officer, sold them the build-and-maintain manual for the KH-ll, the spy satellite whose photographs were of use to President Carter in the late 1970s. In 1977 Christopher Boyce and Daunton Lee, working together, sold to the Russians complete information about Rhyolites, spy satellites then orbiting in pairs to monitor Soviet and Chinese missile tests. In a feeble attempt to confuse ground spies the US military gave the new name Aquacade to the Rhyolite but this did not fool the Russians.

The USAF has yet another spy-plane for the year 2000, the X-30 or TAV, the acronym for Trans-Atmosphere Vehicle. Well-founded rumours say that the TAV will be able to fly at Mach 25, that is, 17,000mph and above, and that it will have a ceiling of 100 miles. As a project, TAV was announced by President Reagan in 1982, but only as a civilian aspiration. People in the aerospace industry at that time dubbed TAV the 'Orient Express' because it could fly from New York to Beijing in 30 minutes. Its uses as a spy-plane are obvious – it would be undetectable and it could gain an amazing amount of photint very quickly.

In the meantime, satellites become ever more important in providing intelligence. They discover so much that often the US Government does not reveal certain information because this would only alert an enemy and force him to take measures to conceal his secrets. Photographs taken from satellites and scientifically analysed confirmed that the Bosnian Serbs had carried out massacres in 1992–94 and hidden the corpses in mass graves. The Serbs buried many of their victims in tunnels and mines, but satellite photos can detect even deep secrets providing human investigators with the information necessary to continue their work.

The ultimate spy satellite – but who can tell what the real ultimate might be? – is HALO. HALO at a more mundane military level stands for high-altitude, low-opening and refers to a type of jump made by paratroops. In the 1990s it means high-altitude large-optics. And, at more than 22,000 miles, HALO is certainly high. To make up for this great distance, at which height photos would have no fine resolution, HALO has seven phased telescopes, which give 49 times the resolution of one telescope. The problems in development have been great and the cost immense, but the US military and its political masters consider that the advantages merit any expense. A number of HALO satellites, spaced along synchronised orbits, are planetary spies that relay real-time intelligence to a ground headquarters. Their powerful telescopes can be aimed precisely at a ship at sea or at, say, a terrorist organisation's base. A sequence of photographs clearly shows changes in the ship's direction or movement around the base. People can be accurately counted and vehicles identified. HALO informs a commander in the field about the progressive movements of an enemy formation.

*   *   *

While the Americans were quick to discern the military value of space and to develop it, the CIA and the other 34 American intelligence agencies were slow to understand that the Internet was crammed with useful information-intelligence when political and economic openness became features of the international scene. For instance, it came as a surprise to CIA analysts to discover that Iranian groups opposing the fundamentalist regime of the cruel ayatollahs were showing information on the Internet that agents formerly had to obtain by covert means. And these resistance groups are *inside* Iran, not those operating in safety from London and Paris, though they too use the Internet.

Former Soviet-bloc countries which for years treated economic statistics as inviolable state secrets, the publishing of which could lead to the death penalty, now broadcast them on the Internet in the hope of encouraging Western financiers to invest. Even transfers of armaments can be monitored and interpreted by reading the electronic bulletin boards of shipping companies.

Electronic bulletin boards are generally a mine of information and they are as easy for 'unauthorised' people to dig into as those with security clearance. Thomas V Sobczak, a security expert with a New York computer company, tells a story that is frightening in its security implications. To test a theory he held about a way of acquiring expert information easily and quickly, he placed a straightforward question on an electronic bulletin board used by aerospace engineers: 'How good is aircraft stealth technology?' (Stealth refers to the revolutionary US bomber.)

The response was greater than Sobczak anticipated. Fifteen engineers and scientists and one US Air Force officer responded, providing data on materials used in Stealth planes, their design and the ways in which radars could probably spot the aircraft. This point was alarming because Stealth is supposed to be radar-proof. Some of the information that Sobczak's question elicited has inspired other researchers to experiment with key questions.

After 1991 the CIA and the other American Intelligence agencies entered the cyberspace age, thus dramatically changing the whole system of intelligence and providing a 'service for users' that once would have been regarded as pure fantasy. The phrase 'revolutionary developments' is often misused but in the case of the CIA's almost complete absorption into the benefits of cyberspace technology it is justifiable.

For instance, beginning in December 1994 the CIA and other US Intelligence agencies began full operation in Intelink, a worldwide computer network similar to Internet but much more exclusive. All 35 agencies feed it and at the end of 1995 it had 3,300 users, all with secret or top-secret clearance to tap into the system. Intelink allows White House staffs, State Department analysts, Pentagon chiefs and operational commanders in the field instant access to 'secrets' on any subject listed on the menu of their computer screens. Before Intelink, CIA sent its daily reports to the White House on a delivery van nicknamed 'the pizza truck'.

The available information is breathtaking in its scope and detail. At the height of the Bosnian fighting the President and his advisors were looking at an animated video showing Croat troop manoeuvres against the Serbs and the Serbs against the Bosnian Muslims. With six spy satellites in orbit, almost instantaneous photographs of any site on earth are available through Intelink. Frequent updates of any military or political situation are sent to everybody involved in decision-making.

The CIA's Langley headquarters holds more than four trillion bytes of secret information, which is said to be the equivalent of documents 35 miles high. Its computer discs occupy two immense floors with signposts so that technicians, riding on electric trolleys, can find their way. Through Intelink, all this information is readily accessible, so that if a planning officer needs to know which of a thousand politicians in Brazil might be turned into an agent, the system will produce a name and, even more, give detailed information about that person. The days of the card-index system vanished overnight with Intelink.

One of the most exciting and useful developments connected with Intelink is the Envision programme. It takes millions of satellite photographs and converts them into virtual reality that verges on *total* reality. Should a covert operative be assigned to a penetrative mission to Teheran he can study that city in detail by 'walking' through its alleyways. He may even study a building at ground level, though how virtual reality photographs at this level are taken remains classified.

In many instances, case officers have studied Envision virtual reality in order to plan a route to and from a selected rendezvous. Armed forces units preparing for a mission can examine every detail – type of terrain, vegetation, natural obstacles, buildings, traffic density. On operations warplane pilots swoop into valleys confident, after having swooped during virtual reality rehearsals, that they can safely fly out again.

What amounts to an open market in intelligence, through Envision, has dangers which have intelligence directors in other countries aghast. The SIS in particular, while noting the advantages, can see problems with security. Indeed, these are obvious. The first is that with 3,300 people entitled to use Intelink there is a good chance of one or more being another Aldrich Ames. No vetting procedure can ensure that every one of the 3,300 is risk-free. Secondly, Intelink is an irresistible temptation for hackers. When Ames was exposed the Operations Directorate took its E-mail address list off the CIA's main computer system for fear that moles could study it to identify case officers.

According to the CIA there are various safeguards. Intelink operates over the Pentagon's Defense Systems Network (DESNET), which has its own lines or leases special lines from telephone companies to send encrypted messages. To penetrate the system, a hacker would need to wiretap a DESNET line, then break the complex encryption and steal another user's password to get beyond the main menu.

During the six months October 1994 – March 1995 CIA security officers caught six agency employees and contractors who, 'for fun', tried to hack into parts of the agency's computer system that were off limits to them. They were dismissed, but there is no such sanction against outside hobby hackers.

I am not convinced by the copious assurances that security is one step ahead of those attempting to steal secrets. My natural scepticism, heightened by the steady flow of traitors, became more specific in the 1980s when the Pentagon formed élite and supposedly secret teams of specialists to crack the nation's defence computer codes. The chiefs believed that the 'Tiger Teams', as they were called, would fail and they wanted to be able to bask in that assurance. To their dismay, the Tigers succeeded every time. After a penetration, computers were reprogrammed or completely redesigned but the Tigers broke in again. When a first attempt proved difficult they planted a 'trap door' in the system which fell open when the thief approached again. Some Tiger teams burrowed into a computer without leaving a single electronic trace. The NSA had spent $100,000,000 to secure the integrity of its computer farm, but after the 'Tigers' had visited it nobody could guarantee that it had not already been compromised.

A nightmare for the security branches of the Western intelligence system is that clever electronic espionage agents, trained in sabotage, could plant a rogue programme or 'logic bomb', that an enemy would activate only in time of war. It would garble communications, fog radar and confuse navigational systems. The 'bombs' would be triggered via satellites. A saboteur would need comprehensive knowledge of the system, but several American traitors working for the Russians have already shown that they can gain access to critical defence installations and they can spend sufficient time there to cause immense damage. Nobody suspected Aldrich Ames for too long. Who else has escaped detection?

*   *   *

Any member of the public can see what a satellite can photograph, without the need to penetrate CIA, the SIS or any other intelligence agency. They can buy a satellite photograph. It will probably not show military secrets, but the Russians have purchased many photographs of specified subjects in the hope of spotting something significant. The French Government is the provider of this remarkable public intelligence through its imaging satellite, SPOT (*Systems Erobatoire d'Observation de la Terre*). It produces photos with a ground resolution of about 30 feet. All those in stock are listed in SPOT's inventory but others can be ordered. The price ranges from about £100 to £1,000. The SPOT photographs are not sophisticated, but those in my collection are clear and detailed enough for my purposes. As a military historian I am interested in First World War battlefields and SPOT photos provide me with information on the old trench lines, mine craters and the fields where fighting took place. As a money-making venture, the Russians are also interested in selling selected satellite photographs to private and commercial buyers.

The only secrets not discoverable from spy-planes, satellites, HALO and, sooner or later, from space stations are those within the minds of enemy leaders, terrorists, drug traffickers and Islamic fundamentalists. This remains the business of humint – human intelligence, as provided by the spies on the ground.

Already there are some fantastic ideas of how minds may be read but then satellites were once considered fantastic. Yesterday's fantasy is today's reality.

11

HIGH-TECH ESPIONAGE: WHEN ALLIES FALL OUT

Information is power. From alliances of nations, to single countries, to corporations and finally to the individual, the principle is steady – the level of power is commensurate with the amount of information held. The businessman's assets are not limited to his cash, securities and stock in hand; one of his main assets is what he knows about his competitors and their products. The responsible lawyer, before beginning any litigation, goes to every possible source for information about the people he will be confronting. A minister of state who attends a summit meeting without all kinds of information about the other ministers sitting around the conference table is asking for disaster. The men and women grouped behind each minister are there to answer any query he might have.

At an even higher level, when a president or prime minister is planning a summit with another president or prime minister, he would like his intelligence advisers to tell him what is in the other man's mind. Will he be springing any uncomfortable surprises and what might they be? At another crucial level, the general preparing defences against an attack – or preparing to make an attack – must know the strength of the forces opposing him and the weapons they will be using. Like his president, he would like information about what goes on in his opponent's mind.

However, commercial competitiveness, diplomatic jousting and military battle are not the only kinds of war. There is an espionage war for information itself. The hunger for information is both the driving force and the objective of this war and it is an unceasing conflict. Through espionage, with its techniques of bribery, corruption, blackmail, theft and coercion, spies seek secrets about technology, banking, commerce, industry, economics and manufacture of 'strategic' products, as well as information about men and women in key positions in government departments, corporations and councils.

There is another aspect to this unremitting and relentless conflict: the 'defenders' need to know what the other side knows about them and, even more critically, a defender is anxious, almost desperate, to know what the aggressors do not know about him and his assets.

What the defender knows that the enemy knows about him is of no particular worry and is really not a liability: he can take it into account when formulating his plans. But what he does not know they know about him, his resources and his plans, is definitely a liability. The enemy could use this 'secret' knowledge to outmanoeuvre him. To give an example at its most serious level: an American president might not know if his Russian counterpart knows that the USA has the technological-scientific ability to destroy an enemy city without bombing it. Meanwhile, the Russian president does not know if his American opponent knows that he is dying of cancer. To the paranoid Russian, such information in enemy hands could provoke an invasion from that enemy.

Technological espionage, which is inextricably linked with industrial, financial, economic, commercial and psychological espionage, is a game of hide and seek of awesome proportions. In the 1990s it was the biggest growth area in espionage. It is not separate from military and political espionage, but clearly linked to it. All technology has both civilian and military uses. It might seem odd that Polish spies would want to steal the chemical specifications of a type of paint, but this particular paint could withstand extreme high temperatures without blistering or peeling. Why would other Eastern Bloc spies be so anxious to place an agent in a British steel plant, since at first glance it hardly appears to be a prime military or technological target? This particular steel plant makes 'Chobham' armour plating for British battle tanks.

Why should German agents working for the KGB gain entry to Neckermann's department store in Frankfurt and photograph all 200 pages of the IBM repair manuals in the maintenance department? Because the information the manuals contained was needed by Soviet scientists who were copying certain American computers. Unable to get hold of the computers themselves, they realised that coded manuals would tell them all they needed – and they were easier to get at than the computers. High-tech manuals, microfiches, programmed magnetic discs, technical data sheets; all these and much more are industrial espionage targets.

For some countries espionage is total: they make no distinction between that carried out for military objectives and that for industrial and business purposes. Everything is for national effort. With the end of the Cold War, national intelligence services turned their attention to industrial espionage to give their own companies every advantage over foreign companies. The governments concerned know very well that this is going on and if, at times, some of them have doubts about the ethics of such activities their intelligence chiefs soon convince them that the secrets of a machine tool manufacturer are just as worth stealing as those of company making laser weapon sights.

Readers of this book will not be surprised to know that every businessman visiting Russia, China, Brazil, Korea and Taiwan will at least have his hotel room bugged and his fax messages intercepted. But they might be surprised to know that every business traveller should make this assumption when also visiting the US and France. France is the most commercially dangerous ally with which to do business.

*   *   *

Technological and industrial spying in the organised modern sense could be dated from 1969 when Yuri Andropov, then the KGB's chief, set up Directorate T. Its sole mission was the theft of Western technology and its staff was recruited from among the nation's best scientists, engineers and academics. Among the directorate's first tasks was the identification of vulnerable targets – men and women who could be bribed, blackmailed or bought.

For the best, fastest and least expensive results, Directorate T chose as its prime area of operations 'Silicon Valley' of California, where the silicon chip revolution had taken place and where, by the early 1970s, the amazing microscopic electronic circuits were transforming the technology of industry. Silicon Valley was wide open to espionage, both military and commercial. California computers, which the Russians had first set eyes on when they examined weapons captured during the Vietnam War, were by now guiding planes, tanks and ships and all the armaments they carried. They were also being put to hundreds of commercial and industrial uses. The Russians were hungry for computer systems.

Into this metaphorical gold mine the KGB's Directorate T sent one of its best agents, a cunning Hong Kong banker named Amos Dawe. He arrived in February 1973 with an enormous amount of money at his disposal. Dawe's cover was his own open history, that of a man who had risen from rags to riches by his own eye for a profit and stubborn determination to be wealthy. He appeared to have succeeded for at the height of his career he controlled 200 companies in six Asian countries with a great total evaluation. Or so it seemed. In fact, he was verging on bankruptcy – his wealth, verified by bribed auditors, existed only on paper.

Among the few people who knew of Dawe's desperate problems was Vachislav Rhyhov, manager of the Singapore Branch of Narodny Bank of Moscow and a senior KGB associate. Rhyhov met Dawe in secret and offered to guarantee his debts and also to finance the enlargement of his empire. Naturally, Dawe accepted the offer. Rhyhov explained the conditions attached to the gigantic loan a week later. Dawe was to go to the USA to buy banks for Narodny and if he did not agree to do this he would have 'problems' with his multi-million dollar loans. Reluctantly, Dawe went into the bank-buying business, even announcing, once he was known around Silicon Valley, that he wanted to buy 20 financial institutions, each in the $100,000,000 range. It was an outrageous plan but Dawe and Rhyhov knew that while US laws prevented foreign companies from making such purchases there was no such prohibition on individuals. Neither the CIA, the Treasury nor any other authority investigated the amazingly wealthy Chinese Amos Dawe.

He was the key figure in a conspiracy to do nothing less than take over the entire financial structure of Silicon Valley and thus penetrate every major high-technology and defence-committed corporation. He made a bold start in 1974–75, buying three banks for Narodny and thus for the Kremlin. The source of the money was concealed by complex banking movements. These purchases gave Dawe access to a large number of boardrooms and their secrets.

Nobody in the USA suspected the great scam, but in Singapore the CIA station chief was receiving reports from his agents about Dawe's association with Rhyhov. He alerted his chiefs at Langley who decided on a classic ploy to wreck the plot, which they named Operation SILICON VALLEY. They leaked the results of an investigation into the affair to Raymond Sacklyn, a Hong Kong-based journalist who ran the story in *Target*, his financial newsletter, on 20 October 1975. According to Sacklyn, the Soviet Government, through its secret services, was trying to wreck the world's financial institutions and that the principal plotters were the Narodny Bank, its manager Rhyhov and Amos Dawe. Picked up and published worldwide, it set alarm bells ringing throughout the American banking system. Dawe, frantic with worry, sought help from Rhyhov and Narodny Bank and from others involved in the conspiracy, but they would not talk with him, other than to say that he was on his own – and all this just as he was in the middle of taking control of a fourth bank.

The scandal affected the reputation of the Narodny Bank itself and at a stroke it had lost the enormous float it had put into the operation. The Dawe empire crumbled, too, and while Moscow Narodny recalled Rhyhov, for his own safety and to discipline him, there was no escape for his agent, Dawe, who disappeared. KGB agents hunted him and in Bangkok a Thai gang, hired by the Russians, beat him almost to death. Having recovered, he went underground again but the hunters – banks and other creditors as well as the KGB – followed him relentlessly. Finally, in 1978 Dawe flew to San Francisco and gave himself up to the FBI, counting on the G-men to protect him. The US Government did not proceed against him but numerous other people did, seeking to sue him for vast sums of money.

A Hong Kong extradition request was granted but in the colony he was acquitted of fraud charges – his Hong Kong friends had arranged the extradition as a way of rescuing him. Stung by this subterfuge, the US Government put pressure on its commercial courts to convict Dawe of embezzlement and to sentence him to five years in prison, a step that would not be possible in many other countries. This was something that Dawe could not face and, in 1982, before he could be apprehended, he disappeared again. In Hong Kong it is popularly believed that the KGB finally killed him, not so much in vengeance but rather as an example to others who might be tempted to swindle the Soviet machine out of billions of dollars. In fact, Dawe was merely following the orders of Narodny Bank, which, in turn, was acting for Directorate T. Rhyhov also disappeared, but that was definitely a sinister KGB-type disappearance; he was held equally responsible for the wrecking of Operation SILICON VALLEY. My information is that Dawe had emergency money hidden in real banks in Europe and, changing his name and lifestyle, he became yet another Chinese living in Canada.

Operation SILICON VALLEY was not a total disaster for the Russians. While it was running they received much secret technological information and they recruited other agents to spy for them in various parts of the USA. Breaking Operation SILICON VALLEY and exposing Amos Dawe was a triumph for the CIA, but the lesson that the Soviet Union was willing to spend huge amounts of money on industrial espionage was not widely enough learned.

*   *   *

The value the Soviet Union placed on microchip technology was dramatically shown in 1982 when Rhode Island fishermen brought up in their nets a silver cylinder weighing nearly half a ton. Under examination in a defence laboratory it turned out to be a previously unknown type of Soviet acoustics buoy, dropped to pick up the movements of NATO submarines. Its electronic brain functioned on a Russian-made computer chip, but this was a circuit-for-circuit replica of an American chip, the TI Series 5400. Without Western technology the Soviet buoy could not have worked. So many similar thefts were discovered that the US Under Secretary of Defence Technology, Richard Perle, went public about them: 'More than 160 Warsaw Pact weapons systems include Western technology. In effect we are exporting through espionage agents the means they use to arm against us.'

Through a 'deliberate error' the Americans proved that their microchips were being stolen. An American engineer with a sense of humour always worked into his microchip design a counter-clockwise superfluous screw. The Russian engineers copying the American design incorporated the giveaway screw, proving that they were rank copyists, not skilled engineers in their own right.

*   *   *

Long before the end of the Cold War, the Polish intelligence service, *Sluzba Bezvieczenstwa* (SB) had been a principal player in industrial espionage, largely through the talents of Marion Zacharski, who was then regarded throughout the Soviet intelligence system as a superspy, though to call him a spy is perhaps to belittle his modus operandi. Zacharski was 'president' of the Polish-American Machinery Corporation (Polamco) a state-owned company established in 1976 to import Polish machine tools into the USA. Polamco was not much of a company but Zacharski managed to sell machine equipment to a top-secret nuclear testing site in Nevada and, in an amazing breach of security, two Polamco engineers, one of them Zacharski himself, were admitted to the site to install the new equipment. What they took out of the site is not known but the giant Hughes Aircraft Corporation knows to its cost that on another occasion Zacharski stole its world-leading radar system.

Zacharski, a personable 29-year-old and a keen tennis player, made friends with a neighbour in an apartment complex in Playa Del Rey, California. The bachelor neighbour, William Bell, was a computer consultant with the Hughes Corporation and the rest, to quote a cliché, is history. In detail, the obliging Zacharski lent the high living Bell large sums of money, thus making him financially dependent on him. The next step was blackmail. Zacharski had chosen his target well and in a steady flow, Bell turned over to the Pole documents and blueprints by the hundred. The more serious thefts concerned the secrets of the US F-15 fighter plane and all details on the Hawk, Patriot and Phoenix missiles. Bell was found out and sent to prison for eight years, but by then the Russians were already testing their own versions of the Hughes developments.

The 'Ding-Dong Affair', as the FBI coded the Bell treason, was bad enough in itself but what made it worse was that by 1979 the FBI knew that Zacharski was a spy, and though agents kept him under surveillance for two years they allowed his entrapment of Bell to continue. In the end Bell himself gave the evidence that led to Zacharski's arrest and conviction as a spy, with the sentence of life imprisonment. Zacharski was not alarmed: he knew that sooner or later he would be exchanged, and he was.

Another victim of the SB was James Harper, an electronics expert who was targeted in the same way as William Bell and lured into becoming an agent by the same method. The KGB and GRU together had been trying for a long time to get their hands on the US plans to strengthen the concrete launching silos of Minutemen missiles, which in the late 1970s were the principal US means of retaliation against any Soviet attack. The additional strengthening was to make the launch pads impervious to a Soviet pre-emptive attack. Harper sold these plans for $100,000 in 1980. For three years, the cautious but confident Harper made a fortune out of selling top-class secrets, those of the new MX missile among them. He even obtained copies of all the manuals concerning the Ballistic Defense Advanced Technology Center in Huntsville, Alabama.

He was trapped in the end by a CIA agent deep in the KGB itself who managed to extricate himself from Russia and return to America with his secrets about secrets. The FBI closed in on Harper, who was sentenced to life imprisonment. Unlike the Pole Zacharski, he could not expect to be exchanged. The Polish operative who had run Harper, a colonel named Zdidzislaw Prychodzien, fared better than his agent: he was presented with a decoration by Yuri Andropov, chief of the KGB.

For Andropov even more than other Russian espionage chiefs, all damage inflicted on the West through the theft of 'secrets' was of equal value. He would have praised an agent bringing back the design of a revolutionary tin-opener, especially if he had gained it in a clandestine way.

*   *   *

In the post-Cold War period, businessmen and women are vulnerable in the ever more sophisticated industrial espionage war because however clever they might be in their chosen field of expertise, they are innocent and ingenuous when they venture abroad on what is, to them, legitimate business. Buoyed up with commercial expectation and relaxing in a luxury hotel of exotic ambience, they lower any guard that they might have had when leaving home. They do not have a password on their laptop computer, they do not use encryption programmes and frequently they leave laptops openly in their hotel rooms. Many countries have agents in hotels frequented by visiting businessmen and other executives.

A cautionary tale concerns two French executives who flew to China to sell an enormously expensive missile-guidance system

Sarah Aaronsohn, a spy for Britain during the First World War. (*Nigel Gribbon*)

The grave of Sarah Aaronsohn at the Cemetery of Zikhron Ya'aqob. Only the name 'Sarah' and the dates of her birth and death are engraved on the stone. (*Nigel Gribbon*)

George Blake arriving in London. At this time he did not know that he had been called home for interrogation and, subsequently, arrest.

Aldrich and Rosario Ames after their arrest in 1994. *(Hulton/Reuters)*

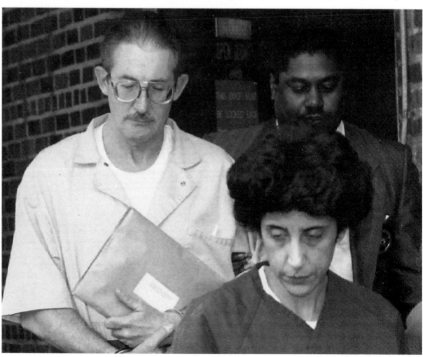

The CIA's headquarters building at Langley, Virginia. The organisation owns many other less public buildings. *(CIA)*

An American artist's impression of a Soviet manned spy satellite with a shuttle approaching. *(USAF)*

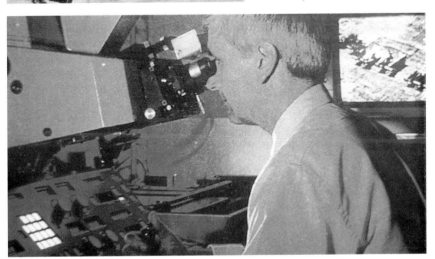

A CIA analyst examining photos taken by a spy satellite. *(CIA)*

Gary Powers, a CIA pilot who was shot down over the USSR in his U-2 spyplane, stands trial in Moscow. After several years' imprisonment, Powers was exchanged for the Soviet spy Rudolf Abel. *(Hulton Deutsch)*

The American SR-71 *Blackbird* strategic reconnaissance aircraft, successor to the U-2. *(USAF)*

'Gordon Lonsdale', a Soviet spymaster in Britain and probably the only Soviet-born spy caught by MI5.

The tin of talcum powder in which Lonsdale had made two secret compartments, containing a microdot reader and negatives.

Peter and Helen Kroger, members of the 'Portland Spy Ring' who were each sentenced to 20 years for spying. *(Hulton Deutsch)*

The 'House of Secrets': the Krogers' house at 45 Cranley Drive, Ruislip, where huge quantities of sophisticated espionage equipment was discovered by the British authorities. *(Hulton Getty)*

The cavity in the foundations of the Krogers' house where a radio transmitter, camera and other equipment were discovered. *(Hulton Deutsch)*

The rear view of the Krogers' radiogram, with tape recorder and headphones connected. *(Hulton Deutsch)*

October 1969: the Krogers board the aircraft that will take them to Warsaw and freedom, after they had served almost nine years of their 20-year jail sentences. *(Hulton Deutsch)*

An early bugging device: a microphone hidden behind a curtain in Germany, c.1925. *(AKG Photo)*

A Russian spy camera, able to work in total darkness, found in the car of Douglas Britten, a Royal Air Force technician who spied for the Russians against Great Britain for money. He was sentenced to 21 years' imprisonment in 1968. *(Hulton Getty)*

Unser Betrieb hat einige neue Artikel aufgenommen, von denen wir uns flotten Absatz erhoffen. Ich wäre Ihnen dankbar, wenn Sie mich über die Lage auf dem Seidenmarkte ein wenig informiren wollten, da sicherlich nach Friedensschluss mit grösseren Importen zu rechnen sein wird und ich gerne auf dem Laufenden bleiben möchte. Ist Ihre Solothurner Fabrik wieder im Betriebe?

Mit besten Grüssen

in Hochachtung

An ordinary spy message written in invisible ink between the lines of type of a business communication. A suspicious investigator has brushed a chemical diagonally across the page and picked up signs of secret writing. He has then brought the entire message to light with horizontal lines of the developing agent.

During the first day of negotiations the Chinese representatives were not merely interested, they seemed desperate to buy what was on offer. That evening the Frenchmen were invited to dinner and they were cautious enough to take their laptops and briefcases with them. When they arrived at the dinner venue, their interpreter advised, 'It would be safer if you were to leave your possessions with the chauffeur. He will be staying with the car the entire evening.'

Next day, the Chinese negotiators' manner had changed. Oh yes, they said, the missile-guidance system was a good one but it was far too expensive. The French side came down to their pre-agreed minimum price but the Chinese were by now yawning. Not until the Frenchmen told their story to officials at their embassy did they realise that the Chinese had obtained the system for nothing. The chauffeur and others had milked their computers and copied their documents.

The embassy officials were exasperated when they found that the French negotiators had not asked them for an approved list of interpreters and drivers. And as for leaving such valuable things in a car – only people out of their mind did that. French officials know about such matters, since their agents, acting as hotel maids, waiters, drivers and tour guides, are accustomed to stealing secrets.

Many companies buy tracker devices which can be implanted in laptops, but at a cost of £4,500 each they are three times the value of the computer itself. Nevertheless the information contained in the laptop can be priceless. This is known to organised criminal gangs which steal laptops and demand ransoms for them. In the USA amounts of up to $750,000 have been paid and it is almost routine for executives to offer rewards of $100,000 for the return of stolen computers.

That espionage concerning computers is a serious problem is shown by the establishment of the Computer Security Research Centre at London School of Economics. In one warning issued by the Centre, businessmen were told that the most common theft of information came from unattended computers in the office: industrial spies often gain access as cleaners or repairmen and make copies on floppy discs at an unattended terminal.

Industrial espionage agents are using age-old entrapment methods. In France, a married businessman fell for the charm of a beautiful young woman and the very next day was shown a video of their passionate evening in bed. It was quite easy to avoid any 'problems' as a result of his indiscretion, he was told. He simply had to co-operate with some new business partners.

*   *   *

But the French go much further than this, and at the highest level. In 1993 *The Independent*, London, disclosed the existence of a French intelligence document which was nothing less than a guide to the industrial secrets which France most wanted to steal from its allies. The 'what to steal' guide had been compiled by the Department of Economics, Science and Technology which, among other things, instructed agents of the *Direction Générale de la Sécurité Extérieure* (DGSE) to penetrate Wall Street banks, giving priority to Citibank, Chase Manhattan and Goldman Sachs. Consultants and lawyers employed by investment houses should also be targeted.

This certainly makes sense, since people in both professions are known to be careless about the security of documents and telephone calls. The Department also called for helicopter technology from the British Westland company and for satellite research. Press revelation about this industrial spying caused the French Government acute but short-lived embarrassment.

They were similarly embarrassed when the US and Canadian intelligence services warned company executives to assume that they would be bugged whenever they flew first class with Air France. The airline indignantly denied that its employees would spy on passengers, but there are many ancillary workers with access to first class seats and espionage agents could be among them. It must be assumed that the CIA and Canadian security services had good reason to issue such serious warnings and that they acted with the approval of their respective governments.

That the French venture into technological, industrial and economic espionage on a grand scale happened at the same time as the end of the Cold War was not mere coincidence. The government of President Francois Mitterand and his various prime ministers were quick to see that the Warsaw Pact countries were breaking apart and that this would be followed by the dismemberment of the Soviet Union itself. These great political developments would mean that only one superpower remained – the United States. As French politicians interpreted the changing international situation, a significant vacuum was opening up. While France could never hope to be a superpower on the American scale it could become the next most important – the 'leader of the rest'. The only possible rivals were Britain, the newly unified Germany and Japan, but each already had a weakness. Britain was in a state of terminal decline following the strains of the Second of World War and because of the British people's confusion about their nation's standing in the world. Germany, though one of the postwar 'miracles', had a foul wartime reputation to live down and the process could take another 50 years. Japan, though triumphant in trade, had also been a Second World War aggressor and though it was not apologising for its barbarism it was not redeveloping its armed forces with expansionism in mind; rather than invade other countries it was buying them up.

As the French leaders analysed the situation, the way was open for French dominance in the political-military, economic, industrial and technological fields. But to achieve this ambition it was necessary to amass 'secrets' of every conceivable kind. The French intelligence services became collectors of 'pieces' (q.v.), which they duly pass on to relevant departments and ministries. While most of this activity is covert, President Chirac, Mitterand's successor, did something overt in his bid for French power – he authorised a series of nuclear tests in the South Pacific and ignored the international outcry that followed each of these tests.

Having drawn attention to France's political will – 'We do not back down in the face of hysterical and ill-informed protests' – Chirac announced an end to the French tests. Late in January 1996 during a speech in Washington, he called for a total world ban on nuclear testing. France would take the lead in this, he said. This was Gallic hypocrisy at its worst.* Chirac did not say that France proposes to take the lead in every way, but it was evident in the display of French military strength in ex-Yugoslavia, especially in Bosnia, and in several

* French political leaders cannot tolerate criticism. When Greenpeace campaigners were protesting about French nuclear tests in the South Pacific in 1985, French secret agents planted a bomb in their ship, *Rainbow Warrior,* and sank it in Auckland Harbour, New Zealand. One crew member was killed in this outrageous affront to the sovereignty of another country. Following strenuous New Zealand protests, France 'disciplined' the agents responsible for the attack – that is, they were exiled to the tropical paradise of Tahiti for three years!

decisions to take independent military action rather than in conjunction with allies.

To achieve their various political, military and industrial objectives, the French Intelligence services were strengthened during the 1990s and given wider fields of operation. No wonder, then, that the Department of Economics, Science and Technology presented its espionage agents with a comprehensive list of 'items required'.

The French budget for intelligence activities, though secret in detail, is said to have been tripled in the years 1995–96. Much of the money must be for technological and industrial espionage for the French refuse to become dependent on whatever the Americans may be willing to share with them.

*   *   *

The end of the Cold War did not bring closer co-operation among the intelligence agencies of the former Western allies. They might be nominally unified in NATO, in the EU and in the Western European Union, but in some ways they distrust one another and operate alone. That there is good reason for distrust was demonstrated in what the British SIS (MI6) labels 'the Assinger Affair', an inter-intelligence scam that destroyed the trust between the SIS and Germany's BND. Assinger is not a real name and we must assume that it is a code-cover for an individual or possibly for the episode.

MI6 and BND had set up a multi-million pound fund to finance the buying of agents from among the Russian generals during the final Soviet exodus from what had been East Germany. It was felt that the Russian senior officers, demoralised and facing loss of status and income, would be soft targets. Obviously, German involvement was necessary in what was essentially an SIS idea, because BND agents could more readily operate in Germany.

Three BND agents, led by the organisation's chief in Nuremberg and with the complicity of a single SIS man, siphoned off much of the fund into secret accounts of their own. The conspirators became greedy for more money and needed the co-operation of somebody within BND's headquarters at Pullach, Bavaria. The officer they approached was either honest or terrified and he reported the matter to the BND's chief of security, Volger Foertsch, who began an investigation.

The SIS knew nothing about the affair until the BND uncovered the involvement of the Englishman. 'Assinger' and his German accomplices were not at this time suspected because they managed to convince Foertsch that the SIS agent had alone stolen the money now known to be missing. He was using it to set up a British spy ring, Assinger said. He himself had been investigating the SIS man and he had heard that he had secretly banked large sums of money in the Cayman Islands, as indeed he had.

Foertsch reported to the Director of BND, Konrad Porzner, who flew to London for an angry confrontation with SIS. He is reported to have accused the Director-General, Sir Colin McColl, of allowing his subordinates to carry out 'James Bond' operations in Germany. But SIS seniors had meanwhile been carrying out their own more thorough investigation and calmly they told Porzner about Assinger and his accomplices in Nuremberg.

Porzner was embarrassed and alarmed because Chancellor Helmut Kohl and his co-ordinator of security policy, Bernd Schmidbauer, would hold him responsible for the débâcle. For internal political reasons, these two had been trying for years to force Porzner from his position. It was unclear early in 1996 what action had been taken against Assinger and his fellow thieves, but two things were crystal clear: the SIS would not recover its money – the damage done to SIS-BND relations would take some time to repair. Full details of the 'Assinger Affair' are unlikely to emerge for years.

*   *   *

As the SIS was trying to come to terms with the 'Assinger Affair', it was horrified by an extraordinary CIA operation concerning Iran. The British had no direct connection with 'Operation AYATOLLAH', but the ineptitude not only of the CIA but the US political establishment as well was alarming. Could the American intelligence organisations any longer be trusted with secrets?

There was nothing secret about Operation AYATOLLAH, it was the best-known clandestine plot the Americans had thought up in a long time. It originated with Newt Gingrich, the plausible but ignorant Speaker of the House of Representatives who managed to earmark $18,000,000 to 'reshape Iran's government'. It had long been Gingrich's ambition to mount a covert operation to bring decency and sanity back to Iran, a society run by terror.

Openly, early in 1995 Gingrich advocated a scheme that 'ultimately is designed to force the replacement of the current regime in Iran'. Later that year, in a speech at a school in Atlanta, he said, 'We have to make Iran a real project.' In October the Gingrich scheme was made public in the columns of the *Congressional Monitor*, the *Wall Street Journal* and on international news services. At this point President Clinton became involved and allowed the powerful Gingrich his covert plan but his great objectives had to be watered down. The CIA would only be allowed to 'alter Teheran's behaviour'.

Gingrich's original plan called for $100,000,000, which would still not have been enough to achieve such a fantastic objective. When it was scaled down to $18,000,000 the CIA showed the amount in its top-secret budget on 31 December 1995. The secrecy lasted for only a few hours.

The Iranian president, Ayatollah Ali Akbar Rafsanjani, angrily announced that a fund of $20,000,000 had been raised 'by public donation' to fight the Great Satan, the label first applied to the USA by Ayatollah Khomeini in 1979. One of Rafsanjani's ministers said that three Iranians accused of spying for the US would be executed, a real blow to the CIA if indeed the men were spies.

It is probable that the CIA leaked information about the Gingrich project in order to kill it, since by February Gingrich himself was perhaps the only person in authority who believed in it. The USA and the CIA could not afford another disaster in Iran. The first was the CIA–SIS coup which reinstated Shah Muhammad Reza Pahlevi in 1953. The tensions that this created in Iranian society caused the Islamic revolution in 1979, an event which the CIA failed to anticipate. It was one of the agency's greatest failures. US embassy staff members were taken prisoner and held for more than a year, during which time the CIA, with the dubious assistance of the Army and Air Force, botched rescue attempts. Finally, the CIA was involved in the misguided and abortive attempt to trade arms for hostages. Operations in Iran left a nasty smell in the corridors of Langley.

Having crippled the Gingrich plan by leaking it, the CIA leaked further information in its desperation to throw it into the discard drawer. A spokesman publicly announced that the CIA was already helping radio propaganda campaigns aimed against the ayatollahs' regime. This would not have been news to the ayatollahs, but they can tolerate a great deal when it is not published. Bringing the propaganda activity into the open was considered offensive.

There was never any likelihood that $18,000,000 spent on whatever Gingrich dreamed up would succeed in 'changing the behaviour of the government' or the government itself. Between them, Gingrich and the CIA provoked the Iranian revolutionary regime into further vitriolic outbursts of anti-American hatred.

The episode once again shook the confidence of the Western intelligence community not only in the CIA but in American Intelligence generally. 'To gain the widest possible publicity for a clandestine project, take the CIA into your confidence', a French official said sourly. This was not quite fair since the CIA's leadership might not have wanted to be involved in the first place, but its subsequent actions were ineptly handled. They could have talked Gingrich out of going public or, failing that, they could have portrayed him as a crazy maverick. Ridicule is a known and proven tactic against influential internal troublemakers.

*   *   *

The SIS was further displeased with the CIA and the DIA when it discovered that the American secret services were operating against them in Bosnia. In place in former Yugoslavia since the war's beginning in 1990, the CIA–DIA teams were reporting to their headquarters in Zagreb, Croatia, that the European Union, and particularly the British, were, in American eyes, permitting the intransigent Bosnian Serbs to get away with murder. The Clinton Administration believed that NATO air strikes should be used to bomb the Serbs to the negotiating table. The commander of the United Nations Protection Force (UNPROFOR), General Sir Michael Rose, was worried that air strikes would endanger his soldiers, firstly by their being close to the bombing sites and secondly because the Serbs would indiscriminately target them in revenge. In particular, Rose wanted no further dangers for his Special Air Services (SAS) men then under deep cover in Bosnia.

The SAS scouts operating from Serb-held territory were spotters both for UNPROFOR artillery and for NATO bomber pilots. But Rose's HQ ordered the SAS teams: 'Do NOT identify targets.' This command was bound to be controversial should it come to light because it was emasculating NATO air power. It should be noted though that General Rose did order NATO air and ground strikes against the Serbs encircling Gorazde in 1994 and wanted to use close air support to protect SAS units there, but he was over-ruled on that occasion by his UN civilian superior, Yasushi Akashi.

Unbeknown to Rose, the CIA–DIA field teams were listening to his communications with his SAS units and reporting back via Zagreb to the Joint Chiefs of Staff and President Clinton. For the impatient Americans Rose was sabotaging NATO attempts to bomb the stubborn Serbs into some kind of peace arrangement. They had good reason for wanting tough action against Serb leader Radovan Karadzic and his generals. For 30 months they had been besieging Bihac, where a weak Bangladeshi battalion was isolated. In addition they had blocked humanitarian aid convoys and looted the trucks. In November 1994 the Serbs subjected Bihac, a so-called 'safe area', to artillery and aerial bombing. At this point NATO intervened, mounting an air strike against a Serb airfield in Croatia. An American Air Force observer at UN headquarters at Zagreb was alarmed when he received reports from DIA agents that the Bosnian Serbs had just taken delivery of fresh supplies of Russian SAM anti-aircraft missiles from Belgrade, capital of Serbia proper. A strong request for an air strike was made but Rose, declining to issue the order, began negotiations about a ceasefire.

In the ensuing days there was much confusion as Rose came under increasing pressure to bomb. The SIS–SAS in combination were listening in to American intelligence briefings and the CIA–DIA partnership was doing all it could to outmanoeuvre Rose. Rose and his staff were determined not to bomb and, in a tactical sense, they held the upper hand, for the only men in a position to identify Serbian targets were the SAS units.

By the end of November Serbian tanks were creating havoc in the suburbs of Bihac. President Clinton could hardly override UNPRO-FOR's commander or even criticise him in public, especially a general from Britain, so his administration offered concessions to the Serbs and soon after it recognised a Bosnian Serb republic. In the meantime, the CIA–DIA pressed on with intelligence operations from which the SIS was excluded. With the US ambassador to Croatia, Richard Galbraith, the agency brought about an American alliance with Croatia, while a military consultancy from Virginia retrained the Croatian Army. Not surprisingly, the man in charge of this training programme was a former senior CIA officer, Ed Soyster. The US Government could claim, with imperfect honesty, that none of its troops were training Croatian soldiers.

The CIA now came into its own, operating in the way that it had in all the wars of Central America during the 1970s and 1980s. In breach of the embargo against supplying arms to the belligerents, the agency dropped weapons and equipment to the Bosnian army at Tuzla on four separate occasions in February 1995. When SIS-SAS reported these drops government sources in London then leaked the news. The row forced NATO to hold an internal inquiry into the air drops. Unfortunately, all four officers appointed to conduct the inquiry were American, leading to allegations that its findings were flawed. They might not have been, but a mixed-nation team of investigators would have inspired more confidence. The findings of the inquiry was that 'the witnesses of the drops had been mistaken'.

The able Rose, his term of duty completed, was succeeded by General Sir Rupert Smith who agreed with the Americans that the Bosnian Serbs would never consent to meaningful talks unless they were both damaged militarily and in morale. He began air strikes against the Serbs in Bosnia in the summer of 1995. The chiefs of the CIA and DIA were delighted, for they regarded this offensive as a victory for themselves. They also saw it as a victory over the SIS–SAS, which was an unfortunate and absurd attitude. The British had done what their own political leaders had ordered and, in the case of the SAS, what the UN in the person of General Rose had commanded. The SIS–SAS in turn were irritated by being bugged by people who were supposed to be their closest allies. The entire episode illustrated an eternal verity that allies often spy on one another.

It also provided another opportunity for the use of hightech surveillance equipment. The SAS reporting to UNPROFOR headquarters and the CIA–DIA eavesdropping on the SAS used the latest equipment. It was so advanced that had the Bosnian Serbs or any other enemy captured it and tried to use it in an attempt to deceive the British or Americans, it would have destroyed its own vital parts.

*   *   *

The only advanced industrial nation lacking a high-tech intelligence capability is Japan. The Defence Agency has proved its ability to

161

intercept elint in its region, but it is without a spy satellite to track, for instance, North Korea's nuclear programme and it sadly lacks a professional corps of analysts to assess data. The country has no organisation like the CIA, MI6 or GCHQ to gather and analyse information and instead relies on a collection of small agencies, each attached to a particular ministry.

Since the 1950s Japan has been dependent on the Americans for information emanating from elint, from satellites and often from humint. Lack of adequate intelligence capability is the price Japan has paid for being an aggressor in the Second World War. Senior officials in Tokyo suspect that the CIA and its linked agencies colour all the intelligence assessments sent to Japan. In 1994 they were sure that the Americans were manipulating data about North Korea's nuclear programme in order to gain Japan's support for a pre-emptive strike against Yongbyon nuclear facility at a time when North Korea seemed ready to go to war against South Korea.

Japan is so far behind all countries of comparable technological development that during the 1991 coup attempt against President Gorbachev the Government was embarrassed by its inability to issue a statement on the crisis. Without independent intelligence it did not know what was happening in Moscow. Also, Tokyo knew nothing of the Bush Administration's covert co-operation with Yeltsin at the time.

With the nation's interests rapidly expanding around the world, shown by the Government's campaign for a permanent seat on the UN Security Council, Japan is ambitious to have its own highly developed high-tech intelligence system to provide better and more timely information.

Meanwhile the Public Security Investigation Agency (PSIA), with a staff of 2,000, does a competent job in counter-espionage and counter-terrorism, and in tracking North Korean agents in Japan. The Ministry of International Trade and Industry (MITI) has a staff of 20,000 analysing trade, commerce, markets and technological developments. Its agents, in 60 countries, are intent on giving Japan every advantage in world business. The Cabinet Research Bureau, the Foreign Ministry and the Prime Minister's Secretariat have intelligence-analysis bureaus, but they are stretched to their limit and have no resources to cover intelligence-gathering.

Everybody in authority wants a Defence Intelligence Agency, as Japan had under another name before the Second World War, but a law would have to be passed to create it. Also, the Diet (parliament) passed a law in 1969 forbidding the military use of space, so Japan cannot have a satellite. Nevertheless, it could get around this prohibition by developing a 'peace satellite.' About 10 years will be needed to put it into orbit. The Japanese have proved devious in bypassing other prohibitions: for instance, the constitution prohibits a standing army, navy or air force, but Japan maintains ground, maritime and air 'Self-Defense Forces'. Each has intelligence resources as well as a combined resource under the Joint Staff Council.

Japan has not fully recovered from the trauma following the nuclear bombing of Hiroshima and Nagasaki. When it does recover, another expansionist phase as well as a desire for vengeance will develop. Western intelligence experts specialising in the Orient are aware of this danger, which is why the Western nations are in no hurry to help Japan develop a high-tech intelligence capability. While not openly protesting about this Western attitude, the Japanese are gaining the information they want through espionage. They are key players in the game of high-tech theft and they have the money to spend.

Obviously there is a contradiction between Japan's stated policies and what it does in practice. When challenged about the respective intelligence services of the Navy, Army and Air Force, Japanese officials disarmingly say that the intelligence activity is at a low level and purely defensive, and that their budgets are small. Western intelligence sections which watch Japan's developments say that the very secrecy surrounding its intelligence activities is worrying.

The Japanese have always been magnificent copyists in industry and commerce. In some ways they have been copyists in intelligence gathering for a century. Wilhelm Stieber, director of Prussian intelligence in the latter half of the 19th century, especially interested Japanese espionage chiefs of the time. Stieber, an intelligent but totally unscrupulous man, demonstrated how the systematic use of prostitution and perversion could be used in intelligence. He established in Berlin the Green House, a high-class and elegant brothel in which every form of sexual perversion could be practised. When Stieber decided to recruit some important man to his extraordinary network he had him lured to the Green House, where he was given free access to its delights. When his victim was hopelessly compromised Stieber blackmailed him with the threat of exposure. It was said that even 'normal' men who entered the Green House came out of it as perverts. The more stubbornly normal were worked on with drugs to weaken their resistance to the professional female and male perverts who staffed the Green House.

The Japanese copied Stieber's Green House and improved on it with their own 'Hall of Pleasurable Delights'. Built in Hankow, China, in a region that was then a Japanese province, it was tastefully furnished and staffed with men and women able to offer every vice, with oriental trimmings. The Hall had two functions – to compromise prominent Chinese men and soften them up for blackmail, and as an intelligence exchange for agents operating deep in China and Russia.

The Hall provided a cut-out on a grand scale. No agent could contact his principal: instead, he went to the Hall, engaged a prostitute and passed his report to her. Getting it to Japanese intelligence HQ was her job. Every prostitute in the place was in the pay of intelligence.

These whores were used in another way – as instructors. They not only professionally entertained the agents but taught them ways in which to seduce ordinary women who might be able to help them in their dangerous work when they returned to the field.

Throughout the century the Japanese have stolen and copied designs for everything from Stieber's brothel to battleships and small arms. In many cases they have improved on the original design. There can be no doubt that Japan has a vast collection of Western and Soviet/Russian high-tech information, amassed through espionage. When it is analysed and put into production Japan could become as immensely powerful in the military sphere as it already is in industry.

*   *   *

The amazing growth of high-tech spying is shown by information given to delegates at a conference of the Co-ordinating Committee for East–West Trade when it met in Paris in 1982. They were told that in January of that year the KGB's Directorate T, responsible for electronic espionage, employed more than 20,000 agents, all engaged in stealing equipment or the plans to build it. The Committee accepted that the figure was not an exaggeration because it had come from a mole who had recently come out of Directorate T. The number of electronic spies has continued to grow.

12

TRICKS OF THE TRADE

To be successful as an espionage agent or as a security operative trying to catch spies, certain knowledge has to be imbibed. It is just not possible to survive in this competitive industry without some basic training. I speak here about the agent or spycatcher in the field, rather than all those essential members of an intelligence organisation such as the forgers, the many analysts, the troubleshooters, the interrogators, the interpreters and translators, the locksmiths, the photographers, cryptographers and many others. Any one of these people might take part in an operation outside the confines of the offices and laboratory when some special need arises, but on the whole they work inside. Even so, I knew an intelligence photographer who spent most of her career in the field; 'field' in her case meant streets and buildings, parks and gardens, mountains and deserts. Many of the 'arts and crafts' described in this chapter are much more difficult to master than they seem to be in film spy stories.

'The House of Secrets'

One of the great British intelligence coups of the 1960s was the exposure of the 'Portland Spy Ring', a group of five ill-assorted people working for the KGB in Britain. They were Gordon Lonsdale (actually Konon Trofimovich Molody), Peter and Helen Kroger (real names Morris and Lona Cohen), Harry Houghton and Ethel Gee.

The Krogers posed as Canadians who had lived for some time in Switzerland, coming to Britain in 1954 in the hope that the climate would be better for Peter's health. They carried on an antiquarian book business by mail from their home in Middlesex. Lonsdale, also posing as a Canadian – and with apparently impeccable proof of his nationality – reached Britain in 1955 and took a furnished apartment near Regent's Park, London, and made many friends and acquaintances. As a director of the Automatic Merchandising Company, he provided himself with excellent cover. When this company failed, Lonsdale found new cover as director of the Master Switch company.

Lonsdale recruited Harry Houghton, a former Royal Navy master-at-arms who, on retirement from the Navy, had found a job with the Admiralty, which sent him to Warsaw to join the staff of the naval attaché. This posting gave him access to all naval classified material. A drunkard, Houghton had public rows with his wife and was returned to Britain where, surprisingly, considering his poor reputation, he was appointed to the Underwater Weapons Establishment, Portland. Here he had easy access to priceless secrets.

At this time, having separated from his wife, Houghton formed a liaison with Ethel Gee, a colleague from the top secret naval base where they both worked. Harry Houghton made a mistake that has led to the downfall of many spies – he drew attention to himself by his extravagance. His annual salary was £750 and his pension £250, but he expensively redecorated his home, refurnished it and bought a new car – and paid for everything in £5 and £1 notes. And as if this were not suspicious enough, he was spending more on alcohol than he received in salary. A low-level investigation commenced by naval security was handed over to MI5 and Special Branch.

Surveillance showed that Houghton and Ethel Gee frequently travelled to London where they met a man soon identified by the watchers as Gordon Lonsdale. Gee would take a package from her shopping basket and hand it to Lonsdale, who would give her a package in return. The transaction was simple to interpret – information being exchanged for money. Nevertheless, Lonsdale, Houghton and Gee were allowed to 'run' for about nine months in order to round up any other members of the ring.

Lonsdale frequently visited the home of Peter and Helen Kroger and sometimes spent the weekend there. A spy ring was definitely at work and experienced speculation indicated that Houghton and Gee procured the secret information and passed it to Lonsdale who took it to the Krogers for transmission to the KGB.

The Krogers lived in a bungalow at 45 Cranley Drive, Ruislip, Middlesex, and when they came under suspicion as spies the house was watched. Chief Inspector Ferguson Smith of the SB made undercover inquiries and established that the home had been made unusually secure. At that time (1960) people were not as security conscious as they became in the dangerous decades of the 1980s and 1990s, but the Krogers' house had extra security locks fitted to the outside doors and special burglar-proof devices to every window. This was unusual, but so far this was not too suspicious since the Krogers were dealers in rare books and manuscripts.

After they were arrested (with Gordon Lonsdale, Ethel Gee and Harry Houghton) the Krogers' house was searched. How illicit objects were hidden in it, the variety of hiding places and the way in which the police searched it provides one of the best examples of spies and spycatchers at work. To begin with, searchers turned each page of every one of the thousand or so books in the house to see if anything was hidden between pages. In the family Bible was specially treated photographic paper for microdots while a book called *Auction Sales* concealed three small pieces of paper on which were figures in Peter Kroger's handwriting. They were found to refer to signal plans.

Behind books on a shelf were two valid New Zealand passports in the names of Peter John Kroger and Helen Joyce Kroger; in all the Krogers had five sets of passports, some forgeries and some genuine, for various countries. Next to the Krogers' bed was a hip flask with secret cavities in the top, one of which contained black powder for dusting the metallic tape of the keying device used to record messages for the transmitter.

Other finds included: a torch with a false battery for holding film; a Britex microscope with slides for mounting microdots; a microdot reader in a tin of talcum powder; Minox, Exaxta and Kodak cameras; several one-time code pads; a great quantity of photographic materials; a high quality writing case with a secret drawer in which were found two forged Canadian passports in false names; and two wooden book-ends in which were sealed $400. Another $6,000, mostly in notes but some in travellers' cheques, were found behind the fibre-glass ceiling insulation.

The large cabinet radio receiver impressed the searchers because it could receive messages from anywhere in the world. It had an aerial 75 feet in length, earphones and a tape recorder. The investigation showed that when Moscow was transmitting the recorder was switched on, so that if reception was poor and the Krogers had some doubt about a message they could play the recording.

Ferguson Smith and his team knew that a transmitter must exist in this spies' house but they could not find it. The bungalow's floor level was three feet above the concrete base, suggesting a cavity. By wheeling the refrigerator into the middle of the kitchen and rolling back the linoleum the searchers found a trapdoor which allowed access to the underfloor space, which was strewn with rubble left by workmen who had installed central heating. When it was cleared out nothing suspicious was found, so a metal detector was used, also unsuccessfully. One searcher now began to tap the concrete base with a hammer. This tactic produced a single absolutely straight crack in the concrete. A few more taps and a rectangular outline showed up. It was a thick concrete lid covering a wooden lid and underneath this was found a large plastic-wrapped parcel. Inside was a steel case holding a high-powered transmitter with a key for transmitting codes at high speed – 240 words per minute, as it turned out.

There was yet another find: the Krogers had a blackout screen for their bathroom so that they could use it as a darkroom.

Some of the spy treasures hidden in Lonsdale's flat at 634 The White House, Albany Street, London, were even more sophisticated than those in the Krogers' home. Two Chinese scrolls hung from a wall in the lounge and each was weighted by a cylindrical bar, with the ends covered in heavy brocade. It was fairly obviously a hide, but how to open it without damage? A searcher pushed the point of a fine needle through the brocade and located a small hole. A little twist and pressure and the head of the bar opened. Inside were $1,800. In a table lighter were found the code signs for a transmitter and some one-time pads of KGB make.

Other finds included: an ordinary-looking radio adapted to receive fixed-time messages from Moscow; $300 in a leather belt; a tin of talcum powder with two secret sections, one of which concealed a microdot reader; and a torch with a 'battery' which had a fine thread so that the head could be removed, leaving space for a film.

In the kitchen was a tin of photographic fixing powder in which the searchers found something that the spies had not intended to keep. It was a receipt for the purchase made out to a Mr Kroger of 45 Cranley Drive, Ruislip, Middlesex. Various coded call-signs were found both in Lonsdale's flat and in the Krogers' home. They were *Lena ya amur*; *Volga ya Azov*; *Esteo*; *Rosa ya Fielca*. On a famous occasion these call signs were transmitted from MI5's communications centre, and back came the response from Moscow: 'Receiving you quite clearly'.

Searchers from MI5 and SB have had even more experience since Lonsdale, the Krogers, Ethel Gee and Harry Houghton were caught and there is little chance of their missing a hiding place during a sustained search. Examination of the Krogers' house lasted for several days.

The five spies were tried at the Old Bailey on 18 March 1961. Lonsdale was sentenced to 25 years in prison, the Krogers to 20 years each, and Houghton and Ethel Gee to 15 years each. It is just possible that had Harry Houghton not drawn attention to himself by spending more than he was known to earn, the Portland Spy Ring would have remained uncovered. Spies so often trap themselves.

Bugging a Car

This is a difficult task unless you have the car to yourself for a few hours. Film spies look along the street to see if they are being watched – which is a good way of making sure that you *are* noticed – then reach under the car and attach a magnetised bug. It may work over short distances if the owners of the car do not sweep the vehicle, which they probably will, but placing a bug inside a vehicle is useless without an external aerial – and that would be rather obvious. The best method is to use a transponder which is passive until it is sparked by radio from a distance. Put your transponder within a bumper bar or ask your special effects branch to camouflage it to look like part of the car. Ideally, any bug must be placed by brush contact unless you can create a crush of people around it by staging a minor brawl as a cover. To be sure that your own car is not bugged, buy a bug detector from one of the companies selling sophisticated surveillance equipment.

Improving your security

You are doing things you should not be doing and you want to know if anybody has picked your locks, neutralised your alarms and then entered your house. Take some dust from your vacuum cleaner bag and gently sprinkle it onto places or objects that an intruder might inspect, on the toilet floor perhaps. It is remarkable how frequently spies will use a toilet in a house they are searching and equally remarkable is that often they do not flush the toilet. Something to do with their nervous tension, perhaps. Brush a light coating of dust on the floor in front of the bowl. Never mind about placing a thread or hair across the door or a drawer; any searcher, no matter how inept, will look for that. Put the thread between the toilet lid and the seat and place a line of small cornflakes under the edge of a carpet which an intruder *must* walk on. They will then inaudibly crush. Do nothing that will prompt the searcher to think that you have anything to hide; nothing is more suspicious than this. Good locks on doors and windows are not suspicious: any citizen might take such precautions, but a deadlock on a kitchen cupboard could invite special attention.

Where to Hide Valuable Property When Travelling

Use the hotel's safe deposit box, where objects of any intrinsic value will be safe but do not expect papers, plans or discs to remain unperused. The hotel management itself will not be interested in these things, but in many cities they will open your box for anybody with a police or intelligence pass. Asian, Arab and Russian cities are especially dangerous and there are hotel managers even in European cities who will telephone their national Special Branch to say, for instance 'An interesting gentleman from Prague has just booked in and has deposited a large packet in our safe. We think he matches the photograph you showed us a few months ago.' In those countries where every hotel room has a Gideon Bible you have a good hiding place – not the Bible in the bedroom but the one you carry with you, already hollowed-out. Nobody ever opens a Gideon Bible, least of all the hotel staff. As for the one in the drawer, take it out and lose it. Morality has no place in espionage.

It is best to carry anything important with you or on you. In the hotel restaurant, should you leave your table to go to the salad bar or the toilet, take your briefcase with you or leave it with your partner. Most of the hiding places in a hotel room are known to the staff and the few that are not generally known I do not propose to disclose. The toilet cistern is not one of them – it is one of the first places in which a spy chambermaid will look. To hide any flat object in a hotel room do not put it under your clothing in a drawer, but stick it to the underside of the drawer.

Where to Hide Valuable Property In the Home

The number of places in which to stash secret or valuable property runs into the hundreds. It is easily possible, though a little expensive, to have a hidden room. Ann Frank and her family lived in one such room in Amsterdam for much of the Second World War. The Jews, a persecuted people for centuries, developed *sliks* or hiding places to the point of a fine art, so that they could remain hidden even during what their oppressors would regard as a thorough search. Drawers can be given false bottoms, a table can have a false top and much can be hidden behind a wall pegboard hinged at the top. Doorknobs are hollow and can conceal films. Most telephone handpieces are also hollow with only a single wire running down the centre. Hollow out the space behind a power point and cover it with the normal plastic plate with the slots for an electric plug. A trapdoor in floorboards usually covered by a carpet makes an excellent hiding place, as does a length of false piping which looks like part of the plumbing, heating system or air conditioning system. Adding on a deeper space or a new wall in front of an existing wall is another possibility. Many older homes already have a double wall. The space beneath stairs offers a wide variety of possible stashes, as do window seats, where many families store linen, blankets and cushions. Often these seats open into an unfinished part of the wall which can be made into a secure hide. I once saw a chest of four drawers with 12 hiding places.

Hiding Places on the Body

What follows is an incomplete list of places on the body that have been used by couriers, agents and other people connected with intelligence or resistance operations and by terrorists. If some of them seem to indicate concealment in desperation, then that reflects the actual situation at the time. The objects hidden included films, photographs, money, compasses, poison phials, benzedrine tablets (for extra energy and to prevent sleep), mini cameras, mini radio transmitters/receivers, diamonds, tiny stabbing weapons, maps, documents, valuable postage stamps and gold.

In a hatband
In hairbuns and wigs
Taped behind the ears
In fake hearing aids
In ear-rings
In hats and caps
In the lining of clothing
In plaster casts on a 'broken limb'
In false buttons (ideal for a compass)
In the lapel or collar of shirt,
    jacket and coat
In false pockets
In a sock pocket
In the hollow heel of shoe
In a tobacco tin, cigarette pack
    or lighter
In a 35mm film cartridge
In inhalers
In a make-up compact
In hollowed-out crutches, cane
    or walking stick or umbrella.
Inside rings, wristlets, neck lockets,
    charms and bracelets
Behind campaign ribbons and
    uniform insignia
In a spectacles or contact-lens case
Under bandages and bandaids
In corsets and girdles, cuffs and
    waistbelts
Inside the fly flap of trousers
In zippered belts
In a jock strap
In sealed **and addressed** envelopes
Taped under the breast, concealed by
a bra
Inside the back of a watch

In a powder container
In the knot of a tie or cravat
In the cheeks of buttocks or
    the rectum
In the vagina
Under the foreskin of penis
In pubic hair
In false caps or teeth
Under false teeth
Loose in the mouth
Under the armpit
Swallowed with string tied to teeth
    to be recovered later
In the nose
In the ears
In glass eyes
In a false external pacemaker or
    battery pack for a pain-reducer
In a pill box
Behind an ornate ID label worn
    on jacket or dress
Inside sanitary towels
In a condom pack
In a baby's nappy, especially if it is
    on the baby
In love beads or as prayer beads
    (Small pieces of plastic explosive
    can be made to look like prayer
    beads; they are moulded
    together when required)
In urine, blood and faeces specimen
    tubes and bags

If some of these hiding places seem to be revolting, then you have
not been in a desperately dangerous situation. If you could not bring

yourself to use some of them perhaps you should rethink your aspirations to be a secret agent.

Should you prefer to be a security operative looking for spies, you might well have to search a suspect. These are exactly the places you need to check. A thorough personal check of a person strongly suspected of being an enemy agent can take all day.

In the house of Helen and Peter Kroger, members of the Portland spy ring (see page 165), were found a Ronson lighter with a false compartment, a tin of talcum powder also with a false compartment and a whisky flask made in three compartments – only the middle one contained whisky. The Ronson lighter contained signal transmission times and frequencies. The searchers found a long piece of electrical cord attached to the radiogram. They traced this wire to a trapdoor in the kitchen floor under which was a deep cavity containing a radio transmitter.

The great Israeli spy, Wolfgang Lotz (referred to again in this chapter), while operating from Cairo kept his radio transmitter in his bathroom scales. Agents from the *Mukhabarat*, Egypt's MI5, found it there. Other spies have hidden radios in the ceiling, behind walls, in secret drawers, in washing machines and refrigerators, and in many other places. There may be some hiding places that have not yet been discovered but I doubt it: a really thorough search takes a house apart. If a security service knows for certain that a person is a spy they will find their radio transmitter.

The Art of Tailing

Most security services consider that a minimum of 30 people are needed to keep a single individual under surveillance 24 hours a day. Israel's Mossad and Shin Bet have learnt to manage with 10 because they cannot afford to employ so many people on a tailing operation. Unless the object is to frighten a suspect into doing something foolish, it is imperative that the target should not suspect that he is being followed and observed. Professional case officers always suspect that this is the position and they learn to live with it. If they can give their followers the slip, they have had a minor triumph and the watchers take it in good grace for they, too, are professionals. If you, playing a lone hand, must tail somebody without assistance and your target *thinks* but is not sure he/she is being tailed, you must be very cautious. Should the target turn around suddenly and see that you have suddenly turned to look into a shop window, you might as well go home.

173

The only course of action in this situation is to walk straight on with everybody else on the pavement, overtake the target and *tail from the front*. Some operatives are skilled at this tactic. Very few individuals who fear they are being followed take any notice of people in front of them, even when they stop to look in a window. A quick, slight glance will tell you if your man is still behind you. You might even let him overtake you once or twice, to buy a newspaper perhaps. It is necessary, when playing a lone hand, to change your appearance as you walk. If you started off wearing a hat, take it off; it is better to begin by carrying a hat, then you can put it on. Take off your jacket and carry it over your arm, put on a pair of spectacles or a scarf or take off your tie.

If you are the person being tailed or suspect that you are being followed, turn and walk back the way you have come, taking note of the people who are now facing you, though this is difficult in a crowded street. Repeat this manoeuvre periodically or enter a large shop and examine the merchandise. Before long you will begin to notice the same type of person, even if he/she is occasionally changing their appearance. It is fairly easy to throw off a tail in a big, crowded store, but not if you are such an important target that the opposition is using 30 operatives to maintain surveillance.

Being Inconspicuous

Many agents of all nationalities have been uncovered because they did something to draw attention to themselves, not deliberately, but just through carelessness, thoughtlessness or the inability to sustain cover. It is necessary to be totally inconspicuous in appearance and lifestyle: there must be nothing 'odd' about an agent and no sudden changes in activity that cannot be accounted for in some simple way.

Many people have contributed to their own entrapment as agents because they made some weakness conspicuous to the sharp-eyed people looking for recruits: they revealed themselves to be womanisers (or 'manisers') or homosexuals, or to be dependent on alcohol or other drugs or to be spendthrifts. All these types of people, if they hold positions of trust or authority or if they have access to information, are potential agents in the eyes of recruiters.

Being inconspicuous in person means wearing ordinary dress, never anything flamboyant or bizarre – unless, and this could happen, you are trying to create a persona as an eccentric. Ordinary behaviour is also essential, just plain good manners without embellishments. One agent started tongues wagging when he so gallantly kissed the hand of every woman to whom he was introduced. 'Who is this man?' was the question on the lips of everybody in social circles. Inquiries, casual at first, became more serious and he was found to be an agent.

The slippery slope to exposure more often then not comes when an agent, and sometimes his wife as well, begin to live beyond their obvious means. They buy expensive cars and wear expensive suits and dresses, she appears in new and costly jewellery, they take expensive holidays and have the money to gamble. Aldrich and Rosario Ames may have been able to continue their espionage had they not flouted the wealth they received from their Russian friends.

The great Israeli spy, Elie Cohen, made himself conspicuous deliberately in order to bend the gullible Syrians to his will, but in the end he overdid it. In one period of five weeks in 1964 towards the end of his stay in Damascus, he sent 31 radio messages to Tel Aviv. This was making himself too conspicuous. Some of his compatriots believe that he was physically, intellectually and nervously exhausted and that he had developed a fatalistic approach to his work, akin to a death wish.

Wolfgang Lotz, as successful a spy in Cairo as Cohen had been in Damascus, lived such an opulent life that it became a factor in his downfall.

Taking Photographs Without Being Noticed

You may safely assume that all the smart gadgets shown in spy films as containing cameras are fakes. Nevertheless, cameras can be concealed in briefcases, handbags, shopping bags, cigarette lighters, smoking pipes, wristwatches and pocket watches, hats, books and many other everyday articles. But actually taking photographs is much more difficult, even with automatic focusing. The camera must be aimed, and just standing it on a counter and pointing it in the general direction of the target will not do. Among the best cameras for taking illicit photographs are the Rolleiflex and Rolleicord, which are quite large with big square viewfinders. Do not attempt to hide the camera but carry it openly as a tourist would, and that is what you are: a tourist. Your particular camera has an additional, false, viewfinder on one side. You aim this viewfinder and yourself – at your attractive companion or anything else that might be worth a shot, but in fact the real lens is pointing at your real target. He suspects nothing because you are not facing in his direction. Your companion, attractive or otherwise, can help in another technique using a 35mm through-the-lens viewfinder, with automatic focus. He or she stands in front of you and you shoot over their shoulder, under their armpit or through their legs. Do not say 'Now!' and have them dodge sideways for a second as this sudden movement may attract the eye of the target, particularly if he is tense. The best way to carry a 'concealed' camera is to do so openly and dress as a tourist, but always carry a spare roll of used film in case some suspicious and overbearing official demands that the film you are using should be handed over. With a little practice you and your attractive companion will be able to appear to be producing the substitute film from the camera. Then remove yourselves smartly from the scene. If you are using a Minox camera to take photographs of plans in a private office, then you are definitely a spy or a criminal and I can suggest nothing to help you.

13
SO YOU WANT A CAREER IN INTELLIGENCE

Many people think they would like a career in what they call 'intelligence', an aspiration that often follows an experience with a spy novel or film in which the emphasis is on drama. In book and film some of the characters are killed and a few may be tortured, but in the end the decent democratic country wins and the 'evil empire', as President Reagan called the Soviet Union and its satellites, is defeated.

Basically, there are two ways of having a career in 'intelligence', depending on a person's ideological orientation. He or she may wish to become a career officer in one of the security/espionage organisations in their own country. It is, after all, an honourable profession and, for most people involved in it, similar to any other career, with 'prospects', a rank and salary structure, duties involving a certain number of hours' work a week and at the end, retirement and a pension. It is this type of 'intelligence' career that attracts most people.

There are always some people prepared to work against their own country, indeed probably a disconcertingly large number of people. That more do not actually do so has less to do with scruples than with ignorance about how to get onto the payroll of a foreign power. Most of those who do turn traitor are recruited by career officers belonging to the 'other side'. Recruiters work to certain guidelines which are based on the experience of the whole history of espionage. Some of these guidelines occasionally appear in training booklets, but a good recruiter does not need to refer to a manual. As I am writing here about people being recruited to operate against their own country, a dangerous step, it is as well to understand beforehand how the recruiter's mind works. It must be said, as another warning, that recruiters often choose as a target somebody who has had no previous wish to turn traitor. This man or woman is lured, trapped or bribed into a life of treasonable espionage. John 'Vera' Vassall (see pages 44–50) is a classic case.

What follows are the principles which are in the minds of the foreign recruiter, let us say a Russian operating out of the Russian Embassy in London. The SVR (formerly the KGB) in Moscow has told him to engage in 'talent spotting'. Apart from this exploratory work the recruiter must keep in mind how he will handle or control anybody he might recommend as a Soviet spy.

Should *you* be tempted by the wiles of some foreign recruiter, this is what *he* has in mind about you:

- I am not buying this man's information, I am buying the man himself because in this way we can totally control him; [*Throughout this section also read him equally applying to her.*]
- What matters to an agent is not the amount of money I can offer him but its regularity and dependability. I must get this across to him;
- This potential recruit may have some useful information but if he is an adventurer I will not recruit him. He will take unnecessary risks and be more trouble than he is worth;
- I am looking for a person driven by personal motives or one who tells me that he does not 'see any harm' in handing documents to me. I should be so lucky!
- I must be certain that my potential recruit is not wholly motivated by ideology because we could have a fanatic on our hands. We prefer someone who believes in our form of government, but there must be some other factors that will balance the risk of fanaticism;
- Before I recruit a person who is apparently a good prospect as an agent I must ensure that he has no vices which will make him a liability, but only those which we can use to manipulate him. Somebody who drinks to excess is dangerous but a homosexual can be controlled;
[*The recruiter will have been taught not to tell a target at the beginning of*

178

an involvement that his vices are known, unless blackmail has become necessary to gain his co-operation. An SIS officer told me, 'A little homosexuality is a good thing in an agent because it can be used to entrap a diplomat with similar tendencies, but I would not recruit a pathological homosexual or a pervert, as Geoffrey Prime was (see pages 61–65)'. Nevertheless, Prime was good value for the KGB.]

- When a potential agent is a person in authority or has rank and status I will pander to his vanity. If he is an academic I will praise his intellect. Praise and flattery interest such people more than money does. When the matter of money comes up I will never refer to payment, but to 'expenses';
[It is well known that academics will take any amount of money in 'expenses' but they can become quite indignant about preferred 'bribes'.]

- If I am close to hooking my potential recruit and he has financial worries, I will give him a little money to tide him over while he makes up his mind;
[Soviet handlers are always warned not to give an agent so much money that he noticeably changes his lifestyle. Some agents have been caught because their handlers have not followed this rule. Aldrich Ames is a classic example of an agent who spent his way into prison.]

- Should my agent be confident that he can produce something really valuable or bring off an espionage coup, I will not offer him the bonus he will expect;
[The thinking behind this is that it is much better to aim for steady good performance from an agent rather than the occasional coup. Some intelligence services reward agents with little more than praise for a job especially well done. The SIS has always been parsimonious, but the French often give an agent a valuable antique which he can sell at some time. This is safer than financial transactions.]

- Before taking on an agent, I will test him to see if he has the discipline to carry out an instruction he might not like;
[For instance, when Ivan Skripov was testing Kay Marshall (see pages 54–56) in Sydney he instructed her to apply for positions in either the British High Commission in Canberra or the US Embassy. ASIO did not want her to do this so Marshall wrote job applications in rudimentary typing, with poor spelling and grammatical errors. Skripov did not see these applications, but Marshall showed him the letters rejecting her for positions. With the test complete, Skripov let the matter drop.]

- I will not attempt to coerce a person into becoming an agent though once I have him firmly in control I might apply pressure to keep him, perhaps by blackmail, so I must find out what skeletons he has in his cupboards.

[Every espionage organisation would much rather not threaten an agent. The SIS, CIA, KGB/SVR, DGSE – all want their agents to believe that they value them and will not fail them. If an agent shows signs of wanting to quit, his handlers will tell him reproachfully that he is not only letting the team down but himself. This is a common British tactic. It is true that most of the important espionage organisations do not fail their valuable agents, and they are even less likely to fail a staff member trapped while spying. Philby, Burgess and Maclean were regarded as staff and found sanctuary, but not happiness, in Russia after their exposure. Blake was sprung from prison and Lonsdale and others were exchanged. But there is no such thing as loyalty to 'expendables' or 'sacrifices'. If anything can be gained by abandoning them or actively betraying them to the enemy, they will be so given up. Anybody contemplating espionage for a foreign power must above all have this in mind.]

While I have mostly given the thoughts of a Russian recruiter of agents here, the approach of recruiters from other countries is comparable. That of the SIS is a little less imaginative, perhaps, and that of the CIA is a little more rigid, perhaps. But there are so many exceptions in the handling of agents. The CIA recruited an agent in Latin America whose value depended on his being able to move freely among the very wealthy – and this meant he had to have the appearance of being wealthy himself. A confessed and obvious snob, he was addicted, according to his case officer, to a form and level of living for which he did not have the personal resources. The CIA considered him so valuable that they financed his lifestyle to provide him with convincing cover. However much they invested in him, it was worthwhile, for he was a superb agent. His handlers also perceived that he had a strong sense of duty so his reliability was never in question: he was not in the game just for the money and the social life. His cover was never blown and after long service he gave up his sponsored spendthrift life only because of ill-health: he smoked too heavily and so contracted lung cancer.

Case officers bear many factors in mind when running an agent and even the intelligent and co-operative Latin American occasionally had to be disciplined. The case officer (or controller or handler) must always dominate the agent in one way or another. In this respect the Russians, surprisingly so given their reputation for being heavy' handed, are more subtle than the Americans. The CIA and its off-shoots have often lost good agents – more in the field of political espionage than in straightforward military spying – by threatening to cut off funds and in some cases actually doing so. An agent who goes into debt because his expenses are not being paid is in a precarious situation and might do something so desperate and dangerous that the 'other side' will notice. In any case, he will be resentful and resentfulness can make an agent vicious. Another comparison between American and Russian handling of agents is that the Russians are much more patient; sometimes they wait many years for results. The British, with the experience of centuries behind them, keep up a steady pressure without being either impatient or overly patient.

Other than the agent, the case officer probably comes under more strain than anybody else. The agent is exposed and visible and operates outside the safety of the organisation for which he works. The case officer is invisible and directs his agent from inside, but he is constantly anxious about his agents. The relationship between the two is the very basis of secret operations.

Christopher Felix, who worked for US Intelligence in Europe in the mid–1940s, likened secret operations to an octopus in an attempt to describe an intelligence organisation's activities. Nobody has better described 'the octopus':

> The tentacles are made up of the chain of human relationships linking the direction of the operations to even the most remote agent. The muscles guiding each tentacle are, in turn, made up of the responsiveness, the discipline, which characterize each of the relationships in the chain. Of all these relationships – which include auxiliary services, such as logistics, communications and administration – there is one which is at the very heart of secret operations. It is the critical relationship, dictating in many cases the success or failure of the operation, between the agent and the case officer.*

A lifetime career in 'intelligence' is quite different from being an espionage agent or spy for a foreign power. Basically, it is approached

* Felix, Christopher *The Spy and His Master*, Secker & Warburg, 1963.

as any other profession might be, in accountancy, banking, medicine, architecture, the civil service or the armed forces. And yet there are differences between all other professions and intelligence. For instance, no other profession demands that a husband keep secrets from his wife – or vice versa – or that a father pretends to his children that he works at, say, 'the Treasury' when, in fact, he is an intelligence officer. All the same, many wives know what their menfolk are doing but forbear to ask them questions about it. Sometimes wives are expected to volunteer for what the security services call 'crowd scenes', perhaps to conceal the placement of a bug in a public place or simply to stand and watch a street corner during a tailing operation that requires a large number of people. I have already hinted at another major difference between the other professions and intelligence: that everybody's involvement in it is covered up by some fabrication.

The USA is more open about a career in intelligence than any other nation, so open that the CIA periodically advertises its need for intelligence officers, a practice which the Russians, Chinese and others consider amazing. MI5 and SIS deplore it. Australian Intelligence finds it bizarre. Each advertisement by the CIA is attractive, offering 'foreign travel, interesting work and the opportunity to develop interests and broaden horizons'. Applications pour in and all are acknowledged though only a few prospective spooks will be called in for interview. For a start, they would need to be graduates of a 'good' university, or be expecting a degree. A language or at least an aptitude for languages is a help.

Even if not replying to an advertisement, an American citizen could write to the CIA seeking employment. All such approaches are considered, though some only cursorily so. Any trained and experienced personnel officer can tell at a glance if a written approach is worth pursuing. If a quick reading is not revealing enough a few inquiries show whether the offer is genuine. An amazing number of journalists and other writers have sought to become CIA or MI5 staff members simply in order to write a book about it later. Only a few succeed.

Personnel staff are worldly-wise people with the experience to sum up a contact instantly. After ten minutes and a few drinks they know even more about their prospect and within an hour they will have leads to work on to uncover what the would-be agent considers deep secrets. It is virtually impossible for a person who is being seriously considered as an agent to keep anything secret.

The SIS and CIA espionage and 'research' departments go to immense trouble to find out about the background of a person who might agree to be an agent, so it is all the more surprising that despite all such precautions misfits do get into the organisations as career staff and cause great problems.

*   *   *

Ambition is necessarily a strong motive for entering a career in intelligence and secret operations. Its drawback is that of all bureaucracies: the desire for advancement clouds judgment, impairs initiative and prevents an officer from risking controversy in favour of conformity and consensus. In short, he takes the line of least resistance for the sake of not damaging his career.

Conformity for the sake of ambition was all too vividly – and tragically – shown in the Aldrich Ames case. It came to light in an assessment made by the CIA, which found that officers had knowingly passed tainted information to the highest levels of the US Government in the late 1980s and into the 1990s that had actually come from agents under the control of the KGB and its successor organisation, the SVR.

CIA Director John Deutsch made the findings of the assessment public, in a remarkable acknowledgement of accountability. Richard Haver, Executive Director of Intelligence Community Affairs, spent a year examining the fall-out from the Ames case. Then, to give the government and the public the confidence to believe that there had been no cover-up, the Inspector-General of the CIA, Frederick Mitz, made a follow-up investigation.

Following all this research, the CIA admitted that information from agents it believed were working for the USA was actually planted on those agents by the KGB and then the SVR. Ames betrayed the agents who were then forced to pass the disinformation back to the US.

The extent of the possible damage was shown by the steps then taken by Deputy Defence Secretary John White who ordered an inquiry, covering the entire Pentagon, to determine the importance the military placed on the tainted threat information in developing new weapons systems, such as the F-22 and ballistic missile defences.

Deutsch said, 'By revealing to the Soviet Union identities of assets [the agents] and American methods of espionage, Ames put the Soviet

Union in the position to pass carefully selected "feed" material to the US through controlled assets [agents]. 'Deutsch, who had taken up the position of Director early in 1995, called the CIA activity, 'an inexcusable lapse in elementary intelligence practice. Nobody could be more indignant than I am.'

He was indignant because certain CIA officers, to avoid controversy and protect their positions, had not reported their strong suspicions that the reports being received were tainted by disinformation. To make the situation worse, this tainted information was passed on in 'blue border reports', the highest level of classification for extremely sensitive information from humint. In December 1996 Deutsch instituted a new 'customer review process'. This means that for the first time policy-makers using the 'blue border reports' will know the source of the information they are receiving.

An 'old boy network' exists as much in American Intelligence as it does in the British service. Various directors have tried to reduce its influence but it appears to be ineradicable. The public might sneer at the snobbishness of the 'old boy' system and it certainly has its dangers. An enemy agent already in the organisation might recommend another accomplice for an appointment and he or she might then more easily pass through the vetting process. Nevertheless, a recommendation from somebody already in 'the firm' and well respected is a strong reason for employing that person.

The idea of friends introducing friends is a tacit security device if only because it helps to create the 'intelligence community', in which accessibility and trust are so important. Some staff are recruited on the recommendation of senior professors who knew them at university and can vouch for their strengths and are not generally inclined to conceal weaknesses. One such recommendation which reached SIS personnel while they were vetting a likely prospect listed many qualities, but the professor's final comment scratched the candidate from the 'probables' list. 'William is an incurable romantic', said the professor. No intelligence service wants 'incurable romantics' in its ranks. Experience has shown that such people talk too much, pose too frequently and dramatise outrageously.

*   *   *

Men and women interested in an intelligence career should be warned that the glamour which they have imagined quickly wears off. The seniors *want* it to wear off, which is why young recruits live through a year or so of mundane duties. They are definitely on probation during this period and some are politely told that they do not, after all, have a career in intelligence, perhaps because assessors may have discerned that a certain probationer's commitment is less than total.

Others lack that indefineable something that makes a good intelligence operative, marginally inadequate commitment perhaps. Some trainee officers on probation just cannot give up certain 'failings'. An SIS officer told me 'I recommended that a probationer be paid off because he would wear the most amazingly colourful ties and socks. People could not help but look at him twice. We want people of neutral, unremarkable appearance who will not be looked at twice. The probationer was warned to tone down his taste in socks and ties but he could not take the advice and he had to go, even though he was intelligent.'

Once accepted and 'in', the new operative gradually feels that he belongs to an élite club, perhaps even to a special world. Confidentiality of activities has this effect. Also, even more significantly, the new officer will have been tacitly indoctrinated into what is permissible in conduct when mixing with friends or at large in the general public. Every staff member of an intelligence organisation is potentially a target for foreign espionage operatives seeking to recruit agents and thus penetrate that organisation. The caution required by a staff member when meeting strangers also has a profound effect in creating an 'us-and-them' outlook among intelligence staff. It is better, security chiefs believe, for their staffs to be over-sensitive to dangers than to be dismissive of them, which is why part of the indoctrination is to make them feel that they stand heroically between their nation and the forces of evil.

The forces of evil were exemplified by the Soviet Union and the Warsaw Pact countries of Eastern Europe. In the democratic West governments, the press and the populace had for years been in stand-by mode, ready to repel the Red Menace, but with the Gorbachev reforms a virtual stand-down was declared. However, the Western security organisations and espionage organisations have not noticeably dropped their guard – nor should they do so. Powerful and malevolent forces remain at work, such as extremist Islam, economically ambitious China, territorially ambitious Indonesia and Japan, as well as international terrorism. In any case, Russian communism remains a powerful threat because many people of the old Soviet Union have found that democracy does not give them what they expected. The Russian military leaders are still suffering from damaged pride: they believe that Gorbachev and his successor Boris Yeltsin abjectly surrendered to the West. Western intelligence organisations are well aware of the many dangers and they are still recruiting staff.

People who seriously contemplate a career in intelligence should be aware that they will be put to more inconvenience and work longer hours than other government employees. Also, they will spend more off-duty time thinking about their professional interests than anybody other than stock exchange brokers. Every so often they are sent on courses either to refresh and update what they know or to learn something new. For instance, it is necessary to keep abreast of the changes in the politics of the volatile Arab world. The security organisations themselves run courses. The CIA Training Division is a huge enterprise with more than 400 courses which can be assembled in hundreds of patterns and adapted for a wide variety of trainees. These students play complex games of strategy and tactics in the military, political, economic, communications and scientific fields. Perhaps the most important courses are those which are intended to teach counter-espionage agents to trap spies in their midst.

Career officers are just as likely to attend courses conducted by business, commercial and industrial groupings, or by foreign think-tanks, institutes, universities or government departments. The intelligence officer sent to such a gathering will not wear an identity label proclaiming JOHN SMITH, MI5 but will use a cover name and company affiliation. During a lecture I gave in London on 'Islam's Many Faces' I saw in my audience – every member of which was required to wear identification – in the front row a woman from 'Standby Index Systems'. I could not help wondering about her professional background, especially when I found no such company in telephone directories. An SIS operative with a sense of humour?

Some career officers will rise through the ranks to become heads of 'desks' – a much-used term even when the 'desk' consists of a suite of offices – of sections and of divisions. They will then find out what it is like to be members of a brotherhood so tight that in comparison it

makes Freemasonry seem open to all comers. By the time officers
reach this elevated status they probably enjoy the clannishness but
some have had to surrender a natural spirit of independence. Like the
Freemasons, this group of seniors is an in-group and they create and
perpetuate a mystique. I once heard of a CIA top-level meeting which
about 20 men and women attended at their HQ at Langley, Virginia. It
was a breakfast get-together called to discuss some matter of critical
importance. They ate a hearty and cheerful breakfast and gossiped
about respective family matters. Finally, without a word being spoken
about the stated professional topic that necessitated the meeting, the
chairman said loudly, 'Well, that's settled then, OK?' and they all
nodded and trooped out with their briefcases.

I cannot guarantee the authenticity of this story but it *sounds* possible, though I would have regarded it as even more plausible if it
related to NATO.

It should go without saying that a career intelligence officer needs
certain qualities, such as patriotism and honesty. If you think that by
becoming a member of CIA, MI5, SIS or NSA you will supplement your
income by padded expense accounts, forget it. The moral imperative
for honest dealing is great. This touches on an equally great irony –
that the whole business of intelligence, even when it is defensive –
that is, in defence of the State – rather than offensive, has much to do
with deceit, cheating, lying, stealing and fraud. Many a career officer
manages to hide all this from himself by saying that deceiving 'the
enemy', cheating them, lying to them and stealing from them carries
none of the stigma that these activities would bear in ordinary life.
Everything is morally justifiable when done in the never-ending fight
against the nation's enemies, whether they are internal subversives or
foreign espionage agents.

Nevertheless, any objective analysis of intelligence must point to
the blunt truth that in order to make the nation secure the standard
moralities are often breached. Would-be intelligence operatives who
cannot square this with their conscience should not apply.

*   *   *

The espionage branch of an intelligence service is the most interesting, but much of the work imposed on an officer after his
probationary period is routine. As an assistant on the Pakistan Desk of

187

MI6 he is the back-up for his colleagues in the field. They might need straightforward non-secret information that is unavailable in Islamabad, or they are passing a warning that a known Islamic *agent provocateur* is on his way to Britain. They want authority to buy some piece of electronic equipment or a high-powered camera. In carrying out these servicing duties, the desk officer acquires a vicarious feel of what life is like in the field, where he will himself arrive within a few years; the period depends on how much he impresses his superiors.

In due course he becomes an assistant case officer abroad, usually in a succession of places. In each instance he generally has advance notice of a posting so that he and his wife – though some case officers are single women – have the time to study the nominated country and to read official literature on diplomatic behaviour and the pitfalls to be avoided. Islamic countries are notoriously difficult postings because Muslims so easily take offence when no insult is intended. A young case officer in Morocco was reprimanded by his superiors for sitting with his legs crossed and the sole of his foot pointing towards a local dignitary. In doing this he was showing the Muslim that he had scant regard for him – at least, this was the way that the Muslim interpreted the sole of a 'dirty' shoe. Before leaving for a posting the case officer and his wife may be required to learn the local language and body language. A case officer cannot meet an agent who speaks only German and take along an interpreter so that the two can converse!

Until he goes 'into the field' – the hunting and military analogies are appropriate – the new espionage specialist has been safe, almost cosseted. Once on the staff of an embassy in Islamabad or Beijing or Tunis, or wherever, he comes under the God-like authority of the ambassador but under the actual authority of the chief of station, with whom he must get on despite the tensions that apparently always arise. He becomes aware only gradually that he is 'different' from the standard embassy employees – but they know it from the beginning. The station intelligence chief is a powerful figure within even the largest embassies because he will have been there longer than the ambassador – as a result of policy from on high – and he knows more.

Some station chiefs are unscrupulous and selfish in providing themselves with cover-plus – the plus means 'special insurance'. The cover itself might be that the station chief is second secretary but the 'special insurance' is that he leaks the information to the diplomatic community that the SIS or CIA station chief is actually the information officer. In the CIA this unpopular practice is known as 'tying the can' (from tying a can to the tail of a cat) and once the host government and its intelligence service hear the can rattling, the stigma is fixed for the first secretary or information officer. In times of tension between the two countries the station chief is high on the list of people liable to expulsion so the poor unfortunate who is carrying 'the can' is the one who has to leave. He can hardly say, 'Wait a minute, I'm not the station chief, that's my colleague John Smith.'*

While the espionage staff at an embassy protect one another, even when they nurse private grievances and even hatreds, they are not so exemplary in their relationships with other staff.

Given the amount of knowledge that a career officer must learn and the expertise that he must develop, he has to be taken on to the staff at a relatively young age. In the CIA the average age for officer enrolment is 25, in the British service it is a little less. Length of the professional career is likely to be 30 years, but there are people who 'can't stand it any longer' and those who 'can't give it up'. It is possible for them to go on a few years but sooner or later everybody learns that absolutely nobody is irreplaceable. Some men and women become bitter and resentful when their services are dispensed with. A few break all the rules and traditions – as well as the Official Secrets Act which every staff member must sign – and write their memoirs. The information that they disclose can be very damaging to agents in place. Peter Wright, author of *Spycatcher*, was one such disaffected retired career officer. The book would never have been published had the British Prime Minister, Margaret Thatcher, taken proper notice of a confidential report which Wright had sent her. In his later book *The Spycatcher's Encyclopedia of Espionage*.** Wright wrote, 'People in MI5

---

* It is interesting when visiting an embassy – any nation's embassy – to try to spot the station chief. It is also frustrating because nobody will tell a visitor if his speculation is correct. Some station chiefs are not to be found in the embassy, but at the consulate or even in the national tourist office. On occasions I have been correct in my assumption that a certain person was the station chief but only because of outside confirmation; at other times I have been wildly wrong. During the Cold War it was possible to know where the greater number of Soviet spooks were stationed in any city – they manned the government Intourist office. Every person employed there was a spy whether dealing with tourists or not.

** Published by William Heinemann, Australia, 1991.

were using the cloak of secrecy to conceal their own illegal, and in some cases, treacherous activities.'

This was one of the essential messages that he was trying to get across to the British Government and people but, as he said, 'the government's "answer" was to try to stop me talking about it'.

Wright was not prepared to conform and simply to go along uncritically with what was happening in MI5. He risked his health, reputation, peace of mind and perhaps his life in order to see reforms brought to the service he loved.

On the whole a career in intelligence is satisfying for those who are prepared to spend 30 years in the trade without public recognition of their services. In Britain the OBE or MBE is bestowed on long-serving members, generally in recognition of 'services to the community'. The CBE goes to more senior people and those who reach the top are almost invariably knighted. The rank and file feel that it is on *their* efforts that directors are knighted.

Good advice to those people entering the intelligence service who hope eventually for a gong is to specialise and make themselves the ultimate authority in some field. Such knowledge can also make a specialist more influential within his organisation.

*   *   *

It is difficult for a retired career officer, or one who has left his organisation or who has been 'dealt out' of the game – as I have heard severance described – to continue the friendships he made during his time with the intelligence service. He/she is no longer one of the club, has no further access to 'secrets' and in many cases they are totally shunned. This is not from any hostility, but because the still-serving fear that the having-served may want to talk about operational matters.

A final mild warning to those eager for an intelligence career: the strains and tensions in certain areas of work are sometimes so intense and prolonged that officers need professional counselling.

Some former intelligence officers find opportunities for espionage even in retirement, when in special circumstances they are asked to go abroad to do the job of an agent, that is, to spy. This usually comes about when no local agent is available or when an organisation needs to check that a local agent is properly doing his job. The case officer cannot safely enter certain areas to carry out a check so 'Old Jim' is asked to do it as an assignment. Western European organisations are in an excellent position to find a suitable person because many of their former members retire to warmer climates, such as Spain, North Africa, southern Italy, Greece, Portugal and other places.

The demands made on an 'Old Jim' can be great. For the sake of discretion I will avoid current examples and go back to Algiers during the Second World War when SIS needed a reliable Englishman in place rather than an Arab or French agent who might profess allegiance to General de Gaulle but in reality be a Vichy spy. As a British expatriate community existed in Algiers, Jim needed a cover that would turn his compatriots against him while making him acceptable to Germans, Italians and others in Algiers, which was a nest of spies. Jim's cover was that of a dissolute, amoral spendthrift but it was not enough for him merely to give this appearance – he had to live his cover. This meant womanising and drinking – which must have been distasteful to a lifelong teetotaller. He was also untidily dressed, loud and rude and his compatriots shunned him. With no known British contacts, he was easily able to mix with foreigners of every class. His cover was so good that after the war several Englishmen denounced him as a German and Italian collaborator. Even then, Jim did not break cover, he just disappeared. His information from Algiers had been invaluable and greatly helped the British-American invasion of North Africa in December 1943.

A surprisingly large number of intelligence retirees are called back for a job which requires a special skill, such as being able to speak Serbo-Croat. Not that such a person would necessarily be required to speak it; MI5 might merely want him to listen to a bugged conversation taking place between Serbo-Croats and report on it and help to analyse its implications. It would certainly be more interesting than spending a day in the garden.

*   *   *

In 1996 the CIA began a recruiting campaign for staff on the Internet, an inevitable development considering the Agency's leaning towards innovation. The approach was challenging and in places couched in language that could have come from advertising specialists in Madison Avenue. For instance:

More than a job, a unique career, a way of life that will challenge the deepest resource of your intelligence, self-reliance and responsibility. You will need to deal with fast-moving, ambiguous and unstructured situations that will test your resourcefulness to the utmost. This is the Clandestine service, the vital human element in intelligence collection.

People interested in such a career were informed on the Internet that they must be US citizens no older than 35, with 'an adventurous spirit, a forceful personality, superior intellectual ability, toughness of mind and a high degree of integrity'.

While these were the essential qualities, 'desirable pluses' included a graduate degree, foreign travel, foreign language proficiency, previous residence abroad and military experience. In order to minimise the number of applications from the 'wrong type' of people, the Internet advertisement warned that every candidate would be required to submit to a thorough medical and psychiatric examination, a polygraph ('lie detector') interview and an extensive background investigation – that is, positive vetting.

Significantly, the CIA disclosed that it was particularly interested in candidates with backgrounds in central Eurasian, East Asian and Middle Eastern languages. With surprising frankness, the Agency declared an interest in people with degrees and experience in international economics and business as well as those with 'special knowledge' of nuclear, biological and chemical warfare. It was made clear that the CIA would not be operating in these areas but that its staff would be countering the activities of other nations involved in such types of warfare. No country was mentioned by name but Iran, Iraq, Pakistan, Libya, North Korea and China are obviously targets.

The advertisement described the CIA as 'the cutting edge of American Intelligence, an elite corps gathering the vital information needed by our policymakers to make critical foreign policy decisions'. Finally, the CIA Career Training Program urged men and women of every racial background and from all parts of the nation to come forward if they felt they measured up to the high standard required: 'We represent America and we want our staff to be representative of America. Come and join us.'

The Agency undertook to respond within 30 days to those people 'we judge could be of further interest'. Starting salaries ranged from $30,671 to $47,025. Aware that these are not high salaries compared with those in commerce and industry, the CIA ended its Internet advertisement with the note that 'there are benefits which cannot be assessed in dollars'.

We will never know how many Americans respond to the Internet advertisement, but it may safely be assumed that the foreign intelligence agencies would examine the advertisement much more closely than any potential CIA staff member.

While the Internet advertisement was genuine, the arch schemers within the Agency had a hidden motive. They hoped that a close scrutiny of applicants would reveal foreign intelligence organisations, operating directly or through American agents, trying to get a toehold in the CIA.

14

PEOPLE WHO SHOULD NOT BE DOING INTELLIGENCE WORK

Claustrophobics and agoraphobics You may have to sit in a confined space such as a cupboard or stationary car for hours while observing somebody or something. Also, should you be caught and interrogated in suspicious circumstances you will certainly be in a small room, generally one without a window. The door will be closed or locked and sometimes the room will have no light. You need a special type of nerve to stand this strain without breaking. In return for being moved to a large cell, many suspects promise to reveal all – and they do. Agoraphobics have a strain of another kind: they cannot stand being in open spaces, but this may be necessary for some spies in some situations. A French spy who was assigned to some espionage task in the great open space of Red Square, Moscow lasted barely a day. He contacted his controller in panic and asked to be relieved. His organisation found him a desk job.

People with excessive self-confidence Confident people can make good spies but those with excessive self-confidence are a menace to themselves and others. They take risks and often act on impulse without waiting for instructions from their controller. Mossad records contain the story of a young married couple, Thomas and Kathy, operating in Cairo. They received an instruction from Tel Aviv about preparing for an operation and it involved recruiting some Egyptian army officer whom they might be able to add to their flourishing net- work. Choosing such a recruit involves patience and lengthy observation, so the instruction from Tel Aviv ended, 'Wait for further instructions.' Thomas and Kathy, enthusiastically self-confident, certain of their judgment, approached a young Coptic Christian officer, Adiv Karolos, in the belief that all Copts – a persecuted minority in Egypt – would be ready to spy against the Muslim rulers. Karolos went straight to his security service, which played Thomas and Kathy for a time to see what they could milk from them. Becoming suspicious, Thomas got Kathy out of Egypt but he, with others of his ring, was arrested. Thomas and two of his agents were hanged in December 1962.

People who can't stand the heat in the kitchen The pressure is on for results in the intelligence spy trade and this applies to the organisa- tions of every nation. Very often the pressure comes from political leaders who need to know, for instance, all possible details of an adver- sary. When Saddam Hussein of Iraq demonstrated that he was a bellicose man, two Israeli intelligence agencies, Mossad and Aman (the military intelligence organisation) worked together to build up a thorough personality profile of the dictator. Much of their informa- tion came from Saddam's daily appearances on television which Mossad-Amen teams closely studied in terms of their target's language, words, and body and facial language. They asked a graphologist to analyse his handwriting, a specimen of which was obtained with some difficulty. The report, copies of which were sent to the CIA and DIA, noted that Saddam was so scared of being poisoned that he used an official food taster to try all his meals – and then he waited an hour for any ill effects to show. 'One of the world's most suspicious people', Saddam changed his bodyguard members frequently and never slept two consecutive nights in the same room. Building up this profile at a time of tension was very hard work and a few of the people who worked on it reported ill with strain.

The chiefs of each espionage organisation demand results, with con- sequent pressure on station chiefs, case officers and recruiters. Following a high-level conference, whether it be in Moscow, Paris, Langley or London, the request goes out for agents to be found in cer- tain target departments abroad. Again a spy scare at home leads to immediate and intense pressure to get to the bottom of the case, to analyse its ramifications and to re-examine security. At such times few staff get any rest.

When an espionage service selects a staff member of a foreign embassy as a target the pressure on that person can become intolerable. This was so for Eliyahu Hazan, a second secretary in the Israeli Embassy in Moscow, who was selected as a target by the KGB. The Russians were ruthless. First, the maid who worked in the Hazans' apartment poisoned Mrs Hazan so that she suffered severe gastric trouble and was rushed to hospital just after Hazan went off to meet a Jewish contact. On his return, Hazan was stopped by KGB agents who, despite the Israeli's diplomatic immunity, took him to a secret police post and interrogated him for hours. During the next week the KGB relentlessly applied pressure to Hazan to work for them. One tactic was to tell him that the maid in his house was pregnant by him. This was not so but the Russians said that the 'scandal' would be made public if Hazan did not sign a statement that he was a volunteer spy for the Soviet Union.

Hazan's breaking point came when one KGB man said, 'If you do not co-operate your wife will not recover from her stomach troubles.' Hazan gave way and agreed to be a Soviet agent. For three days the Russian handlers briefed him, gave him a substantial sum of money for 'expenses' and relaxed their pressure. Ruth recovered but Eliyahu was suffering the torments of the damned. He was so distressed that the ambassador called him in for a friendly talk and Hazan blurted out a confession. He had not done any spying against Israel, but the embassy had him on the first flight to Tel Aviv, escorted by another diplomat. Back home he was instantly dismissed. While no disciplinary action was taken against Hazan he was disgraced and disgrace in Israel can last a lifetime. The lesson of the Hazan case is that if you do not feel strong enough to stand up to extreme pressure you may not have what is required for foreign service.

People who have skeletons in the cupboard It is not advisable to have any role in intelligence, from office staff to covert spy, if you have any secrets that might later embarrass you. You may get through the positive vetting procedure used by MI5 or SIS, CIA or NSA, the Foreign Office, the State Department or any other sensitive department. You may pass the polygraph test without difficulty; lots of spies have fooled the 'lie detector'. If your background is British public school and Oxbridge, your father holds the GCMG and your mother was a former cipher clerk you will probably sail into MI5, even if you are an alcoholic homosexual kleptomaniac.

But you will not keep your secrets hidden away from the 'other side'. Intelligence services have entire departments for ferreting out personal details of the past and present life of potential targets – and potential targets run to millions. Jeremy Wolfenden was not even in government service but a London *Daily Telegraph* reporter in Moscow when the KGB ensnared him in 1962, at the age of 28. They knew he was a homosexual and that he had been in British naval intelligence during his national service days. That rare being, a journalistic innocent, Wolfenden was with a Russian in a hotel bedroom when KGB agents photographed him 'in the act'. They blackmailed him to spy on Western diplomats in Moscow. Bravely, he reported the episode to the British Embassy, whose intelligence officer passed the information to SIS. On his return to London, SIS approached him and urged him to co-operate with the KGB but to keep SIS informed. The British blackmail was less brutal and more discreet, but the pressure was obvious and the hapless Wolfenden, back in Moscow, found himself crushed between the two opposing services. He married an English girl but even with her support he was unable to stand the strain. He drank to excess and eventually became an alcoholic, he picked at his food, his marriage broke down – probably with the help of SIS, which could more readily control a homosexual than a married man – and in the end he collapsed at his Moscow home, smashed his head on the bathroom basin and died. No adequate coronial inquest system existed in Russia and without an impartial, professional investigation and postmortem, some students of espionage will always suspect that an 'accident' was arranged in order to get rid of an embarrassment. There have been many such 'heart attacks'.

People with big mouths Many well planned espionage operations have been endangered or blown because a spy could not keep his mouth shut. Similarly, intelligence organisations themselves have employed boasters or 'big-noters', thus risking the organisation's security. All intelligence chiefs know that one of the greatest of human failings is the desire to appear to be important, to be 'in the know'. The true professional does not boast. He knows that he and his organisation are secure only for as long as nobody knows his basic secret,

hat he is a member of the particular agency. If only one person knows
t, security ends there or it is at least compromised. Staff intelligence
officers know that they must not tell a neighbour what they do for a
iving because he will feel the urge to pass on this interesting informa-
:ion. 'You won't believe this, Jim', he will say on the golf course, 'but
:he guy who lives next to me is with MI6.'

During vetting or screening, recruiters in the field and supervisors at
headquarters are taught to watch for signs of boastfulness in a poten-
:ial spy and equally so in somebody who will be trusted with vital
secrets. Yet recruiters make gross mistakes. The American Naval Intelligence Service (NIS) made one when it took on 25-year-old Jonathan
ray Pollard in 1979 and gave him access to a vast array of secrets. Even
:he most superficial vetting procedure would have shown that while
at Stanford University Pollard, an American Jew, claimed to have been
a colonel in the Israeli Army and that Mossad was grooming him for
espionage 'deep in the American government'. Both statements were
pure fiction, but they would have indicated that Pollard was an unsta-
ple fantasist. There was much else in his life to show that he was
erratic and 'strange'. In fact, he was a Zionist zealot and desperately
anxious to work for Israel.

A Mossad chief, with no more caution than the US Navy Intelligence personnel officer who hired Pollard, accepted his offer to spy for
Israel. His six years in NIS between 1978–84 had taken him deep into
America's secrets. The Navy even issued him with a so-called courier
card, which gave him the authority to withdraw and retain for long
periods classified documents from the archives of the NIS, the DIA and
the NSA: Pollard, just 30 years of age when Mossad took him on in
1984, had the broad authority of senior officers. For nearly a year he
produced enormous quantities of high-grade information for the
Israelis. He was caught partly because he was working so hard for Israel
that even though he had the help of his devoted wife Anne, he was
exhausted and became careless. Anne was even more so: in their apartment they had a stack of American classified documents and when
Jonathan was picked up for questioning she put the papers in a suitcase – with Pollard's name on it! – and asked a neighbour to mind it as
a favour. The neighbour happened to be the daughter of a US Navy
officer – which Anne Pollard must have known – and she reported the
matter to the appropriate authority, the Naval Investigative Service.

At Pollard's trial it was stated that he had given or sold to Israel so many documents that they made a solid pile 10 feet by 6 feet by 6 feet. The Defence Secretary, Casper Weinberger, wrote to the Judge, 'I cannot conceive of a greater harm to national security than that caused by the defendant.' He urged that Pollard be shot or hanged and further stated that even a billion dollars would not repair the damage he had done.

Pollard would have seen this as a compliment for he was still boasting in court: 'I have been Israel's eyes and ears over an immense geographic area stretching from the Atlantic to the Indian Ocean... the nation's political leaders must have known that an Israeli agent [himself] existed in the American Intelligence establishment ... There was a highly co-ordinated effort between the Israeli Navy, Army and Air Force intelligence services.'

On 4 March 1987 Pollard was given a life sentence. This shocked him because he had pleaded guilty in the American system of 'plea-bargaining'. This was supposed to prevent a life sentence being passed but the ploy did not work. His wife, Anne, was sentenced to five years for 'handling classified documents'.

Following what is presumed to have been a deal between the US and Israel, Pollard was released in 1995 and went to live in Israel. According to reliable information, he is not working in intelligence.

Jonathan Pollard wrecked the long-standing trust between the US and Israel and, even more damaging, between Israeli and American Jewry. The American Jewish community believed that Mossad should never have targeted the USA. In any case, the relationship between the two countries was so close that the USA was giving Israel all the intelligence that it needed.

Nobody has satisfactorily explained (a) how Pollard was allowed to work for US Navy Intelligence and (b) why Mossad, believed by many to be the world's most efficient intelligence service, believed that he would make a safe and reliable spy. In their frantic desire to exculpate themselves, the Americans blamed Israel and Mossad for the Pollard débâcle but the original sin lay with their own Naval Intelligence Service in giving this oddball free run of the nation's defence secrets.

Pollard was not the first boaster in the spying game and he certainly will not be the last. And there will be more recruiters who fail to discern in a potential spy the weakness which Fräulein Doktor

Schragmuller, the German spymaster, had identified during the First World War as a compulsive weakness – that of wanting to impress people. She would have had Jonathan Pollard sent to the furthest reaches of the German empire where he could do no harm. And with him would have gone the Israeli and American senior staff who had not seen through him.

15
IS SPYING
OLD–FASHIONED?

Is it all really necessary? Is the vast octopus of espionage, spying and intelligence, whose tentacles stretch across the globe, worth the trillions of pounds spent on its maintenance and further development? Directly or through affiliated countries, every nation spies on every other nation. Every one of them is hungry for 'secrets' – that is information that can have some bearing on attack or defence, on political pressure or bluff, on economic, industrial and technological advancement and therefore corporate and national wealth.

Millions of people are directly involved in the spy trade, millions more indirectly. Intelligence in its many manifestations employs people who might otherwise be out of a job. Many men and women formerly employed by East Germany's espionage organisation, the Stasi, have not found gainful employment since the end of the Cold War brought greater freedoms to Eastern Europe. It ended the East German dictatorship – and threw the Stasi people out of work.

While fear is the spur for espionage, hatred is the whip. There was much hatred between the two superpowers, especially during certain administrations – Stalin, Krushchev, Nixon and Reagan, for instance. Trust was non-existent and hatred flourished. Similarly, certain Islamic countries hate the 'infidel' West and spy on its governments in the hope of bringing about their destruction, later if not sooner.

Hatred of one national neighbour by another – the reciprocal hatred between India and Pakistan for instance – keeps the intelligence services flourishing. The number of spies employed by militarily weak countries is out of all proportion to the size of their populations because they have more to lose – their freedom. Taiwan, under threat from China, is a good example. Other countries, such as Israel are entirely intelligence-oriented. Without a highly efficient intelligence system, Israel perishes.

Internal terrorism costs some countries vast amounts of money in counter-intelligence and counter-espionage activities. The terrorism of the Irish Republican Army (IRA) and its offshoots has led to thousands of deaths in Britain and Northern Ireland and cost the government more than £100,000,000 in the period 1972–96. The security services' intelligence on Irish extremism, in relation to both the Roman Catholic and Protestant communities, improved steadily but it was not good enough to foresee the mammoth IRA bomb which wrecked a great building at Canary Wharf in London, and brought a 17-month ceasefire to a shocking end.

In Israel, Shin Bet's intelligence was not thorough enough in December 1995 to protect the Prime Minister, Yitzhak Rabin, from assassination by an Israeli extremist who 'executed' Rabin for having made peace with the PLO.

Given the fear that still grips much of the world, the high level of terrorist violence, the expansionist aspirations of fundamentalist Islam and the megalomaniacal dreams of maverick rulers such as Muammar Gaddafi and Saddam Hussein espionage is necessary.

Nevertheless, to some extent it has become an end in itself, if only because spymasters are bureaucrats and therefore 'empire' builders. Also, there is so much competition between intelligence agencies that should be collaborating that the chiefs of agencies take on more staff to deal with the competition, which they see as a threat. In Britain, the MI5 chief, Stella Rimington, won a major battle against Special Branch to win prime responsibility for intelligence-gathering against the IRA. MI5 and the SB have often been in dispute over their respective areas of activity though they generally pull together when they sense poaching on their territory by other agencies. The Americans' NSA and DIA have both been known to 'fish' in Ireland's murky waters.

Because of the new openness in national and international affairs, the forces opposed to peace can learn much about the security services. For instance, on 25 November 1995 the British press published profiles of the new chiefs of MI5 and GCHQ, together with portrait photographs. The briefings came from the Prime Minister's office, so the press was not publishing secret information. The world was informed that Stephen Lander, the former head of MI5's counter-terrorism branch, was to succeed Stella Rimington as Director-General of MI5 when she retired at Easter 1996. During his early career with MI5 he worked in most of the five intelligence branches, including counter-espionage and counter-subversion. He was also in the department covering personnel, training and security and was head of the registry of files. After September 1994 he was appointed MI5's Director of Corporate Affairs, responsible for information technology and strategic planning. He was also the principal finance officer. As Director-General of M15 he earns about £92,000 a year.

At the same time, it was announced that David Omand, 48, a deputy under–secretary for policy at the Ministry of Defence, would replace Sir John Adye in July 1996 as chief of GCHQ. He would have a budget of £50,000,000.

The new directors' photographs were published and while Mr Omand looked cheerful and happy to be in front of a lens, Mr Lander's expression was one of disbelief and distaste. It was announced in the Queen's Speech – this is actually the government's policy and programme – in November 1995 that MI5 would in future help the police in intelligence-gathering operations to combat organised crime, so Mr Lander's reluctance to have his photograph in every major newspaper in Britain was understandable.

About the same time, President Yeltsin appointed the Kremlin's former spymaster-in-chief, Yevgeny Primakov, to be Foreign Minister. I have mentioned earlier that espionage is a normal and natural part of Soviet/Russian foreign policy. In giving one of the most important positions in the nation to a KGB director who was also a member of the Soviet Union's ruling Politburo, Yeltsin yet again showed his country's dependence on spying. Primakov, aged 66 in 1996, favours closer ties with enemies of the USA, especially Iraq and Iran. His appointment also signalled a more independent Russian posture in the Middle East, where efforts to bring about a comprehensive peace agreement, maintain sanctions against Iraq and curtail the spread of terrorism could be jeopardised by a revival of Kremlin intransigence.

American, British, French and German intelligence organisations were aware that Primakov was one of three or four men who would succeed the tolerant Andrei Kozyrev, so no panic ensued to gather personal information about Primakov. On his appointment many intelligence analysts were soon hard at work studying its ramifications in order to answer politicians' questions, such as 'What adjustments to our policies must we make in the wake of Primakov's appointment?', 'If Yeltsin falls will Primakov fall with him?' and 'Will Primakov want to change the SVR back to the old-style KGB?'

During 1996 the British and Russians had a precise espionage agenda in each other's country. For the Russian Embassy's staff in London, under their ambassador, Anatoli Adamishim, the main spy targets were:

• The state of the British armed forces in quality and morale, units and numbers, standard of training and weapons under development;
• British-American co-operation in defence and intelligence matters. Even an apparently trivial point such as where British and American intelligence held their meetings could be important;
• The strategy of economic affairs. The Russians were delighted when the British Government began a non-co-operation policy against its European allies following their ban in the import of British beef. Agents were at once ordered to exploit this break in European unity in every way possible;
• Changes and developments in British interests and involvements in the Balkans and the Middle East. The Russians are not interested in giving Britain an easy ride in Bosnia or anywhere else in the Balkans;
• Scientific research in all its manifestations. Some of the greatest developments take place in Britain. The Russians are specially inter- ested in research taking place in British universities and are working at penetrating them.

Overall, in 1996 Russian espionage operations in Britain had changed little in style and objectives since the end of the Cold War. But for the British in Russia some of the targets are different, alarming and critical. The relative difference between the intelligence needs of the British and Russians is perhaps shown in the disparity between the number of people on their respective staffs. At the beginning of 1996 the British Embassy in Moscow had an accredited diplomatic staff of

80 while the Russian Embassy in London had 45. During the Cold War the proportion would have been very much the other way round.

The British Moscow Embassy has only a small number of MI6 members since much intelligence is gleaned from open or 'natural' sources, such as what is read in the Russian newspapers, heard on radio, seen on television and noticed in the streets. Some military information reaches the Defence Attaché in the normal course of his work.

In 1996 the Cabinet Office Joint Intelligence Committee, represented by the heads of all the security and defence agencies, set MI6 these targets in Russia:

- Where are the centres of power in today's Russia? Given the volatile complexity of Russian politics this is an enormous task and it requires positive penetration of Kremlin politics and of party machines;
- Obtain an accurate and full diagnosis of President Yeltsin's health. Yeltsin, though apparently sturdy, has had several 'collapses' and 'heart attacks' and is known to drink too much. It is important to be able to predict whether he might die suddenly;
- Discover the real state of Russia's armed forces. Are they as incompetent and ill-led as their defeat by the much weaker Chechen irregulers seems to suggest? What discord is evident among the Generals?
- To what extent are the Russian authorities genuinely trying to prevent sophisticated weapons and, even more importantly, nuclear material from being smuggled out of Russia and sold abroad. Furthermore, what can we – the Western Allies – do to prevent this trade?
- Provide a list of the names of possible high level defectors.

Gennadi Zyuganov, the Communist leader,was by far the greatest worry for Western intelligence agencies in the months leading up to the Russian presidential election of 1996. Everything that has known about Zyuganov was alarming. His hero was Stalin and he supported the Soviets' crushing of Czechoslovakia's democracy movement in 1968. In several books he accuses the USA, the UN the Roman Catholic Church, the International Monetary Fund and 'international Jewry, among others, of fomenting a conspiracy to destroy Russia's historical greatness'. Zyuganov made it clear during his election campaign that he proposed to 'rebuild the Soviet empire and triumph over the corrupt West'. Zyuganov has much support from all ranks in the disaffected Russian armed forces. The CIA and MI6 need to know exactly how much support.

Many Russians do not want a return to communism but believe Zyuganov when he says that he is a national socialist rather than a communist. Western governments know, through their embassies and intelligence agencies, that Zyuganov is an old-type communist in the camouflage of a socialist. Therefore, in the expectation that sooner or later he will be the Russian president, it is necessary for MI6 and other agencies to know everything about the man – his personality, friends, tastes, idiosyncracies, vices and weaknesses.

In April 1996 a political row over alleged spying developed between Britain and Russia. At first the MGB – also known as the FSB standing for Federal Security Service – accused the British of recruiting a middle-ranking Russian official who was purported to have passed secret documents to MI6.

According to an article in the Russian weekly *Argumenty i Fakty,* the British equipped the Russian spy with a miniature shortwave radio on which he broadcast coded messages to a British contact. Security agents who followed the spy filmed his operations. It must be said that all the material published in the magazine came from the MGB, not from independent journalistic investigation. The paper also said, again quoting the MGB, that the incriminating videotape had been shown to the British Ambassador, Sir Andrew Wood.

The Russian Foreign Office threatened to expel nine British diplomats. Britain countered with a similar threat, in the tit-for-tat style of the Cold War.

For the Russians the matter was then taken over personally by Yevgeni Primakov, the Foreign Minister, who had once been the Soviet spy chief. Under his guidance, officials played down any rift with Britain. In the end Russia expelled only four diplomats, a purely political move by which President Yeltsin hoped to show, in advance of the presidential elections, that he could stand up to the West. This 'show of strength' probably won him some votes. Britain, in turn, expelled four Russian diplomats.

Leaders of the new Russia are sensitive about any information getting out to the West, even when it has no relevance to current defence. In February 1996 the MGB arrested Alexander Nikitin, a former submarine captain, and charged him with espionage and treason. He had been a consultant to Bellona, a Norwegian pressure group alarmed about radioactive contamination from decommissioned nuclear submarines of Russia's Northern Fleet. Bellona published many photographs to support its claim. Further, to show their anger over Nikitin's 'treason', the MGB then hounded his daughter and son-in-law out of Russia, an old KGB tactic. The aim was to deter other Russians from working with foreign pressure groups in the nuclear safety issue.

Ironically, while Russian and British spies operate against each other, there is occasional collaboration between the heads of the services for which they work. For instance, in 1996 the SVR, the KGB's successor, expressed interest in co-operation with Britain on counter-terrorism techniques. Also, according to Tass news agency, the SVR had passed on to British intelligence the 'goodwill' information that the IRA had bought arms and explosives in Estonia. Since this allegation is difficult to check the SVR might well have been making it in order to gain friends in London.

Many people in Western countries vehemently protest about the amount of money their respective governments spend on intelligence gathering abroad and security for its defence secrets at home. The response to their objections must be that money as well as many resources need to be committed. The world is a much more dangerous place since the Cold War ended and intelligence agencies are our first line of defence. Their information can prevent war, an infinitively more expensive and wasteful activity than spying.

It is just possible that there would be less spying, at least among Western Allies, if the various nations voluntarily revealed information which could benefit friendly countries. But in the real world this does not happen. Some valuable information might be exchanged during what seems to be a warm and enduring friendship and then the friends could fall out. One of the former partners could turn that valuable information against the other. Rather than trust one another, even nations with what their leaders call 'historically binding ties', spy on one another.

As I have said elsewhere, the French intelligence services are in the forefront of obtaining secrets by any and all means. At the same time successive French governments have decreed that all French defence secrets must remain wholly and exclusively French. It is permissible for officials and Services chiefs to 'demonstrate co-operation' with allies but that is all.

In mid-1995 rumours began to circulate within the foreign diplomatic community in Paris that French naval security had been breached. It was said that an engineer employed at the great Brest naval base had been arrested for 'spying for a foreign power'. Since the French strategic submarine fleet is based at Brest many diplomats assumed that the foreign power had to be Russia or the United States, the two major nuclear powers.

In fact, it was Britain. The objective was to find out about highly secret French scientific developments to track submarines moving at a depth of hundreds of fathoms. Various governments have spent the equivalents of billions of pounds in efforts to develop this capability. Russian, British and American specialists worked for years to perfect acoustic devices and they worked well until submarines in motion became ever quieter. The great Russian *Akula* submarine, already at a Mark 11 stage, is said to have reached the US east coast without triggering an alarm. This alarmed the Clinton Administration and the Chiefs of Staff.

NATO navies claim some success in tracing deep submarines from satellites, studying the minute ripples on the ocean surface. Another telltale sign is movement by micro-organisms. But none of these tracking methods is assured and certainty is vital. The Royal Navy has quietly boasted that its submarines are undetectable, but the French development, when perfected, would breach this confidence and national defence.

According to French sources, MI6 established not one but several front companies pretending to be technical defence consultancies. MI6 even set up in Paris a publishing house specialising in defence developments. Their legitimacy was not questioned in France where there are many such firms – as there are in Britain. MI6 agents suborned an engineer working on the French tracing system and paid him large amounts of money. This man did not provide equipment but the information he handed over is said to be just as good.

The British operation went much further than recruiting the Brest engineer. At least a score of officials and consultants closely connected to French ministries accepted invitations to write for the specialist journals run by MI6's cover companies. It was the best type of operation because, although the high-powered and very knowledgeable French writers were paid for their work, they had no idea that they were working for MI6.

That the scam paid off in 1995 was largely the result of dummy run in 1992–93 by an MI6 spy team that wanted to be 'discovered'. Posing as engineers, they joined a party of Royal Navy officers who had been officially invited to view a nuclear-powered aircraft carrier under construction. According to French security officers, the British engineers were spies intent on getting details about the steel plates shielding the interior of the ship from the nuclear source. In fact, the Royal Navy already had a quality of steel superior to that of the French. The venture was subterfuge to delude the French into thinking that British intelligence would not again try to penetrate Brest naval dockyards.

For its part, MI6 was mildly surprised that French naval intelligence fell for the ploy. Had MI6 really been trying to find out about the strength of steel plates they would have gone about it in a much more sophisticated way.

According to a British Intelligence source, the Admirality had 'politely asked' the French to consider a joint scheme to work on a submarine tracking system. It was only when this invitation was refused that MI6 was called in to take 'positive and constructive' action. As a result of the elaborate deception a great deal of information reached the engineers and scientists at Portsmouth and at Farnborough, Hampshire, where the closely guarded Defence Evaluation and Research Agency is based.

Much more is likely to come out of the research than a guaranteed way of tracking submarines. According to the same source, 'We have enough raw material to keep the scientists busy for years. If the French had not been so secretive both nations would have worked together for the benefit of each.'

The *Sunday Times* was the first newspaper to break the story in Britain (10 June 1996) and it was suggested that President Chirac would be angry with Prime Minister John Major. Another publication suggested that Britain' s MI6 and France' s DST would be 'at each other' s throats'. This is nonsense. When Chirac next met Major – at a summit meeting in Florence on 24 June 1996 as it happened – he was more likely to have said, 'A good goal for you, John, but the next one will be for us.'

The cost of the intelligence operation against the French must have been considerable but the results justify the expense. To be able to track enemy submarines carrying nuclear missiles and to find ways of making British submarines untraceable is a colossal intelligence prize. MI6 was doing its job.

*   *   *

The first sentence of this chapter asks, 'Is spying necessary?' The answer is yes, more than ever, especially if the security representatives of democracy's law, order and stability (the good guys) are to defeat

Brassey's Book of Espionage

the predatory warlords, terrorists and international organised criminals (the bad guys). The odds are so often in the 'bad guys' favour. For instance, they use digital mobile telephones, each of which scrambles every call in what is known as a rolling code. Under the Global System for Mobile Communications (GSMC) terrorists and criminals comm-unicate around the world without the risk of having their calls tapped.

This is why, in 1996, MI5 and Scotland Yard's Anti-Terrorist Branch, asked the British Department of Trade and Industry to allow them access to encryption keys. These keys are known only to a few people in the telephone companies, which would reveal encryption codes only if the law demanded that they do so.

The most secure form of communication is for a GSMC subscriber in one country to telephone another GSMC subscriber in a second coun-try. It is obvious that case officers and their agents in the field are using digital phones to an increasing extent. They can preserve their secrets in this way. It makes sense for MI5 and other security agencies to be able to intercept calls made by terrorists. In 1996 the organisation was frustrated by the inability of its computers to unscramble the 'bad guys' conversations, which so often deal with operational matters.

*　　　*　　　*

Idealists, pacificists, the Greens and ordinary peaceloving people would like to believe that with 'openness', international co-operation in humanitarian ventures, the end of the Cold War, the growth of common markets and other anti-war factors, the need for spying should decrease. Sadly, this is naive. The perceived need increases. It is not only necessary for a political leader or a general to see what is over the hill; he must also know what is going on under the sea, under the ground and in the stratosphere, to know what his opponents, whether they be real, potential or imagined, are thinking and planning, and to have a very clear idea not only about what is happening now, this minute, but about what will happen in 10, 20, 50 years ahead.

Fear is not only the reason for intelligence, it grows from intelli-gence. Because of this cycle there is no possible end to it.

APPENDIX

BRITISH TRAITORS SINCE 1945

This list of proven British spies forms a useful postscript to my book. That so many spies for foreign countries could work for so long undiscovered in the intelligence services, the armed forces and in secret projects is disturbing, for it indicates a very inadequate level of security. In addition to the people mentioned here were other spies not employed by the armed forces or the intelligence services. Ethel Gee is an example. Furthermore, some men and women known to be spies could not be brought to trial for lack of sufficient evidence. Other cases for which there was strong evidence were not made public for what were considered 'reasons of state'.

Klaus Fuchs (naturalised British subject): Atom and atom bomb projects;
Alan Nunn May: Atom bomb project;
Donald Maclean: Foreign Office and atom bomb project;
Kim Philby: MI6;
Guy Burgess: MI5, MI6, Foreign Office;
Anthony Blunt: MI5;
Leo Long: Military Intelligence;
John King: Foreign Office;
George Blake: MI6;
John Vassall: Admiralty, Foreign Office;
John Cairncross: Foreign Office, MI6, Treasury;
David Bingham: Royal Navy (with his wife Maureen);
Frank Bossard: Aviation Ministry;
Douglas Britten: Royal Air Force;
Nicholas Prager: Royal Air Force and English Electric;
Geoffrey Prime: GCHQ;
Michael Bettaney: MI5;
Hugh Hambleton: NATO;
Harry Houghton: Underwater Weapons Establishment;
Philip Aldridge: Army Intelligence Corps;

213

Helen Keenan: Cabinet Office;
Robin Cloude: Royal Navy;
Percy Allen: Land/Air Warfare Directorate;
Barbara Fell: Central Office of Information;
Leonard Hinchcliffe: Foreign Office;
Michael Smith: Electronics Engineer, sentenced to 25 years in 1993;
Anthony Wraight: Royal Air Force.

The many foreign spies who were active in Britain for long periods before being uncovered include Gordon Lonsdale, (real name Konon Molody), and Peter and Helen Kroger, also known as Morris and Lona Cohen.

CHAPTER NOTES

Chapter 1: Fear is the Spur

While spying is an ancient profession or craft, intelligence agencies are new. In Britain, the first such agency was instituted in 1909. It was probably the first in the world, in the sense that it was actually a government department – of just one room! – and financed by government. As soon as other European countries heard of 'Room 40' they wanted an intelligence agency of their own. Germany and Austria created one in 1913 and Russia in 1917. Surprisingly, France did not possess one until 1937, though it had its military intelligence section before that. The US was without a 'central' intelligence agency until 1947.

Chapter 2: The Language of Spying

It would be difficult for an outsider to follow a conversation between spies, whether it is oral or in writing, especially if they are using double-talk. Miles Copeland gives an excellent exposition of double-talk in his *The Real Spy World*. He groups his interesting examples under 'Introductory Signals', 'Elimination of Provocative Words and Phrases', and 'Names of Persons, Organisations and Places'. Copeland's cover word for intelligence officers was 'merchants'. He also lists signals to be used when arranging meetings.

Chapter 3: The Spy Organisations

Intelligence organisations exist by the thousand, many of them under innocuous cover names. 'Institutes' of various kinds proliferate. The Americans once had 'Research Institute for Indigenous Peoples'. It was a branch of the CIA responsible for espionage in Central America. The branches, sections or directorates within a large intelligence organisation are virtually autonomous and, in some cases, without collaboration with other branches. This militates against the efficient running of the mother organisation but it is commonplace in the CIA and SVR (the old KGB). So-called cultural centres are good fronts for espionage organisations.

Chapter 4: Spying – A World Sub-Culture
Allen Dulles, for eight years Director of the CIA, was aware that the public was so consumed by their interest in espionage that paranoia was causing immense problems for his agency and others. He said, 'People with paranoid tendencies or who have been disappointed in love or in business or who just don't like their neighbors will denounce their friends and foes and competitors or even the local garbage man as Soviet spies.' (*The Craft of Intelligence*, p. 218).

John Vassall: See Vassall's own account of his spying career in *Autobiography of a Spy*. The title would have been suggested by the publishers, for Vassall, while admitting to his treason – he had no option about a confession – still saw himself as a victim, 20 years after he began to spy. Most spies recruited through blackmail refer to themselves as victims: it helps them to put a distance between themselves and their treason. They rarely refer to the people who lost their lives as a consequence of that treason.

Chapter 5: Some Penetrations Work, Others Don't
Colonel Bernard Nut: Details of Colonel Nut's counter-espionage career come to me from a confidential source, but his murder and the motives for it were widely reported in the French press in February 1993.

The Binghams: David and Maureen Bingham, small fry in the intelligence world, were a sad case. There were strains in their marriage even before they began spying and they became more intense after their arrest. The couple did not live together again after David's release from prison and both now live under other names.

Geoffrey Prime: See *The Guardian*, 21 November 1982, pp. 4–5.

Chapter 6: A Country Dedicated to Preventive Intelligence
The foundation of Israel's intelligence system: Information from research I carried out in Israel in the 1950s and 60s.

Eli Cohen: For the full story of Eli Cohen see *Alone in Damascus: The Life and Death of Eli Cohen* by Samuel Seger, published in English in Jerusalem by Seger. Apropos the criticism that Cohen's superiors kept him too long in Damascus see Stewart Steven's *The Spymasters of Israel*, pp. 202–4.

Chapter 7: Three Women in Intelligence and One Who Was Seduced

The KGB and its use of women: according to Oleg Gordievsky and Christopher Andrew, KGB chiefs were 'implacably opposed' to the operational use of women other than as sexual bait, or possibly to recruit other women as agents. Ivan Serov, when Director of the KGB, opposed the employment of women as desk officers. See *KGB: The Inside Story*, p. 366.

Elspeth Shragmuller: for further information on Shragmuller see Nicholas Snowden's *Memoirs of a Spy*, New York (1933). Snowden's given name was Miklos Soltesz and he claimed to have known Shragmuller.

The Nili Spies and Sarah Aaronsohn: in 1974 I spent some months in Israel researching the Nili spies. Much has been written about them in Hebrew, as well as Anthony Verner's *Agents of Empire*.

Yolande Gabay: for further reference see Richard Deacon's *The Israeli Secret Service*.

Rhona Ritchie: four articles in the *Daily Telegraph*, London, on 30 November 1982: 'Ritchie more foolish than wicked'; 'Woman gambled with love and lost'; 'Friends stunned into disbelief'; 'Ritchie walks free'. Also 'The powers of pillow talk', by Bel Mooney, the *Sunday Times*, 5 December 1982.

Chapter 8: Spying as Part of Foreign Policy: Two Great KGB Triumphs.

Soviet and Russian organisations: I note in my book that an entire volume would be needed to list and describe the proliferation of secret organisations. Christopher Andrew and Oleg Gordievsky discuss many of them in their book *KGB: The Inside Story*.

George Blake: 'Steps bordering on the ludicrous were taken on behalf of the Secret Service to cover up the long-term presence of a most damaging Soviet spy inside it.' So says Chapman Pincher in his book *Too Secret Too Long*, p.261. Pincher believes that Blake was a dedicated pro-Soviet communist by the time he joined MI6. He reveals suspicions in MI5 that Blake was recruited into Soviet espionage soon after, while attending a Russian language course at Cambridge.

The Ames Affair: Confidential information. Also a highly readable and well-informed article in the *Sunday Times*, 26 June 1995, 'Traitor-Gate' by James Adams.

Chapter 9: Model Operations Based On Intelligence

Details of these daring and astonishingly successful Israel operations are the results of my own researches in Israel over a period of 20 years.

Chapter l0: A Plethora of American Spies

For public information on the various American intelligence operations refer to: 'Military spies out of uniform: Soldier Spies', *Time* Magazine, 29 May 1995.

Non-official spies: 'Spies for the new disorder', *Time* Magazine, 20 February 1995.

Psychic Imagers: 'The Vision Thing', *Time* Magazine, 11 December 1995.

Espionage in the Cyberspace Age: 'Spies in Cyberspace', *Time* Magazine, 20 March 1995.

Spy Planes and Satellites: See Graham Yost's *Spies in the Sky*.

Chapter 11: High-Tech Espionage: When Allies Fall Out

Operation Silicon Valley: for background see *High-tech Espionage* by Jay Tuck. Tuck is probably the ultimate authority on High-Tech espionage.

French mishaps in China: see Steve Boggan's article 'The cost of keeping commercial secrets', *The Independent*, London, 4 January 1996.

MI6 and BND fall victims to a scam: see Imre Karacs' article 'Millions stolen from under spy agencies' noses', *The Independent*, London, 29 January 1996.

Operation AYATOLLAH and Newt Gingrich's role in the disaster: 'For Crying Out Loud', by James Walsh, *Time* Magazine, 5 February 1996.

CIA and DIA operating against the SIS in Bosnia: See Ed Vulliamy's article 'Why US bugged Bosnia Allies', *The Guardian*, London, 30 January 1996.

The Japanese need for an intelligence agency: various sources.

Chapter 12: Tricks of the Trade

These 'tricks' – though skills might be more appropriate – come from a variety of sources, including spies in the field. They would not wish to be mentioned by name!

Chapter 13: So You Want a Career in Intelligence

Probably the best advice comes from Miles Copeland in his books *The Real Spy World* and *The Game of Nations*. Copeland knew espionage from the bottom up, not merely from talking to people in the game – though he did a lot of that too.

Chapter 14: People Who Should *Not* Be Doing Intelligence Work

From various sources. For more detailed information about Jonathan

Jay Pollard refer to *Every Spy a Prince* by Dan Raviv and Yossi Melman. Similarly, Eliyahu Hazan and 'Thomas and Kathy'. Thomas' full name was Jack Leon Thomas. He married Kathy Bendhof.

Chapter 15: Is Spying Old-Fashioned?

Nearly all writers on espionage ask the question 'Is it really all worthwhile?' It is directed as much to themselves as to others and their consensus is that spying *is* necessary. Equally, there is a consensus among them that what they know of Western spying and Western defences against spies is alarming. There are too many 'black holes', too many potential traitors. One of the biggest of black holes, as I indicated in Chapter 1, is China, the great challenge to come. Nothing that I know leads me to suppose that we are doing enough to meet it.

SELECT BIBLIOGRAPHY

Adams, James, *The New Species: Exploring the Frontiers of Espionage*. Hutchinson, London (1994)

Allen, Thomas B and Polmar, Norman, *Merchants of Treason: America's Secrets for Sale*. Robert Hale, London (1988)

Andrew, Christopher & Gordievsky, Oleg, *KGB: The Inside Story*. Hodder & Stoughton, London (1990)

Bramford, James, *The Puzzle Palace: a Report on NSA, America's Most Secret Agency*. Houghton Mifflin, Boston (1976)

Beesley, Patrick, *Very Special Intelligence*. Sphere, London (1978)

Beechloss, J Bowyer and Talbott, Strobe, *At the Highest Levels: The Inside Story of the End of the Cold War*. Little, Brown, Boston (1993)

Bittman, Ladislav, *The Deception Game*. Ballantine, New York (1981)

Bittman, Ladislav, *The KGB and Soviet Disinformation*. Pergamon-Brassey's, Washington (1995)

Blake, George, *No Other Choice*. Jonathan Cape, London (1990)

Bloch, Jonathan & Fitzgerald, Patrick, *British Intelligence and Covert Action*. Brandon Books, Dublin (1993)

Boar, Roger & Blundell, Nigel, *The World's Greatest Spies and Spymasters*. Octopus, London (1984)

Bourke, Sean, *The Springing of George Blake*. Cassell, London (1970)

Bower, Tom, *The Red Web: MI6 and the KGB Master Coup*. Autumn Press, London (1989)

Breckinridge, Scott D, *The CIA and the US Intelligence System*. Westview Press, Boulder (1986)

Bulloch, John, *M.I.5.* Arthur Barker, London (1963)

Busch, Tristan, *Secret Service Unmasked*. Hutchinson, London (1945)

Cain, Frank, *A.S.I.O. An Unofficial History*. Spectrum Publications, Victoria (1994)

Cave Brown, Anthony, *Bodyguard of Lies*. Star Books, London (1977)

Cline, Ray S, *The CIA Under Reagan, Bush & Casey*. Acropolis Books, Washington (1981)

Cline, Ray S, *Secrets, Spies and Scholars: Blueprint of the Essential CIA*. Acropolis Books, Washington (1976)

Copeland, Miles, *The Game of Nations*. Weidenfeld & Nicolson, London (1972)

Copeland, Miles, *The Real Spy World*. Weidenfeld & Nicolson, London (1974)

Costello, John, *Mask of Treachery*. Collins, London (1988)

Deacon, Richard, *The Israeli Secret Service*. Hamish Hamilton, London (1977)

Deacon, Richard, *The Truth Twisters*. Macdonald, London (1986)

Dulles, Allen, *The Craft of Intelligence*. Harper & Row, New York (1963)

Elliott, Nicholas, *With My Little Eye*. Michael Russell, London (1993)

Faligot, Roger and Krop, Pascal, *La Piscine: The French Secret Service Since 1944*. Basil Blackwell, Oxford (1989)

Farago, Ladislas, *The Game of the Foxes*. Hodder & Stoughton, London (1972)

Felix, Christopher, *The Spy and His Masters*. Secker & Warburg, London (1963)

Fitzgibbon, Constantine, *Secret Intelligence in the 20th Century*. Granada, London (1978)

Godson, Roy (ed.), *Intelligence Requirements for the 1990's; Collection, Analysis, Counter-intelligence and Covert Action*. Lexington Books, Lexington (1989)

Golitsin, Anatoli, *New Lies for Old*. The Bodley Head, London (1984)

Hall, Richard, *The Secret State: Australia's Spy Industry*. Cassell, Melbourne (1978)

Hjersman, Peter, *The Stash Book*, California (1978)

Hood, William, *Mole*. Norton, New York (1982)

Hyde, H Montgomery, *The Atom Bomb Spies*. Sphere, London (1982)

Kent, Sherman, *Strategic Intelligence for American World Policy*. Princeton University Press, Princeton (1949, 1966)

Kessler, Ronald. *Inside the CIA: Revealing the Secrets of the World's Most Powerful Spy Agency*. Pocket Books, New York (1992)

Knightley, Phillip, *The Second Oldest Profession – The Spy as Bureaucrat, Patriot, Fantasist and Whore*. Andre Deutsch, London (1986)

Leigh, David, *The Frontiers of Secrecy*. Junction Books, London (1980)

Levchenko, Stanislav, *On the Wrong Side: My Life in the KGB*. Brassey's, Washington (1988)

Lotz, Wolfgang, *The Champagne Spy*. Valentine Mitchell, London (1972)

Lucas, Norman, *The Great Spy Ring*. Mayflower, London (1968)

MacKnight, David, *Australia's Spies and Their Secrets*. Allen & Unwin, Sydney (1994)

Marchetti, Victor and Marks, John D, *The CIA and the Cult of Intelligence*. Dell Publishing, New York (1974)

Milligan, Tom, *CIA Life: 10,000 Days with the Agency*. Foreign Intelligence Press (1991)

Newman, Bernard, *The World of Espionage*. Souvenir Press, London (1962)

O'Toole, G J A, *Encyclopedia of American Intelligence & Espionage*. Facts on File, New York (1988)

Perry, Mark, *Eclipse: The Last Days of the CIA*. William Morrow, New York (1992)

Pincher, Chapman, *The Secret Offensive, Active Measures: A Saga of Deception, Disinformation, Subversion, Terrorism, Sabotage and Assassination.* Sidgwick & Jackson, London (1985)

Pincher, Chapman, *Too Secret Too Long*. St Martin's Press, New York (1984)

Philby, Kim, *My Secret War*. MacGibbon & Kee, London (1968)

Ranelagh, John, *The Rise and Decline of the CIA*. Simon & Schuster, New York (1986)

Raviv, Dan & Melman, Yossi, *Every Spy a Prince*. Houghton Mifflin, Boston (1990)

Robertson, K G, *British and American Approaches to Intelligence*. Macmillan, London (1987)

Rusbridger, James, *The Intelligence Game*. Bodley Head, London (1989)

Seth, Ronald, *Encyclopedia of Espionage*. New English Library, London (1972)

Suvorov, Viktor, *Soviet Military Intelligence*. Hamish Hamilton, London (1984)

Toohey, Brian & Pinwill, William, *Oyster: The Story of the Australian Intelligence Service*. Mandarin, Melbourne (1989)

Tuck, Jay, *High-Tech Espionage*. Sidgwick & Jackson, London (1986)

Vassall, John, *Vassell: The Autobiography of a Spy*. Sidgwick & Jackson, London (1975)

Verrier, Anthony (ed.), *Agents of Empire: Anglo-Zionist Intelligence Operations 1915–1919*. Brassey's, London (1995)

Verrier, Anthony, *Through the Looking Glass*. Cape, London (1983)

West, Nigel, *Games of Intelligence: The Classified Conflict of International Espionage*. Weidenfeld & Nicolson, London (1989)

West, Nigel, *Seven Spies Who Changed the World*. Secker & Warburg, London (1991)

Wise, David & Ross, Thomas B, *The Espionage Establishment.* Random House, New York (1967)

Wright, Peter, *The Spycatcher's Encyclopaedia of Espionage.* William Heinemann, Australia (1991)

Yost, Graham, *Spies in The Sky.* Facts on File, London (1989)

INDEX

225

Boyce, Christopher 138
Brandt, Willy 44
Brezhnev, Leonid 43
Britten, Douglas 213
BROADSIDE, Operation 71
brush drop (defined) 13
bugs and bugging 22, 169
Burgess, Guy 11, 38, 43, 111, 180, 213
Bush, George 162

Cabinet Research Bureau (Japan) 162
Cairncross, John 213
Cairo Radio 129
careless leaks (defined) 6
Carmen, George 106–107
Carrington, Lord 106
Carter, James 138
case officer (defined) 6
Castro, Fidel 16
Check Point Charlie 37
Cheka 109–110
'Cherbourg gunboats' incident 127–128
Chetverikov, Nikolai 66
Chirac, Jacques 155, 211
Churchill, Winston 6
CIA 4, 27–28, 30–31, 35–36, 39–40, 42, 64, 109, 113, 143, 152, 162
and espionage terminology 6–8, 10–11, 15–17, 19, 21
and Berlin Tunnel 56–58, 113
and Ames case 115–118, 120–122
and military intelligence 133–135
and NOC Programme 135–137
and the 'cyberspace age' 140–142, 191–193
and Dawe case 148–150
and Operation AYATOLLAH 157–159
and Bosnia 159–161
and recruitment/training 180–184, 186–187, 189, 191–193, 196–197
and 1990s Russia 208

CIA Office of Comunications 56
CIA Study Soviet Covert Action and Propaganda 11n
CIAAD 28
CIAOD 28
CIS 28
city drop (defined) 12
Clinton, Bill 135, 158, 160, 210
Cloude, Robin 214
Cohen, Eli 78–88, 175
Cohen, Lona, see Kroger, Helen
Cohen, Morris see Kroger, Peter
Cohen, Nadia 79, 81
Company, the see CIA
Computer Security Research Centre 153
Congressional Monitor 158
contrived leak (defined) 7
Copeland, Miles 10, 15n
Coplon, Judith 6
Corriere della Sera 117
counter-espionage (defined) 7
counter-intelligence (defined) 7–8
country drop (defined) 12
courier (defined) 8
cover role (defined) 9
CPGB 43
Criminal Investigation Department (Palestine) 70
CUKR see SMERSH
cut-out (defined) 9

Daily Telegraph 198
Dali, Colonel Salah 82–84, 87–88
David (Book of Samuel) 2
Dawe, Amos 148–150
de Gaulle, Charles 79, 127, 191
dead drop see drop
deception (defined) 9–10
deep cover (defined) 9
defector (defined) 10
defector-in-place (defined) 10
Defence Agency (Japan) 161
Defence Evaluation and Research Agency (UK) 211

Defoe, Danial 30n
Department of Defense (USA) 7
Department of Justice (USA) 29
Deriabin, Piotyr 32
DESNET 142
Deutsch, John 183–184
Deuxième Bureau 28–29
DGSE 28, 154, 180
DHS 135
DIA 137, 161, 199, 204
Dillon, Douglas 131
'Ding-Dong Affair' 151
diplomatic bag (defined) 10
Directorate K (Russia) 28
dirty tricks (defined) 11
disinformation (defined) 11
Djemal Pasha 94
double agent (defined) 11
Dozier, James 137
DPSD 28, 65–66
drop (defined) 12–15
DST 29, 109, 212
Dulles, Allen 28
Dulles, John Foster 131
Dzerzhinsky Artillery & Engineering
   Academy 111n
Dzerzhinsky, Felix 110

Eban, Abba 130–131
Eichmann, Adolf 85
Eisenhower, Dwight D. 130
El Husseini, Haj Amin 101
El-Ansary, Rifaat 106–107
El-Ard, Sheikh Magid 81
El-Din, General Abdul 82
El-Din, Lieutenant Maazi 82
El-Hafez, Amin 78, 81–83, 86–88
El-Maaz, Eliya 85
'Emily' (defined) 15
*Encyclopedia of American Intelligence
   and Espionage* 16
Envision programme 141–142
Eshkol, Levy, 87
espionology (defined) 16
European Union (EU) 156, 159

F-15 aircraft 151
F-22 aircraft 183
false-flagging (defined) 16
'family jewels' (defined) 16
Farouk, King 98, 104
FBI 28–29, 115–118, 120–121, 149
FCIB 29
Feinberg, Absalom 93
Felix, Christopher 181
Fell, Barbara 214
'Fifth Man' 38, 38n
Fine, Absalom 96
Foertsch, Volger 156–157
Foreign Ministry (Japan) 162
Foreign Office (UK) 7, 105, 107
Frank, Ann 171
Freier, Shalhevet 72
Frenzl, Alfred 6
FSB *see* MGB
Fuchs, Klaus 125

Gabay, Gilbert 98, 102, 104
Gabay, Yolande 98–105
Gaddafi, Muammar 15, 137, 204
Galbraith, Richard 160
GALILEE, Operation 20
Gates, Bob 30
GCHQ 29, 61–65, 162, 205
Gee, Ethel 165–169
Gingrich, Newt 157–159
giveaway information (defined) 16
GLC 50
Goebbels, Josef 6
GOLD, Operation *see* Berlin Tunnel
Golitsin, Anatoli 48
Gorbachev, Mikhail 162, 185–186
Gottfried, Dr Harold 44
'Green House' 163–164
GRU 29, 60–61, 89, 152
Guerrier, Patrick 65–66
Guillaume, Gunter 44
Guriel, Boris 76

Hagana 70–73, 75, 99–100, 102, 104
Haig, Alexander 106

227